A Power User's Guide to FL Studio 21

Master the art of music production and advanced mixing
techniques to create Billboard-charting records

Chris Noxx

BIRMINGHAM—MUMBAI

A Power User's Guide to FL Studio 21

Group Product Manager: Rohit Rajkumar
Publishing Product Manager: Nitin Nainani
Book Project Manager: Aishwarya Mohan
Senior Editor: Rashi Dubey
Technical Editor: Simran Udasi
Copy Editor: Safis Editing
Proofreader: Safis Editing
Indexer: Tejal Daruwale Soni
Production Designer: Jyoti Kadam
DevRel Marketing Coordinators: Nivedita Pandey and Namita Velgekar

First published: October 2023

Production reference: 1080923

Published by Packt Publishing Ltd.
Grosvenor House
11 St Paul's Square
Birmingham
3 1RB, UK.

ISBN 9781803234380

www.packtpub.com

To my mother: "If you can think it, you can be it, so do it." And to my brother: "When the student was ready, the teacher appeared."

– Chris Noxx

Contributors

About the author

Chris Noxx is an FL Studio *Power User* and *JUNO*-nominated (2020 Rap Recording of the Year) producer, composer, and arranger who has charted on global *Billboard charts* over 12 times in the US and Canada (including the US Billboard Top 200, US Independent Albums, US Top Album Sales, US Top Current Album Sales, and the Canadian Hot 100) and has worked with some of the most iconic hip hop artists, brands, and associations of all time using FL Studio.

I'm humbled and thankful for every person who has helped me along my journey, from the support of my close family to my mentors, teachers, and close friends who have all contributed to my evolution as a creative and businessperson. This book is dedicated to you.

About the reviewer

Bobby Yarsulik (or **BSlick** as he is known online) boasts an impressive musical background, having dedicated 28 years to playing the piano and 18 years to music production. For the past 4 years, he has been fully engaged in freelancing as a composer, embracing the freedom of remote work. Accompanied by his wife and three children, he travels full-time in an RV around the US. With over 100k followers on YouTube and 11 million lifetime streams on Spotify, he has established himself as one of the most influential personalities in the online music and gaming scene. His journey serves as an example of harmonizing passion for music with a devotion to family, showcasing the rewards of striking a balance between personal interests and loved ones.

Table of Contents

5

Approaching Melody and Composition Theory   157

6

A Billboard-Ready Production Arrangement   203

Part 3: Best Techniques and How to Appear on the Billboard Charts

7

Chart-Topping Mixing Techniques   243

8

How to Get Records Placed So They Land on Billboard Charts   275

Preface

In this book, we will explore the very essence of music production and unravel the intricacies of FL Studio, unlocking its hidden treasures and unleashing your creative prowess. Whether you're an aspiring producer, an experienced musician, or a curious enthusiast, this guide will equip you with the tools to elevate your artistry to unprecedented heights. As you delve deeper into the chapters ahead, you will find yourself immersed in a world of possibilities. I will share with you the secrets I've gathered throughout my career—working alongside Grammy-winning artists, collaborating with multi-platinum sensations, and witnessing my work climb the global Billboard charts. My experiences have taught me the importance of not only honing technical skills but also understanding the subtleties that breathe life into music, transforming it from mere soundwaves into emotive masterpieces.

Each chapter will ask the reader to take action following the learning to create a record from scratch, mixed and mastered, and ready to send out to artists. Each chapter builds on the Billboard charting framework I've developed over 20 years—from grasping the Billboard mindset to creating signature sounds, creating time-tested drum loops, crafting and adding a hypnotic melody and chords, arranging these using the Billboard framework, mixing and mastering the record, and finally, getting records placed with major artists.

But this book is more than just a technical manual—it's a profound exploration of creativity, innovation, and self-discovery. It's about unleashing the potential that lies within you and crafting records that resonate with the hearts and souls of audiences worldwide.

As you immerse yourself in these pages, allow yourself to experiment, make mistakes, and embrace the uncharted territories of music production. Through trial and error, you will uncover your unique style, your signature sound—a sound that will become your artistic legacy.

With every chapter, you will grow not only as a producer but also as an artist, understanding how to blend technical precision with boundless imagination. As you work your way through FL Studio's powerful features, I encourage you to infuse your own personality, emotions, and experiences into the music you create. It is this authenticity that will set your records apart and forge a connection with your listeners like never before.

I'm thrilled to be your guide on this creative expedition. So, let us set forth on this journey of discovery, where innovation meets tradition, and technology harmonizes with the soul. Together, we will unlock the true potential of FL Studio and unleash your artistic brilliance upon the world. Get ready to embrace the endless possibilities of music production, and remember, your journey has only just begun!

Who this book is for

This book is useful for music producers who are serious about pursuing a career in the music industry as a producer, remixer, composer, or DJ artist. This book will walk you through the step-by-step process of creating Billboard-ready records.

What this book covers

Chapter 1, Delving into the FL Studio Mindset and Workflow

In this chapter, I share my personal experiences with using FL Studio in the music industry, guiding you to master the software effectively. Through practical frameworks, anecdotes, and a focus on creating the correct mindset, you'll learn how to approach FL Studio like a power user.

Chapter 2, From the Piano Roll to the Billboard Charts

In this chapter, you'll discover my proven techniques for consistently crafting professional productions with FL Studio. I'll introduce you to creating an efficient working template and utilizing the FL Studio toolbox to its full potential. From optimizing production workflows to achieving Billboard-worthy records, you'll gain invaluable insights to elevate your music productions to the next level.

Chapter 3, Creating Your Signature Sound

This chapter explores maximizing FL Studio's stock sound kits, VSTs, and plugins to create distinctive, captivating, and original sounds. You'll learn how to leverage these tools, unlocking your creative uniqueness as a producer.

Chapter 4, Working through Drum Programming and Arrangements

This chapter delves into professional drum programming and arrangements. Exploring the **Channel Rack** and **Piano Roll**, you'll learn effective techniques and pitfalls to avoid, ensuring your drum programming hits hard and elevates your records.

Chapter 5, Approaching Melody and Composition Theory

This chapter introduces basic composition techniques using the FL Studio **Piano Roll**. You'll learn how to craft professional-sounding melody beds and counterpoints with ease, coupled with professional drum programming and arrangements. Exploring the **Channel Rack** and **Piano Roll**, you'll learn effective techniques and pitfalls to avoid, ensuring your drum programming hits hard and elevates your records.

Chapter 6, A Billboard-Ready Production Arrangement

This crucial chapter breaks down arranging in the playlist tool using a professional Billboard framework. You will learn about bar counting, transition points, and structuring modern music for recording artists. You will also learn how to simplify arrangements to give your music room to breathe and shine.

Chapter 7, Chart-Topping Mixing Techniques

This chapter introduces mixing techniques using FL Studio stock plugins to achieve professional radio-ready records. You will learn how to enhance sound design and creative compositions through effective mixing methods.

Chapter 8, How to Get Records Placed So They Land on Billboard Charts

In this concluding chapter, I'll guide producers on achieving Billboard-worthy music and leveraging networking platforms for placements with major artists and record labels. You will learn what steps to take after creating your record in FL Studio and how to make the most of your music.

To get the most out of this book

To get the most out of this book, having a solid foundation in FL Studio and music production will be beneficial. Familiarity with the software's interface and basic functionalities will allow you to grasp the concepts more effectively. Additionally, possessing an "ear" for music—a keen ability to perceive and appreciate musical nuances—will further enhance your learning experience.

Software/hardware covered in the book	Operating system requirements
FL Studio 20 or 21	Windows or Mac OS

For optimal performance and a seamless experience using FL Studio, it is advised to have a computer with at least 8 GB of RAM and a minimum of 250 GB of hard drive space. However, to ensure smoother operation, especially when working on larger and more complex projects, I recommend starting with 16 GB of RAM and a hard drive capacity of at least 500 GB. This will allow you to work with larger sample libraries and multiple plugins and handle resource-intensive tasks without encountering performance bottlenecks.

Conventions used

There are a number of text conventions used throughout this book.

`Code in text`: Indicates code words in text, database table names, folder names, filenames, file extensions, pathnames, dummy URLs, user input, and Twitter handles. Here is an example: "Create a drum pattern for your kick, naming it `Drum Kick`."

Bold: Indicates a new term, an important word, or words that you see onscreen. For instance, words in menus or dialog boxes appear in **bold**. Here is an example: "By utilizing the **Scale Highlighting** feature in **Piano Roll** in FL Studio, you can set the key."

> **Tips or important notes**
> Appear like this.

Get in touch

Feedback from our readers is always welcome.

General feedback: If you have questions about any aspect of this book, email us at `customercare@packtpub.com` and mention the book title in the subject of your message.

Errata: Although we have taken every care to ensure the accuracy of our content, mistakes do happen. If you have found a mistake in this book, we would be grateful if you would report this to us. Please visit `www.packtpub.com/support/errata` and fill in the form.

Piracy: If you come across any illegal copies of our works in any form on the internet, we would be grateful if you would provide us with the location address or website name. Please contact us at `copyright@packtpub.com` with a link to the material.

If you are interested in becoming an author: If there is a topic that you have expertise in and you are interested in either writing or contributing to a book, please visit `authors.packtpub.com`.

Share Your Thoughts

Once you've read, we'd love to hear your thoughts! Scan the QR code below to go straight to the Amazon review page for this book and share your feedback.

`https://packt.link/r/1803234385`

Your review is important to us and the tech community and will help us make sure we're delivering excellent quality content.

Download a free PDF copy of this book

Thanks for purchasing this book!

Do you like to read on the go but are unable to carry your print books everywhere?

Is your eBook purchase not compatible with the device of your choice?

Don't worry, now with every Packt book you get a DRM-free PDF version of that book at no cost.

Read anywhere, any place, on any device. Search, copy, and paste code from your favorite technical books directly into your application.

The perks don't stop there, you can get exclusive access to discounts, newsletters, and great free content in your inbox daily

Follow these simple steps to get the benefits:

1. Scan the QR code or visit the link below

https://packt.link/free-ebook/9781803234380

2. Submit your proof of purchase
3. That's it! We'll send your free PDF and other benefits to your email directly

Part 1: Understanding the Basics

This part aims to provide insights into my personal experiences of using FL Studio in the music industry, enabling you to grasp the mindset and knowledge necessary to master this software program. You will benefit from anecdotes of real-life instances where I employed FL Studio and practical strategies for learning, as well as learn how I utilized the software's capabilities to create productions chosen by renowned recording artists. Moreover, we will introduce the fundamental FL Studio concepts and explore their significance in establishing an efficient workflow within the software UI. As we progress, you will be introduced to advanced frameworks, and how you can continue to leverage FL Studio to start creating Billboard ready productions.

In this part, we have the following chapter:

- *Chapter 1, Delving into the FL Studio Mindset and Workflow*

1
Delving into the FL Studio Mindset and Workflow

I'd like to congratulate you on buying this book, for it is a manifestation of your dedication to taking an important step in mastering your skill set as it relates to leveraging FL Studio. It has been said that when the student is ready, the master will appear. In everything you pursue in life, be it related to professional or personal development, you can only build as high as your foundation is deep. This book will provide you with that strong foundation on which you may build. I hope that once you have completed its lessons, you will use it to continue your growth as an FL Studio user, and ultimately, reach the level of a masterful power user.

I hope you are excited to take this journey with me, as I'm excited to share with you the key aspects of its software system, which I have learned over almost two decades, and the experiences it brought to me. I will discuss these topics briefly in the following pages, but I need you to be willing to learn and willing to take action and understand that it is your *why* that will drive your motivation to take action on its contents.

Although this is a book of technical frameworks of the *how* to use FL Studio to create records that work within a Billboard charting framework, we need to ascertain the *why* of your desire to master FL Studio before I can impart the secrets of its formulas to you.

I have broken this book into three parts that represent the keystones in mastering FL Studio. The first part of this book will impart upon you the first key philosophy that must be addressed. This is the most important framework that will set the tone of what you will do with this book, and that is the mindset, or the reason *why* you want to master FL Studio. In the second and third parts of this book, I will teach you the *how*. With the proper mental framework coupled with the technical know-how, only then will you be ready to become a true power user. Ask yourself, is record production simply a hobby you enjoy in your downtime, or is becoming a world-renowned record producer a dream you have a burning desire for? This is a question you must contemplate in your own time.

The *how* is about the actual technical aspects of using FL Studio to get the most out of its powerful work systems.

From my perspective, and the perspective shared with me by some of the most legendary producers in the industry, if you are to truly master FL Studio, you need to have a strong *why* – without this, this book will still impart practical knowledge, but I fear you may not use it to its full potential.

This chapter will focus on sharing my own experiences using FL Studio in the music industry to help you to capture the mindset and absorption of knowledge required to master the software program. You will benefit from the stories and personal experiences I have had using the program, learn about practical frameworks for absorbing knowledge, and how I leverage the software capabilities to complete productions that are selected and used by major recording artists. You will also be introduced to the basic concepts within FL Studio and how they relate to creating an optimal workflow framework within the software UI. You will be introduced to how you should use the foregoing skillsets in sequence when using FL Studio to create productions in an advanced framework.

In this chapter, we will cover the following topics:

- Perfect practice makes practice perfect
- Mindset and using FL Studio
- Making hits that work for the masses
- Using and organizing the Browser and Channel Rack
- Understanding the Arrangement tool (the Playlist)
- FL Studio's Mixer and plugins

Perfect practice makes practice perfect

When I started producing music, I had no musical theory knowledge, no technical mixing expertise, and no real background in software-based production platforms. I didn't know *how*; I only had my *why* I wanted to learn, and it was simple – I wanted to be one of the greatest producers of my generation when I started. This goal made me take action and learn the *how* as I went on, day in and day out. I gained my experience and eventual mastery of FL Studio through daily repetition and trial and error. There were no "how-to" guides at the time, no videos showing tips and shortcuts, and no guru in my ear to tell me the *how*. I learned these processes over almost two decades spent working with the software.

Quite simply, even though you have access to this book, you need to start creating daily habits in FL Studio that will allow you to program your mind to become so familiar with it that it becomes a part of your everyday schedule. You must be teachable and open-minded to grasp the concepts. To be teachable, you must not only be motivated to read this book and act immediately after each chapter but also ask yourself, "*What am I willing to give up to learn about these frameworks?*". If you are motivated to read and apply this knowledge but not willing to change your life to make time for its contents, then you aren't teachable. This is a key point – teachability is where willingness to learn and willingness to sacrifice come together.

I intend to help guide you through a system framework that will lessen your own trial and error (although some trial and error is good for creative experimentation). In this book, I will walk you through each step in leveraging FL Studio's robust system to give you a framework of how successful industry producers make records that work in the marketplace. Although this book is full of tips and tricks on how to maximize your output when using FL Studio, the key point in truly benefiting from this book is that becoming a master of any skill set requires mastering the basics.

Over the last 17 years, I have charted on American and Canadian billboard charts over 12 times, and dozens of times more globally. I have achieved the pinnacle of recognition in our industry with awards and nominations (including a JUNO nomination – the Canadian Grammy equivalent) and have led a career that allowed me to work with some of the most influential artists, songwriters, and producers of all time. This is a direct result of my dedication and "perfect practice" of FL Studio. FL Studio is one of the best **digital audio workstations (DAWs)** ever created, and if you can truly grasp the concepts I'm about to share with you, you are well on your way to becoming a master of FL Studio.

I say this humbly, but I say this to make a specific point as it relates to "perfect practice." A concept I was introduced to very early in my career is, "Listen to those who have been where you are and have achieved what you desire." If you wish to work with legendary artists, chart on billboards, receive awards and recognition from your peers, and be respected as a top creative, then you have come to the right place. In the modern era, there are many "gurus" who teach tips and tricks in their respective fields, yet they have never actually achieved the success they advise on. If you are to truly learn the concepts that work, you need to understand that the saying "practice makes perfect" is a misnomer, for it's "perfect practice that makes perfect." Therefore, this book will be your guide on what practical information you need to create "perfect practice."

I would suggest that if you are to benefit from the framework presented in this book, you should read and reread the book until you fully grasp the concepts. Every time you read the book, you will be at a new place and have a new perspective, as in the case of ingestion of new knowledge, a reader rarely fully grasps all the meta points in a single read. This section is dedicated to setting the mindset that will help you get the most out of what I'm about to share with you. I want to introduce you to a concept that I didn't invent but stumbled upon early on in my career, which helped me take steps in truly mastering FL Studio. That concept is "the four steps of learning."

There are four steps of learning that every person goes through when ingesting a new skill set:

1. **Unconscious incompetence** – the stage where you don't know what you don't know.

2. **Conscious incompetence** – the stage where you are aware you don't know what you don't know.

3. **Conscious competence** – the stage where you are conscious that you must consciously input effort to achieve results.

4. **Unconscious competence** – the stage where all masters of skill sets live. You are unconsciously competent and performing the task as if you could perform that skill set while not having to think it through.

Masters of FL Studio utilize it as an extension of their creative arm. So, it is vital that if you are to gain the full benefits of this book, you must practice each step until you have fully grasped each concept to be able to perform the process of record creation unconsciously competently. This is easier said than done – in fact, you should note that you never truly become a master, as you are constantly mastering your skill set. Perfection is but an idea, and it's subjective in nature. It is the practicing of the correct frameworks that enables you to truly ascend toward the ever-elusive "perfection."

In addition, these mental framework concepts take five minutes to learn but a lifetime to master (no pun intended). You should know that a master is simply someone who has mastered the basics and continues to build upon their solid foundation upward. It is not that one great record you will create that will enable you to have a career in the music industry, but rather the catalog of work that you will create that will define your accomplishments using FL Studio.

When approaching production in FL Studio, it should be noted that there is, technically speaking, no right or wrong way to create records. Some producers will take a purely technical approach while some may take a totally unorthodox approach, but all arrive at the promised land. Ultimately, music is subjective – its beauty is in the eye of the beholder. The framework I will share with you is what enabled me to have success using my creative approach, but it will be your own creativity coupled with this framework that will drive yours.

Now that we have discussed the concept of perfect practice makes perfect, we will now dig further into the power user's mindset by discussing what makes the correct mindset and how it will lay the foundation for your technical efforts.

Mindset and using FL Studio

This section will focus on sharing personal experiences and information shared with me by some of the world's greatest producers, songwriters, and mixing engineers, which are related to staying disciplined and motivated to continue to be teachable when absorbing new information, and about the mindset commonalities successful producers use when executing productions with FL Studio. This section will also include introducing you to the concept of affirmations and how to create and conceptualize them, and ultimately, you will be prompted to create your own affirmations in the *Exercise* section.

Making hits that work for the masses

I started at the same place as most of you reading this book – I had no money and no experience, just FL Studio and a dream. When I ventured out into the wonderous world of Los Angeles and I had finally managed to get around big producers, engineers, and songwriters, I took the approach of listening and learning before I did anything else.

First, FL Studio is an extremely versatile software tool that must be mastered to create great workflows and workflow habits. Most of FL Studio's theory comes from trial and error, but there are lessons in what I shall impart to you that I learned from observing other masters at work. There are two concepts called the **two pillars of practice**, which are as follows:

- The pillar of mastery as it relates to mindset
- The pillar of action as it relates to FL Studio

The pillar of mindset rules the pillar of action. Without the correct mindset, your actions are fruitless.

The pillar of mindset shows that the following applies to each master I learned from:

- They had a chief objective
- They believed that the objective was possible, even if it was farfetched and outrageous
- They programmed their minds to focus obsessively on their goal by thinking about it daily
- They took daily action toward the goal
- They understood that discipline trumps motivation, for motivation *gets* you going but discipline *keeps* you going
- They had a ferocious appetite for learning everything they could about FL Studio
- They experimented creatively and technically
- They aren't afraid to take risks in creation
- They are perfectionists in their own right

Before I share with you the first key lessons that will set the tone of this book, we need to focus on the concept of affirmations, or narrowing down your *why*.

Successful musicians, producers, engineers, songwriters, and the like all use affirmations to train their subconscious minds to set in motion the action and discipline they will need to start and complete the objective they wish to attain. Think of affirmations as your destination and the technical frameworks of this book as the directions. Affirmations should be recited regularly and updated as goals change. The truth is your subconscious mind doesn't know whether you are capable of achieving a goal or not. That's why it is important to affirm within yourself that you can and will attain your goals.

For the purpose of this book, we will focus on affirmations that are related to your skill set as a producer or composer, and the goals someone in this profession may have. It's important to write down your affirmations and verbalize them in private regularly. I say this because most people who don't share the same mindset of setting goals will think you are crazy! If your goals aren't crazy, they aren't big enough. It's important when writing affirmations that you frame them when you write them as something that has already been accomplished. When writing an affirmation, you want to write it as if you have already achieved the goal, not as if you want to achieve the goal. We want to affirm that you are heading there, not simply dreaming of heading there.

For example, a bad affirmation would be, "*I want to be the best music producer ever.*" The reason this affirmation isn't powerful is because it implies you want to be, not that you are. An example of a good affirmation to the contrary would be, "*I'm excited and happy knowing I'm the best music producer ever.*" This implies you already are, and not simply wishing you are.

This is *very* important! So please, take note and practice writing goals and objectives correctly – it absolutely matters, and whether through coincidence or serendipity, you will see your goals unfold if you internalize these objectives through repetition. I want to make it clear, there are a lot of books and seminars that purport simply wishing your goals into existence; this is a misnomer. When you have identified a goal, it must be followed by these:

- A genuine internal feeling of excitement
- Consistent action toward achieving that goal

Without these two components, you are simply just writing words on a page, and it won't help you internalize the techniques taught in this book. If you are writing goals and affirmations and you feel doubt, negativity, or frustration, that just simply means you need to dial back and focus on the next logical step instead of the objective you feel doubt over. This is important as when you feel doubt, you internally don't believe you will get the goal, and you won't! On the contrary, if you feel motivated, positive, and accelerated when you write a goal down, you're in the sweet spot and you need to follow through with taking action.

Again, let's simplify the concept of affirmations by following these steps:

1. Write your objective down as if you have already achieved it.
2. Consciously repeat it to yourself every day.
3. Feel excited and motivated when you repeat it.
4. Take ruthless action until it is achieved.

Remember, objectives are moving targets – you can only go as far as you can see, and when you get there, you will be able to see a little further. Let's look at some further affirmation examples you can use or modify as they relate to this book:

- I'm thrilled and excited that I have mastered FL Studio and have worked with some of the biggest artists and songwriters in the industry
- I'm grateful that I have earned Grammy Awards and nominations using FL Studio in my genre
- I'm humbled that I've been able to create a career using FL Studio that allows me to earn a fantastic living for myself and my family

Now that we have explored the concept of affirmations and the art of setting goals, we will discuss the concept of viewing growth through the lens of what I call the mental balance scale.

The mental balance scale

Mental balance is simply the idea of taking action on your goals, objectives, and clearly defined affirmations that you must be balanced in your approach to both the *how* and the *why*. Although this sounds simple in nature, the truth is (and this may go over your head), the most important part of mental balance is actually your *why*. The conscious mind nourishes the subconscious, which in turn exerts its influence on your actions and thoughts within your reality.

As we discussed in the *Perfect practice makes practice perfect* section, without a strong *why*, you won't put in the required effort to learn the *how*. The concept of mental balance is a "conventional thought" or "conventional wisdom." To be super successful, I need you to start thinking outside of the box, outside of conventional wisdom. Your status as a producer, composer, or arranger using FL Studio is a culmination of all of the thoughts and habits you have created to date. If you continue to think and do what you always thought and done, you will continue to get what you have always got!

All of the most notable producers I have worked with in the business know this, and they continue to be teachable even after all of the success they achieve. They continue to set new goals, they go as far as they can see, and when they get there, they know they can see a little farther. The art of goal setting is knowing that there will always be another step, another aim, another objective once you complete an affirmation. The most successful producers I have worked with, in most cases, aren't musical geniuses, they weren't Mozart when they started, but they dreamed big. They had a powerful *why* that drove them to learn the *how* as they progressed in their careers.

The truth is with FL Studio, you don't need to be an expert in musical theory, playing instruments, or composing when you start. FL Studio is a powerful tool that gives you everything you need to make your ideas come to life. It is practicing with the correct mindset that will enable you to master the software and become a great musical theory expert, instrument player, and composer.

Now that we have covered the basics of mindset as it relates to becoming a true power user, I'm going to show you the *how*.

Using and organizing the Browser and Channel Rack

In this section, you will learn what the Browser and Channel Rack are and how to use them efficiently to create optimum workflow capabilities.

The Browser represents the organization and sound selection palette. This contains all of the FL Studio stock sounds and menu options and will contain the custom workflow folders we will create in this section. The Channel Rack is the tool you will use to plug in sound files (kicks, snares, hi hats, and sound design) to then create rhythmic patterns. The two are intimately connected, as sound files in the Browser will ultimately go into the Channel Rack.

We will now explore both the Browser and Channel Rack in detail in the next sections.

Exploring the Browser tool

This figure is a screenshot of the FL Studio software system:

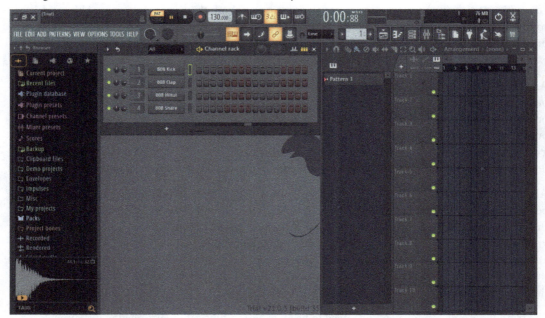

Figure 1.1: On the left, you will see the Browser, and in the middle, you will see the Channel Rack

The Browser on the left side window is the library to all of your sound kits. Organizing the Browser from the Windows folder externally is key to setting up an optimum workflow. The objective of organizing the Browser is to find the location of your go-to sounds and sound kits that you can begin to memorize through your workflow to create "clicking" habits through repetition, and to organize your go-to sounds into custom folders, which saves you time searching FL's robust sound kit sections each time you want to start a new production.

For this book, I will be focusing on using the stock sound kits that FL Studio provides, but as you grow as a producer, you will likely purchase or create your own sound design that you will incorporate into your FL Studio workstation folder.

Now, let's start our journey of learning how to master FL Studio by following these steps:

1. When you open FL Studio, you will see an option selection on the left side of the window, as seen here:

Figure 1.2: Packs folder within the FL Studio Browser

Clicking the **Packs** tab will open up FL Studios' stock selection of sounds, which you can use to start making the bare bones of how your production will sound.

2. To create your own folders that generate tabs in FL Studio, right-click on **Packs** and click **Open** to start using the Windows Explorer tab externally from the software in the location you have installed FL Studio, under the Image-Line folder. Then, you will be able to access the Patches folder, as seen here:

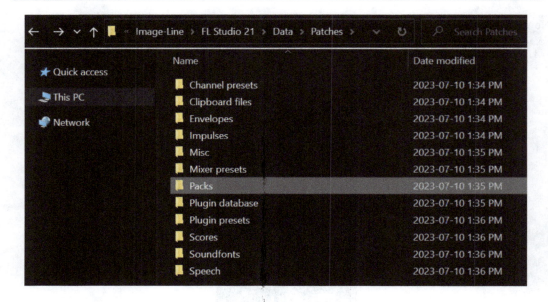

Figure 1.3: Windows Explorer folder, Packs

Note

In Windows 10, the application formerly known as Windows Explorer underwent a transformation and is now referred to as File Explorer. Please note that the terminology and naming may vary depending on the specific version of Windows being used.

By default, FL Studio gets installed in your main drive, under the `Image-Line` folder. You will then click through the `FL Studio 20 | Data | Patches` folders. This is where all of your sound kits will be installed and ready for organization.

3. Once you have accessed the `Patches` folder, you can create your own folders from within to start organizing the sounds we will create in later chapters. For this example, I've chosen to name the new folder `Power Users Drum Kit`:

Figure 1.4: Power Users Drum Kit folder within the Image-Line install folder

The potential is limitless for how you want to organize your Browser – you may only have one or two folders, or you may have many – it's up to you what makes sense in your own toolkit and preference.

4. Once you create the folder, you will now see it populate within FL Studio under the **Packs** tab in the Browser:

Figure 1.5: Power Users Drum Kit within the Browser

In *Chapter 4*, we will create drums and WAV sounds so that you can begin to formulate your own unique sound, and ultimately, revisit strengthening your workflow templates to include drums, VSTs, and mixing plugins. For now, we are simply getting you used to organizing the Browser to fit this specific workflow habit.

In addition to creating custom sound design, you may find specific sounds you already have or ones that are within FL Studio and are your favorite – you can simply copy and paste these files into your custom folder to shorten the workflow by "clicking" within the DAW, as I have done here:

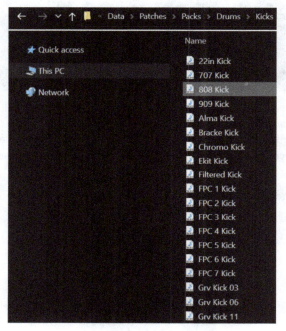

Figure 1.6: Windows Explorer | FL Studio 20 | Data | Patches | Packs | Drums | Kicks

In *Figure 1.7*, we will locate the 808 kick contained in `Data | Patches | Packs | Power Users Drum Kit`:

Figure 1.7: Windows Explorer folder | FL Studio 20 | Data | Packs | Power Users Drum Kit | 808 Kick

The reality is you do not need a million different kick sounds to create great records. In fact, most of the high-level producers I know typically only use a small number of drum sounds in every record they create (although they mix them according to what type of feel and vibe the record permits – we will discuss this in *Chapter 4*).

5.   You can start adding your go-to sounds in your custom folder by locating your sound file in the specific FL Studio stock folder, copying the file, and simply pasting it into your own custom folder – this will populate the file in your FL Studio Browser under the **Packs** tab:

Figure 1.8: The Power Users Drum Kit within the Packs folder within the FL Studio Browser

Viola! You have now created your first workflow benefit by moving your favorite kick into your first custom folder. This allows you to avoid going through each pack in the Browser to find it the next time you wish to use it in a production.

> **Important note**
>
> In *Chapter 2*, we will delve into utilizing the Piano Roll for crafting custom sound designs and enhancing your workflow practices.

Exploring the Channel Rack

The Channel Rack is one of the most important tools within FL Studio that you can master – it is where you will add your VST's instruments, and where you will add drum sounds. I use the Channel Rack to create the backbone of my drum sequencing, and ultimately, the foundation for what the track can become. To begin optimizing the workflow and using it efficiently, we need to create a preloaded template with your go-to sound already loaded. This will save you time when you are experimenting with new ideas or just want to explore your creativity.

The following figure shows the Channel Rack. This is located in the main window when you open FL Studio and, by default, populates the center of the screen:

Figure 1.9: The Channel Rack within the FL Studio Browser

To start loading sounds into the Channel Rack, simply right-click the desired sound in the Browser and click **Open in new channel**, as seen here:

Figure 1.10: The Open in new channel selection

You may ask, if we are organizing files in the Browser, why don't we just preload everything into a channel rack template? To avoid confusion, understand that a channel rack template is a basic foundational template, and we just want to have our basic sounds loaded – your custom folders may end up having hundreds of different sounds contained within them as you grow your sound design library. So, this is to keep your setup simple and give you the best place to start a new record.

To create a template, we are going to simply add the desired sounds into the Channel Rack. This will import the sound into the Channel Rack. You can do this for as many sounds as you like. Once you have added the desired sounds into the Channel Rack, click **FILE** | **Save as…**:

Figure 1.11: Clicking FILE | Save as… within the FL Studio main page window

This will bring up the project folder within the FL Studio Window Explorer. Name your template to your liking, and save the template FLP file. This will now act as your go-to workflow template. Clicking **Save** will add this FLP file to your Projects folder, and it can now be used for future projects:

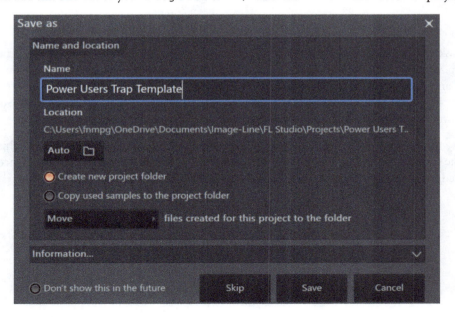

Figure 1.12: FILE | Save As, creating a template name

You can get creative with the different templates you want to use. For example, you may wish to create a hip hop template, or a trap template that only preloads specific sounds for those types of productions. I recommend keeping it simple and adding to your templates as you become more comfortable with your production skill set. For example, I have named this template `Power Users - Hip Hop Template`:

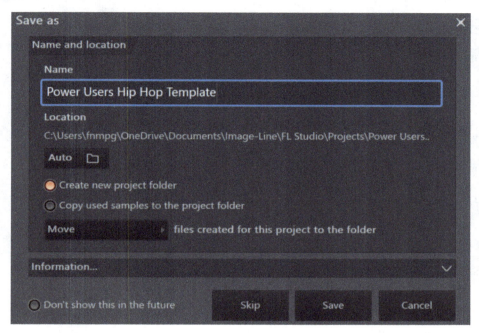

Figure 1.13: FILE | FL Studio | Projects | Save As | File name

Now, let's talk about how the Playlist tool works, and what we can do with it to create full productions!

Understanding the Arrangement tool (the Playlist)

The Playlist tool is where we will create the arrangement for your production. Accordingly, FL Studio's arrangement tool is essentially the function that enables you to combine all the various elements of your song into a unified framework. Organizing the pieces of a puzzle to create a complete image comes to mind. You can drag and drop your different patterns (such as your drums, bass line, melody, etc.) into a timeline that represents the duration of your song using the Playlist tool. From there, you can easily edit and arrange the various components of your song to produce a full track that flows smoothly from beginning to end. In other words, the Playlist tool is essential for transforming your unique musical ideas into a finished, polished piece of music. In *Chapter 6*, I will show you how we set up templates that the pros use to structure songs within the Playlist tool. For now, let's dive into the basics of how it works.

The Playlist tool is located on the right-hand side of the FL Studio window. The playlist tool shows a grid with the option to place different channel rack loops into a "track" segment.

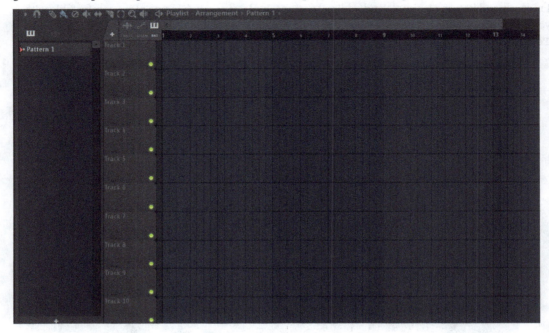

Figure 1.14: Arrangement window

When you use the FL Studio Playlist tool, we typically create patterns for each element of your production, such as your drums, bass line, and melody. Once you have your patterns created, you simply drag and drop them into the Playlist tool window. From there, you can arrange the different patterns in the timeline, using the mouse to move them around and adjust their lengths as needed.

Within the Playlist tool, you can also add different automation clips to control things such as volume, panning, and effects, and use the Mixer window to adjust the levels of each individual element in your song. It may take a little practice to get the hang of it, but with a little bit of patience and experimentation, you should be able to create a fully arranged track that sounds great.

The reason we create templates for workflow optimization is to ease the burden of creating arrangements from scratch each time we start a new project in FL Studio. It can be complex, and a formula should be followed.

To get the most out of the FL Studio Playlist tool and maximize the workflow in it, it's important to take some time to really plan out your song structure ahead of time; this is why, in *Chapter 6*, I will give you the exact templates to have your workflow maximized for the greatest return on time and input.

A great working template will help you to organize your ideas and create a cohesive flow that keeps your listener engaged. When you have the basic idea of your song structure, you can start experimenting with different patterns and sounds to find the ones that work best together.

As an example, and as we will discuss in *Chapter 6*, the new formula is 4-bar intro – 12-bar verse – 8-bar hook – 12-bar verse – 8-bar hook. In *Figure 1.15*, this will appear as such in the Playlist tool.

In *Chapter 6*, we will create a modern pop/billboard formula arrangement template that is time-tested and works. As a quick example, let's use this bar framework to input blank blocks into the playlist tool. The finished arrangement using this formula will appear as follows:

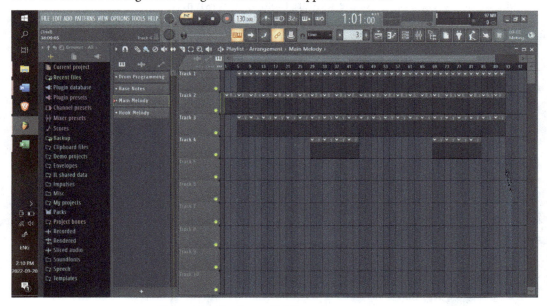

Figure 1.15: Playlist tool | full song arrangement

Creating working templates as saved project files will make it easy to start manufacturing records like clockwork. The key here is to establish workflow habits that allow you to focus primarily on being creative and filling each of the blocks in the playlist with catchy chords, hypnotic melodies, and funky bass lines.

Now, let's talk about the FL Studio Mixer and its mixing plugins. These are the tools that you will use to get the most out of your sonic crafting; whether we are adding things such as reverb to create space, or delay to add rhythmic echoes, these tools are your bread and butter for crafting unique sound design with FL Studio's key plugins.

FL Studio's Mixer and plugins

The FL Studio Mixer is the equivalent of your **Solid State Logic** (**SSL**) board in the classic studio setup – this is where you will load all of your sound kits and VSTs to start mixing and mastering sounds. In addition, this is where you can get creative with stacking mixing plugins, such as reverb and delays, to create unique sounding tracks and sound designs. Let's walk through getting your mixer template set up.

Setting up a mixing template

First, look in the top-right corner of the software toolbar, as shown here:

Figure 1.16: Software toolbar | Mixer tool in yellow

Click the highlighted button on the toolbar to open the mixer:

Figure 1.17: The mixer

Now that we have the mixer open, I'm going to share the first hack, and it's a hack because it goes against conventional wisdom. In the **Master** channel, you will see (in *Figure 1.17*) that FL Studio automatically loads up the **Fruity Limiter** plugin (highlighted in red in *Figure 1.17*). This plugin limits the volume of the overall Master track. Although you may end up experimenting in your mixing with this as an overall mastering plugin, when crafting ideas, it's a good idea to turn it off or delete it totally. The reason is when you are sound designing your draft production, you may want the kick and snare to go above 0 in the volume mixer to get that heavy feel, as it can get in the way of letting those sounds really shine. Just click the circle button next to the plugin, and it will turn it off.

Let's click the input button off, as seen in *Figure 1.18* in the highlighted red circle:

Figure 1.18: The mixer's Fruity Limiter plugin

Now that we have a "clean" mixer, let's walk through the mixer settings from a basic view:

Figure 1.19: The mixer's current channel selection

Let's walk through each of the **Mixer** applications as seen in *Figure 1.19*. These are all of the tools contained within the mixer and how they function:

- **Current channel**: This is the highlighted section in *Figure 1.19*, which allows you to add and insert specific plugins into the section you have selected.

- **Master channel**: The **Master** channel is where you will add plugins to affect the entire track. This is used for mastering the finished product and adds the desired plugin to all tracks in the mixer. I don't recommend adding plugins to this when you are simply drafting productions for the purposes of creativity.

- **Inserts**: Inserting plugins into a channel on the mixer will add the desired plugin to the selected sample sound. For example, the Reverb or Delay plugin will be added to the sample.

- **Mute and Solo feature**: When you add plugins to a specific channel, you can mute and unmute the effect by clicking this button.

- **Panning feature**: As suggested, this allows you to pan the inserted sample sound left or right.

- **Reverse polarity**: This can be used to change the frequency of the selected sample sound. Reversing polarity is a technique that lets us flip the phase of an audio signal. It's like turning the waveform upside down, and a cool way to experiment with your sound and create interesting effects.

- **Swap left and right channels**: This will allow you to swap sample channels left and right.

- **Stereo separation**: Select Mono or Stereo for the selected sample sound.

- **Volume**: This is used for adjusting the sample sound volume up or down.

Now that we have gone over each of the high-level functions of the Mixer, it's important to recognize that these will come in handy when we are practicing the mixing techniques discussed in *Chapter 7*. For now, get familiar with them inside FL Studio, and feel free to experiment with how they work.

Next, let's discuss adding sounds to the Mixer so we can start to craft the sonics of each individual sound layer using the FL Studio plugins and tools.

Adding sounds to the mixer

Let's talk about how we can start adding sounds to the mixer. First, click on the desired sound you want to load into the mixer. For this example, I have chosen to use an **808 Kick** sample. Now, right-click on the selected channel you want to load into the mixer and right-click the channel to bring up the drop-down menu. Then, click **Route selected channels to this track**:

Figure 1.20: Mixer, channel selection, 808 Kick

Once we have loaded the kick sample into the mixer, let's explore how to add plugins to it to start getting our mixing template ready for sound design and overall mixing. This drop-down menu will show you a selection of preinstalled FL Studio mixer plugins:

Figure 1.21: The mixer, channel selection, 808 Kick, plugin input

There are a few key mixer plugins we are going to add to our workflow template; these are referenced in the *FL Studio key plugins* section.

For kick samples, the main plugin we want to load is **Fruity parametric EQ 2**. This will allow us to stretch the kick sound to give it the heavy feel we are looking for when making pop or rap records:

Figure 1.22: EQ 2 plugin as loaded in the mixer

When it comes to kick samples, don't overcomplicate their mixer plugins. The key is that the kick is simply the driving sound in the track that keeps the rhythm section intact. As a general hack, making kicks "heavy" with the EQ 2 plugin is as simple as moving the number **2** filter slider to 74 **Hertz (Hz)** in a general direction. Each kick sample sound you use will have a different natural feel to it, and you will want to slide it around to find the punchiest spot for it to fit in the overall track, but as a point of general direction, this is where it should be:

Figure 1.23: EQ 2 plugin

Now, let's load up our snare sample into the mixer. Once we have loaded it into the mixer channel, the two key plugins we want to add to its mixer stack are **Fruity parametric EQ 2** and **Fruity Reeverb 2**:

Figure 1.24: Mixer, slot channel input for plugin tools

I will walk you through more on specific plugins in the sound design and creating a signature sound in *Chapter 4* – for now, let's get familiar with the amazing stock plugins that FL Studio gives you from the outset.

FL Studio key plugins

FL Studio has a lot of base plugins. These are the plugins you should learn, experiment with, and get familiar with. The truth, and the overall high-level knowledge of my framework, is to keep things simple. Even today, I have an onslaught of third-party software plugins, but I still use these FL Studio stock plugins in every one of my productions. These seven plugins are the keystone in my stack.

Each one of these can be used to get creative with chords, melodies, and drum sounds – each of these is the base for sound designing in FL Studio:

- **Gross Beat** – This is used primarily in rap and hip hop productions to augment chords, melodies, and leads to create unique sound design and rhythmic outputs. Used by almost all of the most successful producers who use FL Studio, it's a great tool for accessing sidechaining, slowing samples to half-time, gating, and more.

Figure 1.25: Gross Beat VST

- **Fruity Delay 3** – FL Studio has a few different Delay plugins. This is by far the best and most flexible plugin they have for delay effects.

Figure 1.26: Fruity Delay 3 VST

- **Fruity Reeverb 2** – This is the better, more flexible, and more advanced version of its sister, Fruity Reeverb. This will allow you to add reverb on your samples loaded into the Channel Rack, and I use it all the time to this day.

Figure 1.27: Fruity Reeverb 2 VST

- **Maximus** – This is an interesting plugin that acts as a limiter but can be used in a non-conventional way to add bass to 808s, guitars, and drum sounds.

Figure 1.28: Maximus VST

- **Fruity Love Philter** – This is by far the best and most versatile filter plugin in FL Studio. This allows you to get creative with filter effects and augmenting samples.

Figure 1.29: Fruity Love Philter VST

- **Fruity Parametric EQ 2** – This is the only EQ I use today, and I have used it since I started producing back in the mid-2000s. Other third-party EQ software exists that other producers may prefer, but I really like this plugin for its simple UI and straightforward mixing usability. For example, each frequency range can be easily mixed and augmented using the visualizer, whereas using hardware-based EQ tools requires a greater sensitivity to ear and pitch.

Figure 1.30: Fruity Parametric EQ 2 VST

- **Fruity Flangus** – This is a Flanger plugin that allows you to add a flanger effect to your samples and VSTs. I use this on chords, snares, hi hats, and bass sounds for added effect.

Figure 1.31: Fruity Flangus VST

FL Studio offers a plethora of plugins and mixing tools you may want to explore further as you become more proficient in using the software system. But as I have said before, keep your production workflow simple – most of the modern-day pop music that is created stems from really cool and hypnotic scoring and mixing that creates the feel of a record. Mastering these specific plugins will give you all you really need to start creating records that will work in the marketplace and lead you on your journey to becoming a true power user of FL Studio.

Summary

Throughout my journey of learning music production and mastering FL Studio, which has spanned almost two decades, I have come to realize the importance of daily habits and repetition in becoming a true master of any skill. In my experience, teachability requires not only the motivation to learn but also the willingness to make sacrifices. I have developed a framework for learning that consists of four stages: unconscious incompetence, conscious incompetence, conscious competence, and unconscious competence. It's crucial to master the basics and engage in perfect practice to achieve success in music production.

I would advise anyone looking to learn to read and reread this book until they fully grasp the concepts. Additionally, I have introduced a concept called "the four steps of learning," which can help streamline the learning process.

We also learned how to use the Browser tool and Channel Rack, learned about the basics of the Playlist tool, workflow techniques, and frameworks, and worked through FL Studio's mixer and plugins. These concepts act as the foundation for the frameworks I'm going to share in *Chapter 2*, and I'm excited to start sharing some very specific technical frameworks.

We can now move on to *Chapter 2*, where I will share with you the secrets of how I make records work within the marketplace using creative approaches to sound design and score techniques – the real secrets!

Exercise

Exercise A. I challenge you to write down your own affirmations; take the examples from this chapter or create totally new ones as, without direction, you're just driving to nowhere. Always have a destination, a goal, a reason *why* you want to learn something if you are serious about it.

Exercise B. I challenge you to create a series of custom sounds using the techniques described in this chapter and create a folder within your own Browser to start developing a signature sound.

Exercise C. I challenge you to create a mixing template using your custom drum sounds with the plugins mentioned in *FL Studio's Mixer and plugins* section.

Part 2: Creating Music with FL Studio

In this part, you will explore a series of essential techniques and concepts to master the FL Studio toolbox and elevate your music production skills to a professional level. Throughout this journey, you will be introduced to various aspects of music production, each part focusing on distinct elements. You will understand the nuances of approaching the FL Studio toolbox to craft Billboard-worthy records and unlock the full potential of FL Studio's stock sound kits, VSTs, and plugins as you learn how to leverage these tools to create unique and captivating sounds. We will dive into the art of drum programming and arrangements and learn how to structure your arrangements using a Billboard framework, incorporating bar counting, transition points, and arrangements that breathe life into your recordings.

In this part, we have the following chapters:

- *Chapter 2, From the Piano Roll to the Billboard Charts*
- *Chapter 3, Creating Your Signature Sound*
- *Chapter 4, Working through Drum Programming and Arrangements*
- *Chapter 5, Approaching Melody and Composition Theory*
- *Chapter 6, A Billboard-Ready Production Arrangement*

2
From the Piano Roll to the Billboard Charts

Congratulations! You have just been introduced to the concepts of how a strong mindset and the art of setting goals will be the driving factor in your ability to master FL Studio and create records that can chart on billboard charts I recommend you read and reread *Chapter 1* to fully grasp the high-level concepts covered in it. As I mentioned previously, you can only build as high as your foundation is deep.

Now that we have established that your foundation must be based on a strong mindset, I can now show you how to master FL Studio to realize your goals, dreams, and desires as a creative entrepreneur. After all, being a producer, composer, or record producer is mostly a career choice that falls into the self-employed category. In the old days, record producers tended to get in-house jobs at major record companies, but those days are gone, and nowadays, very few producers get these types of roles with major labels, it will be up to you to truly move forward in your career. I will say, its up to you to make your career happen, but if you should listen to what I impart to you, take action, and dedicate yourself, I promise you will go further than where you are today in your career.

The industry is full of pitfalls and winding roads that only experience can guide you through. You will learn by fire, and every adversity that you overcome will make you stronger. My hope is that by reading this book, you will have the necessary skills to master FL Studio and gain a mindset that you can achieve and be anything you want to be in your career. Whether that's simply being a better creative or the greatest Power User of all time, it is what *you* want to get out of life that is important. It is in this chapter that we will form meaningful connections about how I use FL Studio to create records that captivate fans, get the attention of multi-platinum and Grammy Award-winning artists, and help market products and multimedia content. Now that we have a good grasp of what your *why* is, let's talk about your *how*!

In this chapter, we will cover the following topics:

- Using the Piano Roll
- How to use the Piano Roll's features to your advantage
- How to create chords and melodies that work
- Building MIDI templates in the Piano Roll
- Using the stamp tool to create chords
- Optimizing workflow in the Piano Roll
- Workflow optimization hacks

Using the Piano Roll

The **Piano Roll** is FL Studio's internal MIDI keyboard that is used to create chord and melody structures and scoring. The Piano Roll has some incredible features that allow you to use FL Studio's intuitive software to draw, click, and paint notes into the scoring system. It also contains features that allow you to use algorithmic tools to create base note sequences and leads, as well as edit note lengths in bar sequences.

Now, it's time to show you how using the Piano Roll with certain frameworks can take you from FL Studio to the Billboard charts. When it comes to creating records, the Piano Roll is where you will create all of your melodies and chord progressions within FL Studio. I will explain how to use Piano Roll with a power user's mindset to create hypnotic and attention-grabbing melodies and chord progressions. For now, I will walk you through the basics of what it is and how you can get the most out of it as a tool for creative input.

Opening the Piano Roll

To locate and open the Piano Roll, look in the upper right-hand corner of the admin bar at the icon with the piano notes (see the highlighted icon in *Figure 2.1*):

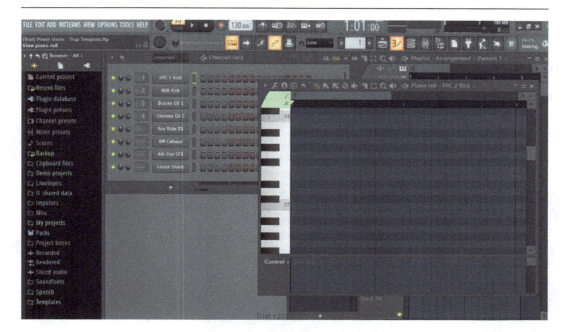

Figure 2.1: Viewing the Piano Roll from within the Channel Rack

The Piano Roll will open and show piano keys and **OPTIONS** in its top taskbar:

Figure 2.2: The Piano Roll

In *Figure 2.2*, middle C is represented by **C5** (as highlighted).

How to use the piano roll

The Piano Roll is an integrated tool to click and compose notes to create topline melodies and chord progressions. In addition to clicking on notes, you can connect a MIDI keyboard or simply use your typing keyboard to compose within the Piano Roll.

To sync a MIDI keyboard to FL studio, you will need to have an external keyboard, install its software separately (if any), and click the **OPTIONS** tab, as shown in *Figure 2.3*:

Figure 2.3: Settings | OPTIONS

Once you open the **OPTIONS** tab and click **MIDI settings**, FL Studio will open a pop-up window where your MIDI keyboard will populate, as shown in *Figure 2.4*:

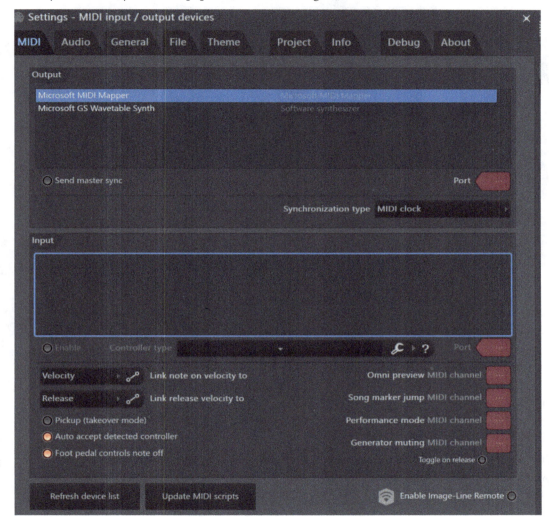

Figure 2.4: Settings | OPTIONS | MIDI input / output devices

Simply sync the keyboard, and FL Studio should begin to integrate directly into the Piano Roll.

In *Figure 2.4*, under the **Input** window, you can see **(generic controller)**. When you click this, FL Studio will show you a list of MIDI players that can be easily synced to the software.

Figure 2.5: The MIDI input selection window

If you are using a MIDI interface (whether it be a keyboard or drum machine), it's easy to integrate this into FL Studio. Once synced up, you can now use your preferred MIDI interface directly in the Piano Roll. Using the keyboard, you can simply type when the Piano Roll is open, or when you select a sound or VST within the Channel Rack, it's simple and easy within the Channel Rack. Once we open the Piano Roll with our preferred sound or **VST** (also known as **virtual software technology**), we can start adding notes with your mouse. I will discuss this in greater detail in the *Getting started with the Piano Roll* section.

During my career, I have used both a MIDI keyboard and a computer keyboard – it's more of a preference per your understanding of music theory and piano-playing skill set, but for me personally, I use a combo of the computer keyboard to write ideas and then augment notes with the clicking feature. This may seem counter-intuitive, and it does limit your playing ability when trying new things creatively, but it makes your laptop or computer a music-composing powerhouse if you can master it. A lot of "trap" producers simply click in notes and use their ear to find the best melodies and chords they like. There really is no right or wrong way to approach music; after all, it's more about keeping your productions simple and leaving room for the artist to record over the finished product.

Getting started with the Piano Roll

To get started, choose your preferred method to use the Piano Roll (the MIDI keyboard, clicking, or the computer keyboard), and let's find a VST to play with in it.

To add a VST into your Channel Rack to start composing in with the Piano Roll, right-click in the Channel Rack and you will see a drop-down menu. Click **Insert | FL Keys**:

Figure 2.6: Insert | Insert Open | VST Plugins | FL Keys

This will bring up another drop-down menu and populate all of FL Studio's stock VSTs. If you have implemented third-party VSTs into FL Studio, you will see these VST's populate your VST folder as well. For this example, we will load up the **FL Keys** VST. This is FL Studio's stock piano VST.

Now that we have loaded the FL Keys VST, we can begin playing with it in the Piano Roll.

Figure 2.7: FL Keys loaded on screen

To open the Piano Roll for the FL Keys VST, and future VSTs in the Channel Rack, right-click the **VST** button and click **Piano Roll**:

Figure 2.8: FL Keys | the Piano Roll open selection

Once we have opened the Piano Roll for this particular VST, we can start to dive into how to use it to create melodies and chord progressions. Let's open the Piano Roll feature in the selected VST FL Keys:

Figure 2.9: The Piano Roll open selection

Now that we have loaded a VST and opened the Piano Roll, lets walk through all of the amazing things you can do in the Piano Roll to maximize creativity and get rid of writer's block (or "beat block" as it is known in the producer community).

Recording in the Piano Roll

There are two definitive ways to input notes into the Piano Roll – mouse-clicking and recording from a MIDI interface or using the computer keyboard.

In order to use a MIDI interface or computer keyboard, go to the top of the FL Studio window and find the red record button. Left-click this icon, and you will be prompted by FL Studio to ask where to record the notes. Now, click the **Everything** menu option so that we can start recording the Piano Roll right away:

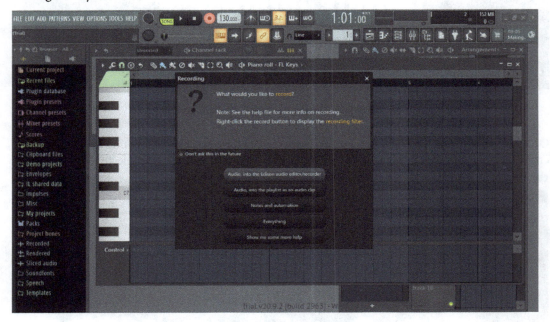

Figure 2.10: The recording selection

When you click **Everything**, you can use the record button when the Piano Roll is open. I recommend using the 3-2-1 feature to introduce the four-count metronome to prompt you before live recording kicks in. Although *Figure 2.11* says **3.2.1**, but the recording will start on a four count for the avoidance of doubt – plus, when you get into in-studio sessions, this is jargon that you and the engineer will throw back and forth at each other. The following screenshot shows the Rec in 3-2-1 prompt:

Figure 2.11: The menu bar and recording option

You can now play and input notes directly into the piano by using your MIDI interface and computer keyboard, for example:

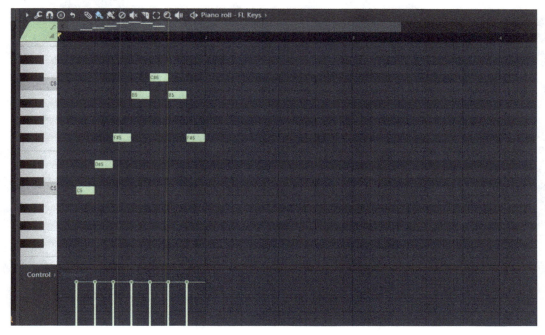

Figure 2.12: The Piano Roll note selection

Now, let's go over the top taskbar with the Piano Roll.

Figure 2.13: The Piano Roll top task bar menu

Within the Piano Roll, the taskbar gives you different tools that allow you to add and edit notes, create riffs, randomize notes, quantize, and work within your Piano Roll composition. There'll be more on this in the *Quantizing notes* section. To keep things simple, the main buttons you need to master are the **draw**, **paint**, **slice**, and **zoom** buttons, which are discussed next:

- The drawing tool allows you to place a single note when clicking a corresponding **Piano Roll** keynote:

Figure 2.14: The Piano Roll short note input

To lengthen a note, simply hover over the end (or edge) of the green key, and by clicking it, you can drag the note to the desired length:

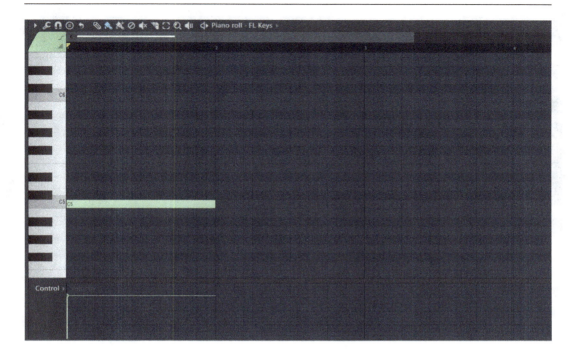

Figure 2.15: The Piano Roll long note input

When scoring using the Piano Roll, a note can be scored as short or shorter notes (staccato notes) or longer notes (legato notes), depending on your preference when creating chord or melody leads.

- The paint tool(s) have two selections and work in a similar fashion to the drawing tool; however, the highlighted **Paint Brush** allows you to add additional notes when holding the left mouse key on the desired keynote:

Figure 2.16: The long Piano Roll note input

- The slice tool within the Piano Roll allows you to cut off note lengths, similar to hovering over the desired note, by left-clicking the mouse and dragging the length left or right to find the desired note length:

Figure 2.17: The slicer tool on the long Piano Roll note input

- The zoom feature comes in handy when you compose loops over a four-bar or eight-bar length. Rarely will you need to do this, unless you create complex loops, and this is pretty self-explanatory, as it is a tool that simply allows you to zoom in and out of the window screen. A trick when using the zoom tool is to simply hold down the *Ctrl* button on your keyboard and use your mouse wheel up or down to zoom in and out.

Now that we have described the basics of painting, drawing, slicing, and zooming in and out, let's discuss some of the additional features that FL Studio within the Piano Roll tool can bring to your production workflow.

Some useful features of FL Studio

When you click the right arrow at the beginning of the taskbar, as shown in *Figure 2.13*, there are many different options and selection tools. To keep things simple, you can experiment with all of them as you spend more time in FL studio, but in my almost 20 years of using the software, the most important two drop-down items in its menu are the **Tools** and **Snap** tabs.

Within the **Tools** tab, the key selections that we will use are **Riff machine...**, the **Chop...** selection, and the **Quantize...** tab.

Figure 2.18: The Piano Roll menu | Tools

First, we will discuss the **riff machine**.

The riff machine

This tool will help you randomize piano notes to create potential melodies, chords, and rhythms when you have writer's block. When you select this option, the Piano Roll will randomize notes within itself, based upon a pre-selection tool, as shown in *Figure 2.19*. This will allow you to randomize notes, chords, or progressions.

Figure 2.19: Piano Roll – riff machine

Because the riff machine will randomize notes, it is important to remember that you should customize these notes once they have been implemented, as they are typically useful for creating a starting point rather than a Billboard-charting loop.

When you use the Piano Roll, notes will automatically be quantized to the lines within the **Piano Roll** window.

Figure 2.20: The menu bar | Line selection

This is great for drum programming and finding perfect placement of notes per music theory timing, but there may be times when you want to move notes off grid for a creative approach (for example, when you traditionally recorded piano players in big studios, not all notes would be quantized, as is done in software-based recording and production techniques). The **Line** button can be altered by simply hitting the *Backspace* button on your keyboard.

The Chop feature

In FL Studio, the Chop feature in the Piano Roll allows you to split a MIDI pattern into smaller, individual notes or groups of notes, making it easier to edit and arrange your melody or rhythm.

The Chop tool can be used for many different creative approaches, but in modern music production, it is mostly used for hi-hat and rhythmic augmentation. As an example, in modern trap or pop music, most hi-hat patterns will have a triplet roll – we will use the Chop tool inside FL Studio's Piano Roll to manipulate our MIDI patterns to create triplet rolls. Let's discuss how to do this now.

First, open the Piano Roll for the pattern you want to chop by clicking on the small icon that looks like a piano keyboard on the left side of the pattern. Now, select the Chop tool in the Piano Roll toolbar or by pressing the *C* key on your keyboard:

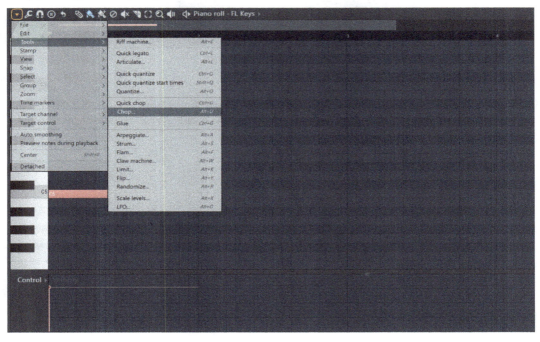

Figure 2.21: The Piano Roll | Tools | Chop…

This will bring up the Chop tool interface. You can use the Chop tool to split MIDI notes by time lengths, using its **Time mul** knob. You can also adjust the width of the chop by dragging the edges of the selection of the green MIDI note, as shown in *Figure 2.23*. Let's look at the Chop tool in *Figure 2.22*:

Figure 2.22: The Chop tool

You can now edit and separate a MIDI pattern into smaller pieces and arrange them in any order you desire by using the **Chopper** feature in the Piano Roll, as shown in *Figure 2.23*. For this example, I have highlighted the chopped sequence in red:

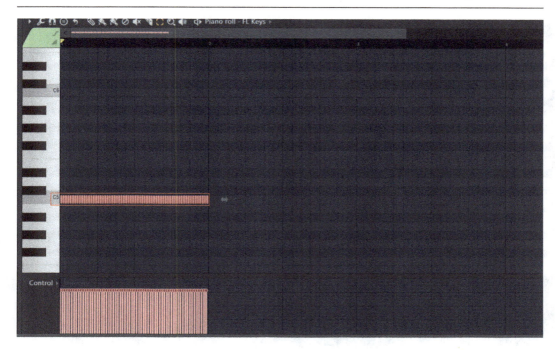

Figure 2.23: The Piano Roll | a chopped sequence

This can be helpful to write intricate rhythms or melodies with intricate patterns.

Now, let's talk about using the Quantize tool to space MIDI patterns within FL Studio's Piano Roll tool.

Quantizing notes

Let's discuss the basics of quantizing. **Quantizing** is what allows the software to properly align each note to the closest bar within the Piano Roll. To do this, let's look at a generic note progression unquantized and recognize how each note is slightly off the bar points in *Figure 2.24*:

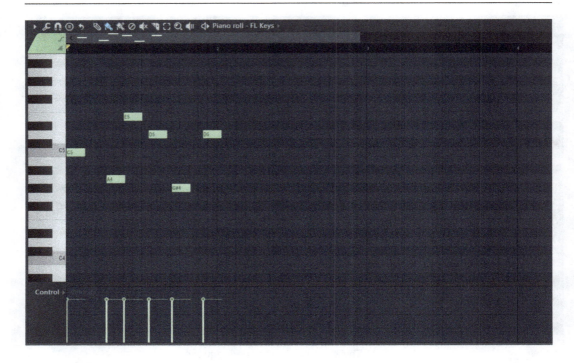

Figure 2.24: The Piano Roll | note inputs

To quantize these notes so they fit the bar sequence perfectly, click the top taskbar arrow, and select the **Tools | Quantize…** option:

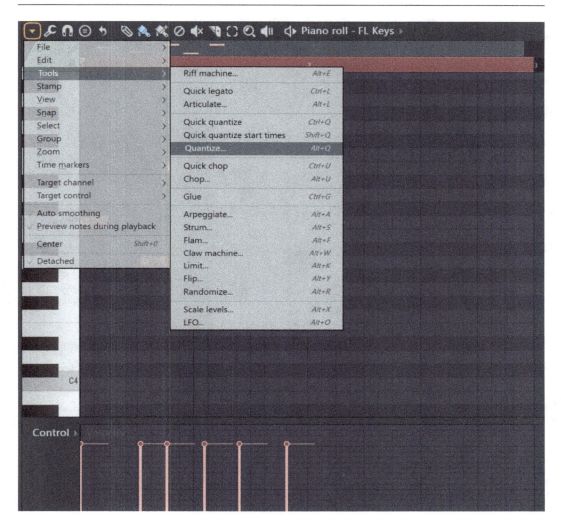

Figure 2.25: The Piano Roll | Tools | Quantize…

When we click the **Quantize…** option, it will give us the option to use the **Start time** sliding button (highlighted in red in *Figure 2.26*) meter to bring each note to the closest bar point:

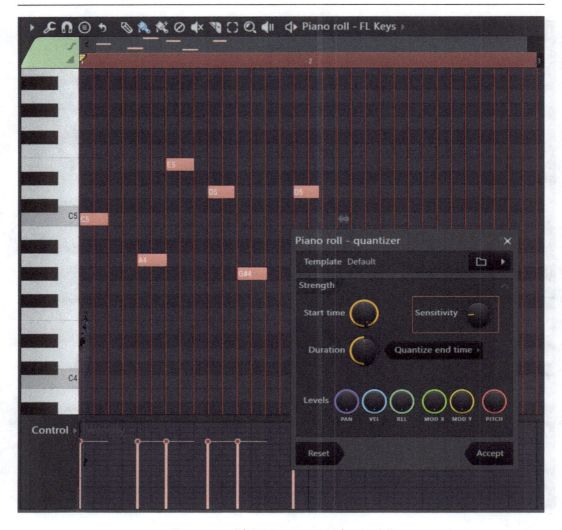

Figure 2.26: The Piano Roll | the Quantizer tool | notes fully quantized

We have now quantized each note to successfully bring them on to perfect bar alignment.

> **Tip**
> Quantizing is great to align notes, but there are some occasions when you may opt out of using this tool for the sake of having a creative approach to where notes land on a bar sequence – ultimately, it's up to you to figure out what you think sounds best.

Now, it's time to share with you some secrets on how to use the Piano Roll at a high level.

Piano Roll hacks – the Billboard producer's template

Now that we have discussed the basic overview of the Piano Roll, you should be able to load a VST and a drum sound into the Channel Rack, be aware of how to click and record in the Piano Roll, and understand quantizing. What I have described so far is just simplifying your approach to FL Studio – you can do a lot more with the Piano Roll, but I don't recommend trying to master every single facet of the software to get the most out of your productions. I could easily extrapolate out each feature of the software into its own book – the key to mastery is mastering the basics. To be honest, I've never needed to go farther than what I have described in this chapter, simply because FL Studio is a tool to input creativity into. It is not about how in depth you are with every single tool in FL studio but understanding the basics of how to use the software. With that being said, I'm going to give you some real secrets now.

Producing records from a perspective of Billboard framework is the key to creating productions in FL Studio that actually work in the marketplace. The first thing we need to discuss is that most producers tend to over-complicate records. Remember, unless you are scoring for a film or advert, commercial records are created with the intent that an artist or songwriter is going to record verses and chorus (or "hooks") over your production. This means, we need to leave the track open, yet hypnotizing and ear-catching. Here's the key – you have great sound design, great mixing, and a vibe and feel that is unique to you, but we are all use the same notes and chords. Always remember that when it comes to music, there is nothing new under the sun. It's how you approach records that makes the difference.

Modern pop music typically follows a formula. Creating workflow efficiently when creating records every day needs to follow this formula. As we discussed in *Chapter 1*, over the last decade, music arrangements have changed. The typical intro-verse-hook-verse-hook-verse is becoming less and less popular. This equates to a 4–8 bar intro, a 16-bar verse, and an 8-bar hook, which is repeated. Songs nowadays in the rap genre are less than 2:30 seconds long, sometimes shorter. The new formula is a four-bar intro – a 12-bar verse, an 8-bar hook, a 12-bar verse, and an 8-bar hook. Keep this in mind when you are creating underlying loops and progressions.

For now, I want to provide you with some secrets to create loops in the Piano Roll, what progressions work time after time, and what you can do to start creating records that will chart on the Billboard charts.

Understanding music theory in modern pop music

To start crafting billboard-ready records in FL Studio, I'm going to introduce you to the concept of pop chord progression theory. This hack uses a solid chord progression as a foundation for you to build on as you progress through the production of the track. Creating melodies that work is a framework of modern music theory in current pop music trends, offering a baseline to create sure-fire formulaic productions. In the *Creating melodies that work* section, I will discuss this in greater detail.

Introducing pop chord regression theory

Throughout history, simple and hypnotizing chord progressions have popular music. The difference between popular music chord progressions and chords you may hear in other genres of music (such as classical or jazz) is that music that makes the Billboard chart follows a simple chord theory rule. Chord progressions should offer simplicity, and make records memorable, catchy, and enjoyable for the listener. This is one of the keys to creating Billboard-charting productions in FL Studio.

The C-A minor-F-G pattern is a classically used progression that hundreds of hit songs have used in various combinations. To create this chord progression in FL Studio, we will use the Piano Roll to click out these notes using the FL Keys VST:

Figure 2.27: The Piano Roll menu – chord inputs

Another combination of these historical chord progression could look like this:

Figure 2.28: The Piano Roll menu – a second variation of chord inputs

Chords can be rearranged and made in similar but different patterns to create new tones and moods as you experiment with your composing theory. As simplistic as this chord theory is, it works. You can get creative on how you arrange notes following this succinct pattern.

Now, let's talk about creating melodies that work.

Creating melodies that work

Open the Piano Roll and select the draw tool. Once we have this window open, we will create an eight-bar loop:

Figure 2.29: The Piano Roll draw tool

For my example, we will use the mouse to create this eight-bar loop – when you've grasped the concept, you can get fancy and use a MIDI interface.

Now, before we dive into what works and what doesn't from a creative standpoint, keep in mind that music is subjective. However, there are certain things (including note patterns) that just work, have always worked, and will always work.

One of the greatest songwriters of all time, Harlan Howard, once said, "*A hit song is just three chords and the truth.*"

In addition, I recommend that you get creative with the loop in *Figure 2.30* – play around with it, try different things, but stick to it as a framework.

There are two main ways I approach creating leading melodies that work:

- Starting with base notes as a foundation
- Starting with high octave notes as a foundation

We always want to use middle C (**C5** in FL Studio) as the base point for our melodies. Let's start with using the base note formula. As shown in the following screenshot, click middle C by adding four note patterns:

Figure 2.30: The Piano Roll – note input

Using this approach, we will start with a baseline to build on of the MIDI pattern; this can also be approached through both long notes and short notes as follows:

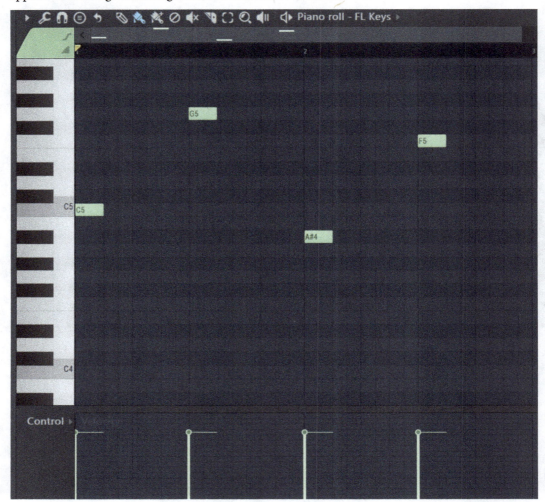

Figure 2.31: The Piano Roll – staccato note input

Once we have built a base foundation, we want to start experimenting with high octave note patterns. These notes will make the track standout and act as the melodic points combined with your base notes. I like to place these in a sequence of four notes per each grid block, as shown in *Figure 2.32*:

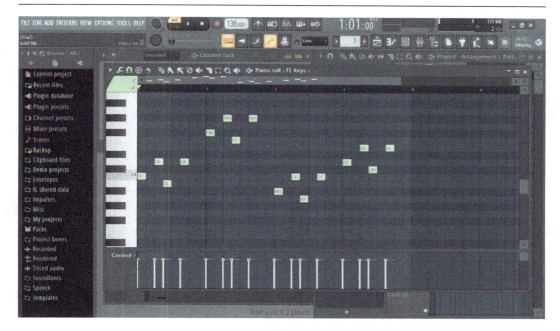

Figure 2.32: The Piano Roll | a staccato four-note input pattern

FL Studio is a great tool for flexibility as it relates to playing around with ideas in the Piano Roll. You can start with a simple pattern and start moving notes around up and down keys to find the best combination.

The theory behind creating great records is keeping your loops and melodies simple – you don't want to over-complicate the base of the track so as to confuse a songwriter or artist when they record a reference or song to it. As a matter of music theory, most traditional hit songs follow a formula of the same chord progression or a combination of those chord progressions in nature – the reason being that we as humans respond to certain combinations of notes in a very specific way! For example, major chords tend to produce a feeling or vibe of happiness, whereas minor chord progressions tend to create tension, aggressiveness, and anxiety. You may have noticed that most hip-hop or rap uses minor chords, and most pop or country uses major chords. This is done specifically to fit the niche of that particular genre. The C-major progression has been tried and tested in pop music for decades and is a go-to for most producers when formulating ideas.

The most important piece of advice I can give you as it relates to composing within FL Studio is to keep it simple. Every record needs room to breathe and space for a songwriter or artist to add their creative input. There exists a framework that we covered in the *Using the Piano Roll* section that describes the three- and four-chord pattern that pop music has used for decades to captive listeners, and we will now dive into this in greater detail.

The reality is that creating hypnotic and memorable melodies and chords will drive your productions forward, while your drum programming and arrangments with hold a rhythm and keep the listener attentive. Even though songs are only a few minutes long, have you ever noticed that you can get lost in one where it felt like time almost didn't exist? Music is a powerful tool that directly affects the subconscious, which is a higher level of the mind. What I want to share with you is how we can use the Piano Roll to directly grab the attention of your fans and listeners by using certain age-old techniques that I have used and witnessed others use.

In *Using the Piano Roll* section, I introduced you to the concept of the Piano Roll and its flexibility within FL Studio. Now, we will discuss how to use it as a frame of reference to create and follow a Billboard chart-ready formula.

Building MIDI templates in the Piano Roll

A MIDI template is a pre-scored series of notes within the Piano Roll that, over time, you will accumulate for workflow optimization. These are note or chord progression scores we will build following the formula of creating melodies that work and ultimately saving the scores as MIDI files, so we can drop and drag in and out of the Piano Roll tool when creating new productions. In this section, we will go through each step to starting creating MIDI templates.

Let's open up FL Studio and load into the Channel Rack the FL Keys VST (for this example, you can use any playable VST, but starting chords or a melody on a simple piano VST can help save time when creating future productions in FL Studio):

Figure 2.33: FL Keys | the Piano Roll window

For the exercise we will discuss in this section, we will create a chord progression that you can use to create template frameworks using the MIDI export feature in FL Studio.

First, let's score a typical chord progression in the Piano Roll to use as our MIDI template. This MIDI file will be put into a folder in your channel browser so that you can start building out a chord library you can use in subsequent productions. To do this, let's score a chord progression:

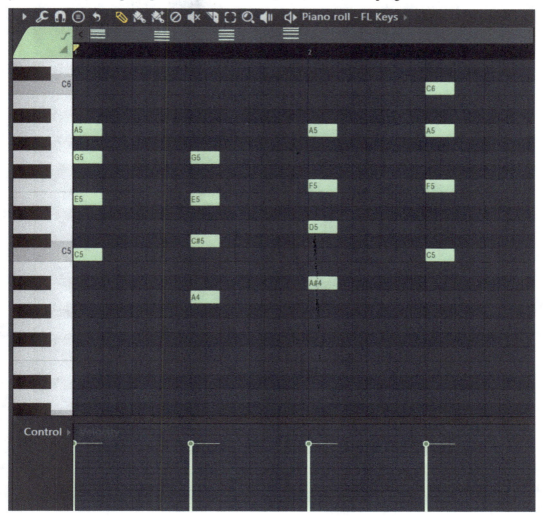

Figure 2.34: FL Keys | the Piano Roll | a chord progression example

FL Studio's software allows you to score a MIDI sequence by simply using the Piano Roll, by accessing the **Piano Roll** option and then clicking **FILE** | **Export as MIDI file…**, as shown in *Figure 2.35*:

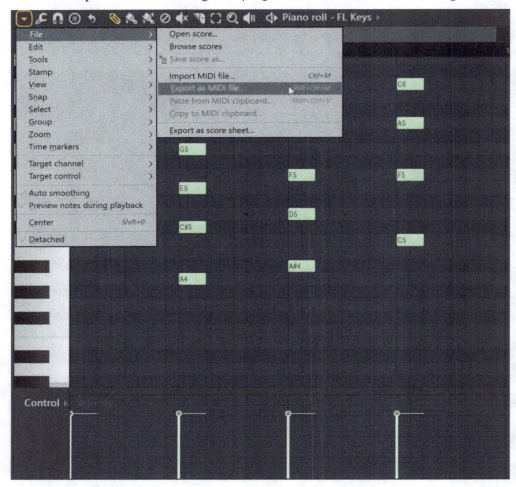

Figure 2.35: The Piano Roll | the drop-down arrow menu | File | Export as MIDI file…

Now that we have a MIDI template, we can drag and drop any VST plugin with this MIDI sequence in FL Studio – you can follow the same advice given in the *Exploring the Browser tool* section of *Chapter 1* to create a custom folder in your browser to start organizing MIDI files.

To be clear, there are hundreds of chord combinations you can create using the Piano Roll scoring system. Ultimately, experimentation will lead you to find what you like best. Certain chord progressions create a feeling of calmness, while some create a feeling of tension or action – it is up to you to explore and experiment when you create productions in FL Studio.

Now that we have covered the basics of MIDI templates in FL Studio, let's dive into a specific tool that can be useful when working with MIDI clips – the stamp tool.

Using the stamp tool to create chords

The stamp tool in FL Studio is a feature of the Piano Roll that allows you to quickly paste certain note combinations within a pattern. This allows you to copy and then paste the chord combination to use in the next note range easily as a workflow hack. It is represented by a small icon of a stamp or a rubber stamp, and it is located in the top-left corner of the **Piano Roll** window in the **Piano Roll** taskbar. This tool allows you to choose certain chord combinations and place them within the Piano Roll scoring system. This is a useful tool to start creating progressions without knowing about music theory.

To use the stamp tool, you first select the notes that you want to copy. Then, click on the stamp tool icon and drag your selection to where you want to paste it. The stamp tool will create a new set of notes at the location where you dragged and dropped the first note, with the same pitch, length, and other properties as the original notes. You can also use the stamp tool to quickly create repeating patterns or sequences of notes by copying the first stamped chord combination. For example, you can select a single note and use the stamp tool to quickly create a repeating pattern by dragging it across the Piano Roll.

In *Figure 2.36*, the highlighted red box identifies the stamp tool. Let's click this to see how we can start choosing our initial chord progressions:

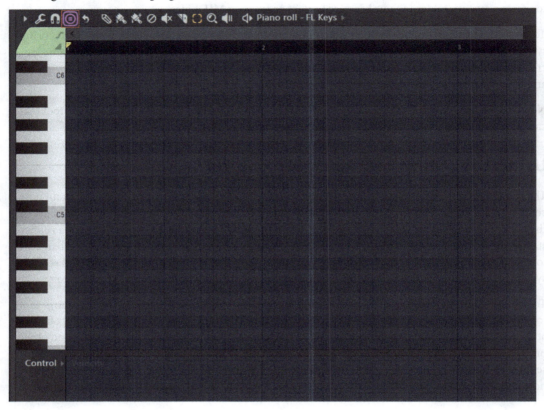

Figure 2.36: The Piano Roll | the stamp tool

When we click on the stamp tool, we will see the options of what chords FL Studio has pre-loaded to use as a starting point when scoring in the Piano Roll:

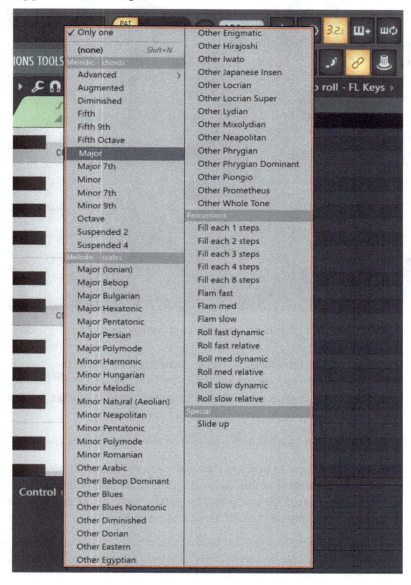

Figure 2.37: The Piano Roll | the stamp tool | the stamp tool chord options

Let's click on the **Minor** chord option and input it into the Piano Roll:

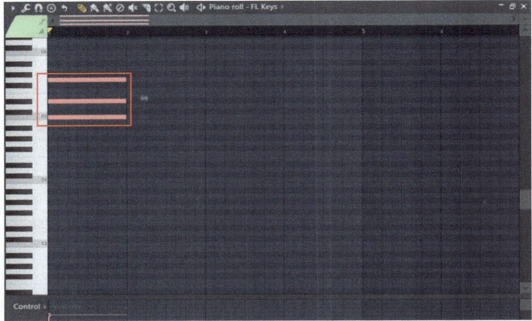

Figure 2.38: The Piano Roll | the stamp tool | the stamp tool minor chord using middle C

From here, you can build off this foundation to create chord progressions in the Piano Roll. This is a useful tool to create frameworks and export MIDI files for later use, and it will help you to create a library of chord options. In addition, you use this technique on a per-production basis and simply save progressions you really like once you have completed a track.

The stamp tool in FL Studio's Piano Roll is useful for several reasons, including the following:

- **Saving time**: The stamp tool can save you time when you need to duplicate a set of notes and paste them in another location within the same pattern. Instead of manually copying and pasting each note, you can use the stamp tool to quickly duplicate the first note combination using copy and paste to duplicate them in the new location.

- **Creating patterns**: The stamp tool can also be used to create repeating patterns or sequences of notes, by selecting a single note or a set of notes and dragging the stamp tool across the Piano Roll. This is a quick and easy way to create complex patterns that can be used in your music.

- **Streamlining your workflow**: The stamp tool is a useful feature that can help streamline your workflow by allowing you to quickly duplicate notes and create patterns. This can help you focus on the creative aspects of your music-making process and reduce the time you spend on repetitive tasks.

Overall, the stamp tool in FL Studio's Piano Roll is a very useful feature to craft specific progressions, create repeating patterns, and streamline your workflow.

Now that we have discussed the power of the Piano Roll, let's discuss how we can use these frameworks to maximize workflow to spend longer on composing, generate ideas, and avoid writer's block.

Optimizing workflow in the Piano Roll

We maximize workflow by creating **Project bones** templates and saving them to our `packs` folder. Project bones is a feature in FL Studio that allows you to save and reuse specific parts of your project. These can include mixer track settings, pattern settings, plugin settings, and so on. Essentially, Project bones allow you to save a "skeleton" or framework of your project that you can reuse in future projects or share with other users. Project bones include everything from your MIDI patterns in the Piano Roll to mixing presets. Creating Project bones is an effective export tool that allows you to save your workflow templates for future use and composing.

In this chapter, we have discussed how to get the most out of the Piano Roll. There are two distinct ways we can optimize future workflow when composing melody and chord progressions:

- The first is by using the MIDI export theory, in which we export a specific Piano Roll pattern into a MIDI file, save it in our browser, and drop and drag it into future projects

- The second is by creating Project bones (as it is called in FL Studio), which we will discuss in this section

We can create Project bones by following these steps:

1. Open the Piano Roll for the instrument you want to create a template for:

Figure 2.39: The Channel Rack | Insert | FL Keys

2. Set up the Piano Roll with the desired MIDI pattern – here, I have composed a basic chord progression and included a tempo of 130 BPM:

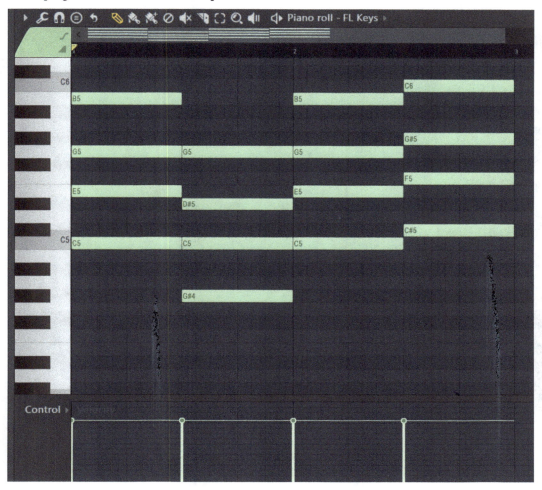

Figure 2.40: The Piano Roll | a chord MIDI pattern

3. Now that we have created the template, go to **File | Export | Project bones** (`.fsc`)(a `.fsc` file is a "Score" file) to save the template, give the template a descriptive name, and select a location to save it:

Figure 2.41: File | Export | Project bones…

4. To use the template in a new project, go to **File | New from template** and select the template you created:

Figure 2.42: File | New from template

The new project will open with the Piano Roll template you created, ready for you to start working.

Now that we understand the concept of using Project bones and how they work, let's take a closer look at how they can be used to enhance your workflow and save time when working on future projects.

Workflow optimization hacks

There are a number of tactics you can use to increase workflow in FL Studio. This book gives you the frameworks you need to familiarize yourself with the software's features and operations; as we have established, perfect practice makes practice perfect! Once we have a grasp of how to use all of FL Studio's tools, we can use these quick hacks and tips, such as picking up keyboard shortcuts, using hotkeys, and adjusting the user interface to your preferences to maximize your workflow. Secondly, think about how you can best organize your computer when you develop your own habits and production approaches.

Let's talk about some of the keyboard shortcuts that will help you increase workflow overall. These are as follows:

- *F1*: Help
- *F2*: Rename a selected channel or mixer track
- *F3*: Open the mixer
- *F4*: Open a playlist
- *F5*: Open the step sequencer
- *F6*: Open the Piano Roll
- *F7*: Open the browser
- *F8*: Open the plugin picker
- *F9*: Open the mixer track properties
- *F10*: Open the MIDI settings
- *F11*: Full-screen mode
- *F12*: Open the plugin database
- *Ctrl + C*: Copy
- *Ctrl + V*: Paste
- *Ctrl + X*: Cut
- *Ctrl + A*: Select all
- *Ctrl + Z*: Undo
- *Ctrl + Y*: Redo
- *Ctrl + Shift + C*: Copy the state of selected mixer tracks
- *Ctrl + Shift + V*: Paste the state of selected mixer tracks
- *Ctrl + Shift + X*: Cut the state of selected mixer tracks
- *Ctrl + Shift + A*: Select all audio clips in a playlist
- *Ctrl + Shift + Z*: Redo
- *Ctrl + Shift + Y*: Redo
- *Ctrl + Shift + F*: Toggle smart disable for all plugins
- *Ctrl + Shift + L*: Lock all playlist tracks
- *Ctrl + Shift + M*: Mute all playlist tracks

- *Ctrl + Shift + U*: Unmute all playlist tracks
- *Ctrl + Shift + P*: Show the plugin picker
- *Ctrl + Shift + I*: Insert score data
- *Ctrl + Shift + S*: Save all
- *Ctrl + Shift + O*: Open all recent files
- *Alt + F4*: Close FL Studio
- *Alt + Enter*: Toggle full-screen mode
- *Alt + Tab*: Switch between open windows
- *Alt + left arrow*: Move back in browser history
- *Alt + right arrow*: Move forward in browser history

In addition, for music producers, FL Studio's compatibility with sound kits, sound design, and VST plugins opens up a world of creative options. The use of a variety of sound kits and sample packs is one of the most important benefits of interoperability. Because FL Studio supports a number of file formats, including WAV, MP3, and OGG, you can easily incorporate these sounds into your compositions. Because of this integration, it is possible to combine sounds from various sources, pitch-shift and lengthen them to produce totally new sounds and textures, or even use them as a base for more intricate sound creation.

FL Studio offers a variety of integrated plugins and effects in addition to sound kits that can be used to produce your own sounds. The **Patcher** plugin, for instance, enables you to mix numerous plugins and effects in a variety of ways to build custom processing chains that are specific to your project. A potent synthesizer, the **Sytrus** plugin can produce a wide variety of sounds, from vintage analog tones to cutting-edge digital soundscapes. Even more sophisticated synthesis capabilities are offered by the **Harmless** and **Harmor** plugins, enabling the creation of elaborate and complicated sounds with ease. You can use external software instruments and effects without any hassle, thanks to the smooth integration of VST plugins in FL Studio. Because of this compatibility, you can utilize both FL Studio's built-in plugins and your preferred VST plugins, significantly enhancing your creative options. Also, FL Studio is compatible with the majority of third-party plugins on the market because of its support for numerous plugin types, including VST, VST3, and AU.

Overall, FL Studio's interoperability of sound kits, sound design, and VST plugins is an effective tool for composers and music producers. This interoperability offers a wide range of creative opportunities, enabling the production of original music of a high caliber. Music makers can easily combine sounds and plugins from many sources with FL Studio's support for a variety of file formats and plugin types. This allows them to compose music that is both original and of high quality.

Last but not least, employing effective time management strategies such as goal-setting, task prioritization, and break-taking can help you remain concentrated and productive throughout the creative process.

There are various techniques to streamline productivity with FL Studio's Piano Roll, including learning keyboard shortcuts, personalizing the user interface, and utilizing templates. You can explore and carry out tasks inside the Piano Roll quickly by using keyboard shortcuts, and you can organize and access frequently used functions more effectively by personalizing the interface. Certain settings, patterns, or chords can be saved as templates and used again in subsequent projects. You can increase your productivity and creativity when using FL Studio's Piano Roll by putting these tips into practice and developing solid time management skills.

Summary

In this chapter, we learned how to use the Piano Roll to create MIDI patterns, build templates, and take advantage of FL Studio's features to produce effective melodies and chords. We emphasized the importance of mastering the Piano Roll to enhance productivity and creativity to maximize music production and how we can use FL Studio's featured tools, such as Project bones, to increase workflow.

Now that we have discussed how to use the Piano Roll, let's walk through how to start creating a signature sound!

Exercise

Creating a Custom Workflow Template in FL Studio: In this exercise, you will create your own custom workflow template in FL Studio using Project bones and the Piano Roll. This exercise will guide you through the process of creating and exporting a custom template that you can use in your future projects. We will follow these steps:

1. **Setting up Project bones**: First, open FL Studio and create a new project. Set up your mixer and arrange your patterns as you would for a typical project. Next, select the elements of your project that you would like to save as a Project bone. This could include mixer track settings, pattern settings, and plugin settings. For this exercise, let's focus on the Piano Roll.

2. **Creating a custom workflow template in the Piano Roll**: Once you have selected the elements you want to save, go to the Piano Roll for one of your patterns. Here, you can create a custom workflow template by setting up your preferred grid, snap settings, note lengths, and so on. Take your time and adjust everything to your liking.

3. **Saving your custom workflow template**: Once you have set up your custom workflow template, it's time to save it as a Project bone. To do this, click on **File** | **Export** | The **Project bones...** option in the drop-down menu, as shown in *Figure 2.43*:

Figure 2.43: File | Export | Project bones…

This will open the **Project bones** window. Click on the **Add** button to add your custom workflow template to the list of Project bones. Give it a name that is descriptive of its contents, such as `Custom Piano Roll Template`. Once you have saved your custom workflow template as a Project bone, you can reuse it in future projects or share it with other FL Studio users.

4. **Exporting your workflow template**: Finally, export your custom workflow template so that you can use it in your future projects. To do this, go to the **File** menu and select **Export | Project bones…**. This will open the **Project bones export** window. Select the Project bone that you just created, and choose a location to save the file. Make sure to save it in a location that is easy to access in the future, such as your FL Studio `packs` folder.

Congratulations! You have now created a custom workflow template using Project bones and the Piano Roll in FL Studio. You can use this template in future projects to save time and streamline your workflow.

3
Creating Your Signature Sound

Now its time to start building a library of signature sounds that will represent you and your productions in the marketplace. And yes, you can buy or license sounds from third-party websites and producers that are incredible and have led to multi-platinum hits, but wouldn't it be amazing to have a one-of-one signature sound? That's what we are going to do here. In fact, I'm going to show you how to do this by exclusively only using FL Studio's stock sounds (sounds crazy, I know!) but the reality is, all of those amazing sounds you hear on third-party websites are just a combination of stock sounds and custom layers created by other producers. This in essence is called "sound design."

Leveraging the art of creating sound design will impart upon you a few different forms of skill sets, not limited to just banging drum sounds, unique synth patches, or arrangement tweaks. Learning how to create sound design with bare minimum pallets will in fact enable you to sell producer sounds kits yourself and pitch specific sound design to trailer houses, advertising agencies, and filmmakers.

To get you excited, and give you a hint of what happens in the upper echelon of the business, I personally own and run a company that sells and pitches sound design cues to these types of clients for major film and advertising projects. Each cue can generate thousands of dollars every time it is used in a single placement.

To that end, we will cover the following topics in this chapter:

- Why should you create a signature sound?

- Crafting your signature sound with FL Studio's stock sounds

- How to create drum kits that hit hard

- How to create signature hi-hat sounds

- How to create custom synth and instrumentation kits

- How to create a sonic branding tag (a mnemonic) or producer tag

- Creating arrangement style

- Mixing for a creative feel (not the same as mixing for release)

Why should you create your own signature sound?

Every major producer and composer follows a similar formula but can be studied from a distinct point of sonic identification when you listen attentively to the nuances in their work. In the mid-2000s, Scott Storch used similar drum sounds and played Middle-Eastern riffs to create a signature sound, Timbaland used big sounding percussions sounds and baby crying samples to create his signature sound, Dr. Dre used minimalistic drum sounds with piano riffs and transitional elements to create his sound, 808 Mafia uses their signature hi-hat triplets and 808 bass hits within a specific arrangement, and so on. Every producer has their own sound – it's what ultimately sets you apart from the crowd. After all, the music production community is extremely overcrowded and opportunities are limited. Let's talk about what creating a signature sound is, and what it is not.

A signature sound is a collection of customized drum sounds, VST patches and synth sounds, arrangement nuances, and melody and chord approach frameworks. What a signature sound is not is a specific template where every single production sound is exactly the same to the point of being uncreative in your approach to creating records.

The magic is in the nuance of how you approach creating a signature sound. What makes it work is perfect practice. Repeating your own formula and frameworks as taken from this book will get you to a point of unconscious competence when it comes to creating records.

Let's break down how to start building a signature sound.

These are the components that make up a signature sound:

- Drum sounds
- Customized VST patches (or layering synth patches)
- Transitional sounds
- A producer tag or sonic brand tag
- Arrangement style
- Mixing for a creative feel (not the same as mixing for release)

To avoid any doubt, each element can be expanded upon long after you have finished this book, and building your signature sound collection is always an evolving aspect of staying up to date on your sound as you expand your creativity and as modern music and pop culture change.

A great example of this is when you listen to early 2010s trap music, you will notice that the 808 bass sound (which was originally created by Drumma Boy, and then altered and crafted by Lex Luger and Southside) had a very heavy mid-range feel to it. In today's trap music, the use of a more distorted and staccato sound is used. This new modern 808 sound offers more of a grunge sound and represents the point in pop culture at which rap music is today.

Another general rule of thumb when it comes to sound design is the use of samples or re-invigorating eras in music – producers will typically sample eras that existed 20 years before today's date. For example, you may notice that samples used in pop music today are from the early 2000s, whereas samples used in the early 2000s relied heavily on an 80s sound.

When it comes to drum sounds, there is a balance of fitting in with what is current and how you can augment or predict trends. If everyone uses the same sounds, music gets boring – even established producers get caught in the pattern of copying the new generation, and although they add their own spin to it, it is always better to try to set or predict trends.

The most successful producers are typically the ones who change or set trends in their generation. As a general rule of thumb, there is no rule per se on what you can use – it will be up to you to decide whether you want to follow trends, augment trends (by using what's current and adding your own flavor), or set new trends with totally new snare sounds. When it comes to trend-setting, a lot of that has to do with your position in the marketplace. If you are the "it" producer of that year, typically, people will copy your style and thus create a new trend. As a general rule of thumb, becoming the "it" producer has everything to do with relationships in the industry. Major labels that sign producers to publishing deals and JV agreements have a vested interest in that producer getting placements, and typically, you see these signed producers dominate the charts for no other reason than the labels attempting to recoup their investments. A major label system is a machine that supports its signed artists and producers based on the methodology that it controls the marketing and visibility of a specific song or album based on budgets that indie artists typically can't compete with. This is neither good nor bad, but just how the industry has operated for decades. Occasionally, producers will break through with a new artist, but with the production market having such a low barrier to entry with the internet at beat-selling marketplaces, it has become increasingly even more competitive to do so – but not impossible, even if you have all of the odds stacked against you. More on this in *Chapter 8*!

Now, let's discuss how we can overcome and beat the competition by creating our own signature sound that will set us apart from everyone else. That starts with creating your signature drum sounds. These will carry your productions throughout your career, and having the right kick or snare will set you apart from everyone else. So, what drum sounds will we need to create to start our signature sound? Drum sounds can be defined as kicks, snares, claps, snaps, hi-hats (both open hats and regular hats), and percussion sounds (e.g., bongos, sticks, hits, etc.).

Now, let's get into how you can start crafting your own signature sound using FL Studio's stock sounds!

Crafting your signature sound with FL Studio's stock sounds

FL Studio is a powerful digital audio workstation that includes a sizable sound and sample library. Using FL Studio standard sounds can be a useful approach to creating a distinctive and recognized sound, even though many producers might disregard them in favor of third-party plugins and sample packs. The stock sounds that come with FL Studio are extensive and contain anything from vintage analog synths to contemporary electronic drums and percussion. By opening the **Browser** tab on the left side of the screen or the **Browser** window in the Channel Rack, you can access the incredible stock sounds that FL Studio has to offer. The **Browser** tab, which can be customized to incorporate your own unique sounds and folders, is a fantastic tool for searching for and organizing sounds.

Layering FL Studio stock sounds with additional sounds or samples to get a distinctive hybrid sound is one way to use them. For instance, to produce a unique drum sound that nobody else has, you may layer a stock kick drum with a third-party snare sample. Similar to this, to give your tracks a distinctive texture, you could mix a stock synth patch with a sample of your own voice or a field recording.

Using FL Studio stock sounds as a jumping-off point for sound creation is another approach to making use of them. A stock sound can be modified to match your unique requirements by changing its settings and parameters. By altering the filter cutoff and resonance of a pre-made bass patch, for instance, you can radically change the sound and make it work with your track.

Moreover, FL Studio has a number of integrated effects that may be used to further sculpt and tinker with the basic sounds. **Equalization** (**EQ**), compression, distortion, reverb, and other effects are among these. You can build distinctive and captivating textures that give your music depth by playing with these effects and applying them to the stock sounds. It's important to remember that while FL Studio stock sounds are excellent tools for creating your own distinctive sound, it's crucial to experiment with a range of sounds and samples.

Finally, using and leveraging FL Studio standard sounds is a useful strategy for creating a signature and distinctive sound. The possibilities are unlimited, whether you layer them with other sounds, use them as a foundation for sound design, or add built-in effects to shape and alter them. To find your unique distinctive sound, don't be scared to experiment and explore the enormous library of sounds that comes with FL Studio.

The **Mixer** is one of the most powerful tools in FL Studio we can use to start augmenting FL Studio's stock sounds to create your own signature sound. One of FL Studio's primary features is its **Mixer**, which enables musicians to mix and master their songs to generate music with a professional-quality sound. Let's look at how to master FL Studio's **Mixer** so you can use its standard sounds to create distinctive signature sounds:

1. **Understanding the Mixer:** The FL Studio **Mixer** is a complex tool that allows you to control the various elements of your track, such as volume, panning, EQ, and effects. Before you start using the **Mixer**, it is important to have a good understanding of its different parts. The **Mixer** (as shown in *Figure 3.1*) is divided into channels, with each channel representing a different element of your track, such as a drum loop, a bassline, or a vocal track. Each channel has a number of controls, including volume, panning, and mute/solo buttons. You can adjust these controls by clicking and dragging on the sliders or buttons.

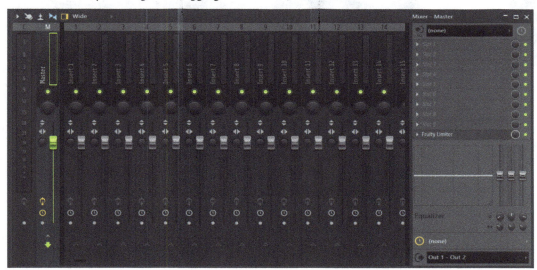

Figure 3.1: Mixer

2. **Using EQ to shape your sound**: EQ is a powerful tool that allows you to shape the frequency spectrum of your track. FL Studio comes with a built-in EQ plugin called **Parametric EQ 2**, which is a great tool for creating signature sounds. **Parametric EQ 2** (as shown in *Figure 3.2*) allows you to adjust the volume of specific frequency bands using sliders. You can also adjust the width of each band and choose from different filter types, such as low-pass, high-pass, and band-pass filters. Experiment with different EQ settings to shape the sound of your track. For example, you can boost the low-end frequencies of a bassline to make it more powerful or cut the high-end frequencies of a vocal track to make it sound warmer.

Figure 3.2: Parametric EQ 2

3. **Adding effects**: FL Studio comes with a wide range of built-in effects, such as reverb, delay, and distortion. These effects can be used to create unique signature sounds for your tracks. The **Settings** window allows you to adjust the various parameters of the effect, such as the decay time for a reverb effect or feedback for a delay effect. Experiment with different effect settings to create your own unique sound.

    To illustrate this point, it's important to note that every individual plugin possesses a unique array of customizable settings that offers opportunities for fine-tuning and enhancement. A prime example of this concept can be found in the **Parametric EQ 2** plugin, where we can delve into the intricacies of its functionality and observe how these settings can be manipulated to achieve desired sound outcomes. This process not only empowers us to shape and mold the audio to our liking but also highlights the potential for creative exploration within the realm of sound design.

4. **Using automation to create movement**: Automation is a powerful tool that allows you to create movement and variation in your tracks. FL Studio allows you to automate almost any parameter in the **Mixer**, including volume, panning, EQ, and effects. You can then use the pencil tool (shown in *Figure 3.3*) to draw the automation curve. For example, you could automate the volume of a synth lead to create a sweeping effect or automate the filter cutoff of a bassline to create a pulsing effect.

Figure 3.3: Pencil tool

5. **Using sidechain compression**: Sidechain compression is a popular technique that allows you to create a pumping effect by ducking the volume of one element of your track in response to another element. For example, you could use the kick drum channel as the trigger for the sidechain compression on the bassline channel. Adjust the settings of the compressor to achieve the desired pumping effect. You can adjust the threshold, ratio, attack, and release settings to fine-tune the compression.

6. **Using the Mixer to create space and depth**: The **Mixer** can also be used to create space and depth in your tracks. By using panning and reverb, you can create a sense of space and place each element of your track in its own sonic environment.

To use panning, simply click on the panning knob in the **Mixer** and drag it left or right to adjust the position of the sound in the stereo field. This can be used to create a sense of movement in your track or to separate different elements of your track. In *Figure 3.4*, I have highlighted the panning knob to show you how you can do this directly in the **Mixer** plugin with sound routed to that specific channel:

Figure 3.4: Mixer | panning knob

Reverb can be used to create a sense of space and depth in your track. FL Studio comes with a built-in reverb plugin called **Fruity Reverb 2**, which is a great tool for creating realistic-sounding reverb.

Figure 3.5: Fruity Reverb 2

7. **Mastering your track**: Once you have mixed your track using the FL Studio **Mixer**, it is time to master it. Mastering is the final step in the production process and involves making final adjustments to the overall sound of your track. FL Studio comes with a built-in mastering plugin called **Fruity Limiter**, which is a great tool for mastering your tracks. **Fruity Limiter** allows you to control the overall level of your track and apply compression to make it sound louder and more polished. In *Figure 3.6*, we can see **Fruity Limiter**:

Figure 3.6: Fruity Limiter

Mastering the FL Studio **Mixer** is a key skill for any music producer. By using EQ, effects, automation, sidechain compression, and the **Mixer** itself, you can create unique signature sounds that stand out from the crowd. Experiment with different techniques and settings to find the sound that works best for you.

Now that we have discussed a solid foundation of FL Studio's stock sounds and how we use the **Mixer** and mixing plugins to augment and creatively change stock sounds as a baseline to craft our signature sound, it's time to dive deeper into sound design and creating your own unique drum sounds. Specifically, let's take a closer look at creating kicks that really hit.

Creating drum sounds – kicks that really hit

When it comes to creating kick drum sounds, there are two main types of kick sounds that you will create:

- The first type of kick is what we call a "generic" kick; this is a kick sound that can work with any production style because it simply is a well-rounded and balanced sound that fits with 808 basses, traditional bass guitars, and sub-bass noises.

- The second type of kick is what we call a "textured" kick. Textured kicks are drum noises that have a bit of attack to them, a specific sound that accompanies the underlying kick sound. Timbaland's production catalog is full of textured kicks. They sound unique and are extremely creative in sound design nature. However, these need to be used properly to be able to fit within the bass range of certain frequencies. Certain textured kicks won't gel sonically with certain 808 bass sounds, sub-basses, or bass guitars.

Let's find a great FL Studio stock kick that already achieves a base of what we want.

Adding a generic kick

After going through FL Studio's stock kick sounds, I have chosen **Jung Kick**. It offers a balanced and well-rounded starting place for creating a custom generic kick noise we can use in our productions. Let's add it to our Channel Rack:

Figure 3.7: Browser | Packs | Drums | Kicks

Jung Kick has a good feel to it, it's generic, and can fit into almost any type of track. The key to making this a go-to kick is giving it that heavy bottom you hear in modern production styles. Every producer needs a go-to generic kick with heavy bottom!

Now that we have loaded it into the Channel Rack, we are going to add this sound to the **Mixing Channel** slot 1:

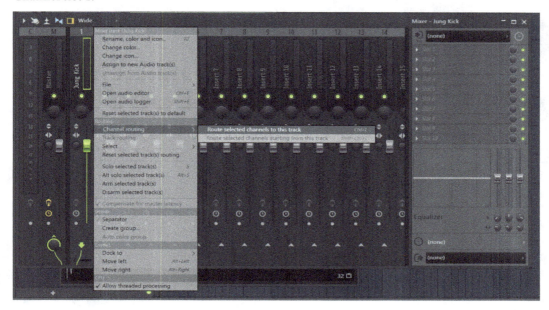

Figure 3.8: Jung Kick channel routing | Mixer

Now, let's proceed to add **Fruity Parametric EQ 2** to the mixing channel of the kick. To do this, we will select slot **1** to add the plugin tool:

Figure 3.9: Mixer | slot 1 | insert plugin | Fruity Parametric EQ 2

As I discussed in *Chapter 1*, we want to give the stock kick sound a "noxx" boost by using the **2** key and moving it to approximately 114 hertz. This adds bottom weight to the lower frequency range of the kick and will make it shine.

Figure 3.10: Fruity Parametric EQ 2 | editing key slider 2

Now we want to add a little top to the bottom-mid range frequency. This additional technique will depend on the specific kick noise you use. As for **Jung Kick**, we want to add a little more punch to its mid-low range frequency. We do this by moving the **3** key to 219 hertz and making the EQ slightly tighter at 23%:

Figure 3.11: Fruity Parametric EQ 2 | editing key slider 3

Now to add **Fruity Parametric EQ 2** to our **Channel Browser** for future use, we are going to export this file as a one-off in the Channel Rack directly into our Power User Drum Kit as we did in the *Using and organizing the Browser and Channel Rack* section of *Chapter 1*. To do this, we simply export the .wav file (wave sound) with the mixing plugin enabled as a single sound in the **Playlist** tool:

Figure 3.12: File | export .wav file | Power User Drum Kit

Great! We have now created a signature generic kick – simple, I know, but trust me, you only need one great generic kick to start building a great sound design library and signature sound.

Now that we have a baseline kick that you can use in almost every production you start, let's dive into how to make textured kicks.

Adding textured kicks

Remember, textured kicks are nuanced, and only really work with specific types of production styles. I don't recommend using them for every type of track, and encourage you to start your productions with your generic kick sound.

The key to textured kicks is layering top-end sound on top of your generic kick sounds to create a crispy or attack-led hit. This can be accomplished with numerous top-end sounds depending on what you want to accomplish with your sound design selection. I recommend starting with percussion sounds, things such as clicks, bells, or a specific snare sound. Remember – I'm giving you a formula. What you choose and how is what will make your signature sound unique.

Let's go to the Channel Rack with our newly created generic kick from the *Adding a generic kick* section.

We are going to use the kick in the Channel Rack and then the mixing channel. This ensures that the **Fruity Parametric EQ 2** mix is already active, so we don't need to re-create the kick noise.

I've found **Ambass Snare** as a perfect top range to add on top of the kick to give it a textured feel:

Figure 3.13: Browser | Packs | Drums | Snares | Channel Rack

In the Channel Rack, we want to enable the kick on the one bar and add the snare on the one bar so that they play when you hit the *space bar* in sequence as a single sound, as seen in the red box in *Figure 3.13*.

Now, add your snare sound to the Channel Rack and add it to **Mixing Channel** slot 2, as seen in *Figure 3.14*:

Figure 3.14: Mixer | slot 2 | insert Ambass Snare

Add **Fruity Parametric EQ 2** to the mixing channel into the snare sound channel:

Figure 3.15: Mixer | slot 2 | insert Fruity Parametric EQ 2

Now we are going to remove the bottom range of the snare so that it fits on top of the generic kick. This requires a bit of playing around depending on the sound – a general rule of thumb is to place slider key **1** at 52 hertz, at 68%:

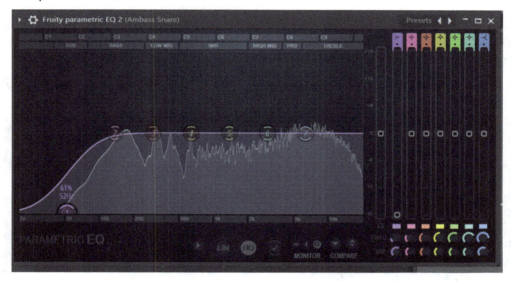

Figure 3.16: Fruity Parametric EQ 2 | edit slider 1

Now that we have removed the bottom range of the mixing frequency, we are going to add some punch to the low-mid range:

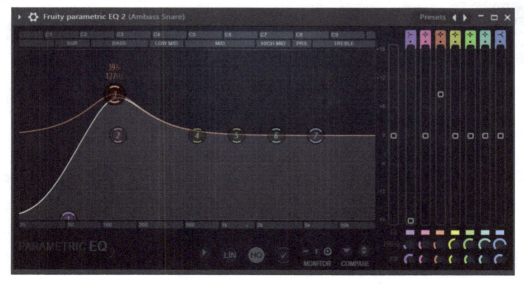

Figure 3.17: Fruity Parametric EQ 2 | edit slider 3 | 127 hertz | 39%

Perfect! Now hit the *space bar* to hear what you have created. This is your first textured kick sound!

Adding more texture to kicks

This can be done by incorporating additional snare sounds and following a similar EQ technic, or by leveraging FL Studio's mixing plugins to add more feel to the snare (the top end of your textured kick). We are going to add a second layer of texture to the kick to be spaced using the FL Studio delay spacer.

We are going to use the **Fruity Stereo Spacer** preset setting to widen the kick in stereo to give it a larger, special feeling:

Figure 3.18: Mixer | slot 2 | add Fruity Stereo Shaper

Perfect – now, we want to find and select the preset entitled **Fruity Delay 2**:

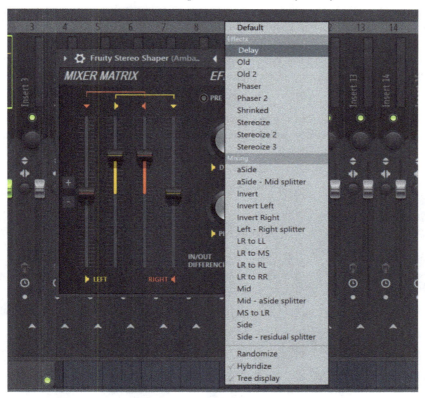

Figure 3.19: Fruity Stereo Shaper | preset selection | Delay setting

This will give the sound wave a spaced feel in the left and right headphones, increasing the range of the kick's overall sound. It should be noted that this doesn't work every time you fit it into a track because of competing bass sounds, but if you are creating kicks, this is a great way to get creative and build up a collection of usable sounds in the future.

Now, we have created a textured kick with stereo space!

Creating drum sounds – snares that pop

Creating a custom snare follows the exact same framework as creating and layering kick sounds. The only difference is we are going to only use other snare-like sounds instead of including kick sounds. To make a wide range of custom snares, we can get creative by blending and layering certain FL Studio stock snares with claps, percussion sounds, and hi-hats. The general snare sound design theory follows a framework that uses snares layered with claps, snaps, and percussion sounds to add texture to the main sound.

From a pop culture standpoint, at the time of writing this book, common snare sounds have evolved in the 2020s to mainly use short or small-sounding snares. This includes snare sounds such as claps with little to no tail, rim shots, small snares with little to no reverb, and so on. The 90s used big snare sounds that were mainly sampled from 60s and 70s records, whereas the 2000s used a lot of clap sounds from hardware and keyboards such as the Korg Triton. The 2010s saw the use of the classic Roland TR-808 drum machine sounds, typically used in the 80s for funk and pop records, mainly claps and variations of that.

Now, let's start a fresh project we can use as a blank canvas to create our first custom snare. First, let's find an 808 snare sound, something generic used in tracks today. Once we have found that snare, we will follow the same procedure we followed in the *Adding a generic kick* section and add it to the Channel Rack and then to the mixing channel:

Figure 3.20: Channel Rack | Mixer | Channel routing | 808 Snare

Now let's find a clap sound and follow the same procedure that we followed in the *Adding a generic kick* section. We will use the **Pap Clap** sound for this example:

Figure 3.21: Channel Rack | Mixer | Channel routing | Pap Clap

Now that we have two layers added to the Channel Rack and mixing channel, let's load up **Fruity Parametric EQ 2** to the **808 Snare** mixing channel.

Now, to add a little power to the snare sounds mid-range to give them a strong pop, move key **3** to 244 hertz (not every snare sound will be exact to this framework, so use your ear to find the best spot, but as a general suggestion, 244 hertz adds a huge amount of volume to the low to mid-range):

Figure 3.22: Channel Rack | Mixer | Channel routing | 808 Snare | Fruity Parametric EQ 2

As a matter of personal preference, I typically don't remove the low end in snare EQing because I like a heavy-sounding snare. You may wish to follow this framework or do the opposite – it's completely up to you.

Now, for the clap sound, which is the designated second-layer sound, I don't like to do too much to this kind of layer – it should just sit on top of the snare sound as is. In addition, I don't like to remove the bass range from clap sounds as they are already light-sounding. This goes for most claps, snaps, or click-and-clack percussion sounds.

What we can do is add creative mixing elements on top of the second layer to give it a more interesting feel.

Plugins that work well with second-layer claps, snaps, and percussion elements are **Fruity Flanger**, **Fruity Phaser**, and **Delay 2**. I don't recommend adding two levels of reverb unless you want a very specific layer evoking the sound of a big space.

Let's add **Fruity Flanger** to the mixing channel:

Figure 3.23: Channel Rack | Mixer | Channel routing | Pap Clap | Fruity Flanger

Great! Now, here is where you will use your own creativity to choose the preset you feel works best with the clap. In my experience, if I use a flanger plugin on a second layer, I shrink it to 30-40% of its total output for the specific sound – as a general rule of thumb I would do this for the phaser plugin as well. As seen in *Figure 3.24*, I modified the plugin output from slot **1** of **Fruity Flanger** to keep the settings the same within the plugin but to control the overall master output. This can be a matter of preference, and I encourage you to try experimenting with the plugin and the slot output.

Figure 3.24: Channel Rack | Mixer | Channel routing | Pap Clap | Fruity Flanger | restrict plugin output knob

I encourage you to experiment with all of FL Studio's plugins and their presets when creating your signature sound. As a tip, plugins such as **Delay** are tricky ones for drum sounds – most snares shouldn't have a noticeable stack of delay echo unless the specific style warrants it.

Now that we have created a layered snare/clap sound that is custom to your signature sound, follow the same framework as discussed in the *Exploring the Channel Rack* section of *Chapter 1* and export it as a .wav file to your Power Users Drum Kit in the **Browser**.

Now we have a kick and snare, let's talk about hi-hats.

Crafting signature hi-hat sounds

Hi-hats for the most part are simple – it's only when you want to try to recreate a live-sounding hat or perhaps add a level thickening to it where it makes sense to get creative with layering these types of sounds.

But because we are creating a signature sound, let's walk through how to create a custom hi-hat sound.

Let's look through the **Browser** and find a hi-hat we think has potential. To create a signature sound for a hi-hat, I want to let you know that there are a few types of hi-hats we will create, which are commonly used in our sound design. These are as follows:

- Flat hi-hats, what we use as the main driving hat in our rhythmic patterns
- Open hi-hats, which we use to create lift and add transitional ear candy in a hi-hat rhythmic pattern and percussion, which compliments and adds texture to our hi-hat patterns

There are various types of hi-hat sounds in the marketplace, everything ranging from recorded live drum kits to synthetic sounds created from drum machines such as the Roland TR-808. There is no rule of thumb when it comes to picking hi-hat sounds, although if you study popular culture and the preceding decades, you may notice a pattern of certain types of hi-hat sounds representing certain eras. See these examples:

- In the 1980s, the Roland TR-808 drum machine hi-hats and drum sound were prevalent in most pop music productions.
- In the 1990s when hip-hop became mainstream, the use of sampling live-recorded drum sounds became prevalent.
- In the 2000s, the use of the Korg Triton and its relevant keyboard stock sounds became the prevailing hi-hat sounds of choice.
- In recent years, pop culture follows a trend of using all of these sounds in a very concentrated way. Trap music borrows from the Roland TR-808 sounds, yet some records choose to use live-recorded-sounding hi-hats too.

When it comes to creating a folder of signature-sounding hi-hats, I recommend having not just one main or key focal point of reference but creating a multitude of go-to hi-hats that may fit in different forms of production styles, like having live-recorded-sounding hi-hats for certain productions, in addition to having 808-sounding hi-hats for more trap- or urban-focused productions in FL Studio.

To get started, we will browse through FL Studio's stock hi-hat sounds and create a kit of "live-recorded-sounding" hi-hats. Again, when creating a hi-hat folder, we want a short and dry-sounding hi-hat and an open hi-hat. Percussion sounds can be added for texture to each type of sound or can be used sparsely in addition to these main driving sounds.

Let's dive into our **Browser**. These hi-hats already have a great live feel to them, and we will use these as our base foundation to create a signature hi-hat sound. In the stock drum kit sounds, the **Bracke CH1** sound represents a short and dry hi-hat we can use to start off:

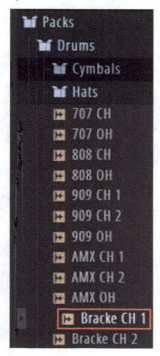

Figure 3.25: Browser | Packs | Drums | Hats| Bracke CH 1

Now, load the **Bracke CH1** hi-hat into the Channel Rack as we discussed in the *Using and organizing the Browser and Channel Rack* section in *Chapter 1*:

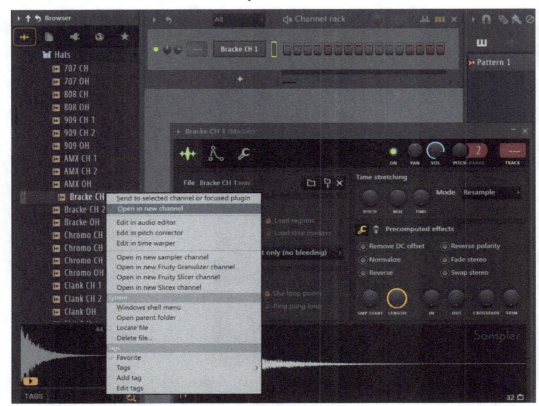

Figure 3.26: Channel Rack

Now, we are going to find another hi-hat noise to add to the Channel Rack for additional texture:

Figure 3.27: Browser | Packs | Drums | Hats| Glotch CH

Place a note by clicking both of the hi-hat sounds in the Channel Rack on bar one:

Figure 3.28: Channel Rack | Bracke CH 1| Glotch CH

In this example, I have left the volume range the same on both layers. I have done this as a matter of preference, but I do suggest you use your ear to combine layers based on the specificity of each sound used.

Now let's add the first hi-hat to the mixing channel:

Figure 3.29: Mixer | Bracke CH 1| Glotch CH

Now, what works well with hi-hats in my experience is either leaving them bare or adding a flanger or phaser to them.

> **Important note**
>
> Reverb plugins can work – but I don't recommend them as a first stab in experimenting with this type of sound. The hi-hat should fit into your overall mix as a rhythmic carry, and shouldn't be drowned out too far by a strong reverb, if any. Presets that work well for hi-hats include **Fruity Stereo Spacer** (for creating stereo spacing), **Fruity Chorus** (for adding texture), and **Fruity Flanger** (for creating motion-moving sidechaining).

Now that we have added the base hi-hat to the mixing channel, let's add **Fruity Flanger** to its mixing channel in the **Glotch CH** channel and use the **The Mover** preset to create a swinging stereo sidechain effect for the layered hi-hat:

Figure 3.30: Mixer | Glotch CH | Fruity Flanger | The Mover preset

This is a simple framework that introduces the concept of layering and adding plugin effects to hi-hat sounds, which you can use to get creative when making hi-hat sounds. There is no particular rule of thumb, but heed my suggestions when it comes to preferencing certain plugins over others unless the overall production has room for delays and reverbs.

Now let's look at open hi-hats. Whereas straight hi-hats are for holding down rhythm and carrying the track, open hi-hats add an accent to certain rhythmic patterns. There are certain stock open hi-hats in FL Studio similar to straight hi-hats that fit certain types of productions. For reference, FL Studio uses the tag *OH* for open hi-hats in its stock collection. Let's create an open hi-hat by using the 808 OH sound and right-click to open the **Open in new channel** button now as seen in *Figure 3.31*:

Figure 3.31: Browser | Packs | Drums | Hats | 808 OH

Now when we layer open hi-hats, we can take the approach of layering a second open hi-hat or finding a crisp attack layer that will slightly add an attack frequency to the base open hi-hat.

In my experience, certain open hi-hats can blend well with each other, and you should experiment as you build your sound design library – but be careful not to just add two open hi-hats together with the thought that anything can be layered. I recommend finding quick-attack hi-hats to add layers to the base open hi-hat. In the example in *Figure 3.32*, this is what we will do. So now, let's find another hi-hat to give the 808 open hi-hat an attack layer. The **Stud CH 1** hi-hat is a quick, crisp, and quick-attack hi-hat that makes a good addition to the 808 open hi-hat; let's add this as a separate instrument to the Channel Rack now:

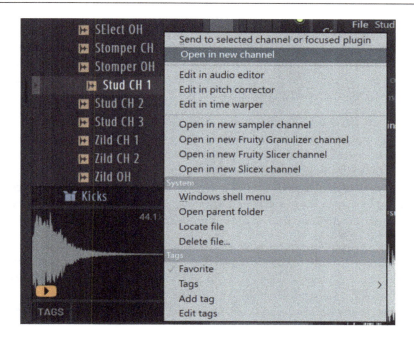

Figure 3.32: Browser | Packs | Drums | Hats| Stud CH 1

As this is a simple layer framework, we do not need to add the sounds to the **Mixer** unless you want to experiment with adding plugins to each sound. I will note that open hi-hats should be dry in most cases. You can experiment with stereo shaping or playing with the volume panning, but as a general rule of thumb, open hi-hats fit well when centered and dry.

Now that we have gone through the base frameworks for creating hi-hats, let's talk about how we can use FL Studio's stock VSTs to make custom sound designs and synths.

Creating synths and custom sounds

Before we dive fully into creating custom synth and patches, I want to tell you there are a few different ways to approach this. In my career, I have created both patches and layered synth sounds when experimenting with instrumentation development and signature sound frameworks, and recommend doing sound design via synths and melody sounds on a track-by-track basis. This may sound counterintuitive, but I'm going to explain why.

You certainly can spend hours, days, weeks, or longer creating custom synth patches by tweaking presets inside of FL Studio's VST plugins if you desire – but remember, I'm giving you tips for being a Power User. In *Chapter 1*, we talked about having goals and taking action – RUTHLESS ACTION! Ruthless action is heading toward your high-level goals, so never confuse activity with accomplishment. Accomplishment is achieving your goals.

This means your end goal is to pump out hits, not overcomplicate your day-to-day in FL Studio as a sound designer specifically. Of course, if you end up going the route of just creating patches to sell online in third-party marketplaces, you can do that, but this is a guide to creating billboard-charting records, so for the sake of your workflow, get in the habit of learning how to create custom synths and patches on a track-by-track basis.

For example, you may never use all of the wonderful patches you create, for reasons such as them not working for the type of records you are making, them not being good, and no one liking your tracks because you keep using some weird sine synth with a flanger in it. The market will tell you what works – that's just the reality of selling art. The reality is the best way to create a signature sound as it pertains to custom synth and melody sounds is to work through each track by first creating what the chord progression or melody top line is, and working backward to try and make it stand out and unique so that it doesn't complicate the rest of your production.

Now, there are a few key components to creating interesting-sounding synths in your tracks. In your toolkit, you have access to multiple VSTs that generate synth and orchestral sounds, which you can layer, and you have mixing plugins, which you can add on top of those mixing channels to tweak or add flavor to the synth or instrumentation you may use in your production. For example, **Fruity Flanger**, **Gross Beat**, **Fruity Reverb 2**, and **Fruity Delay 3** all work well for creative mixing and adding sonic uniqueness to a sound wave.

So, with this in mind, let's load up a new project and add the **FL Keys** VST to the Channel Rack as a base work tool for creating a melody we can use as an example. Now let's create a basic chord progression:

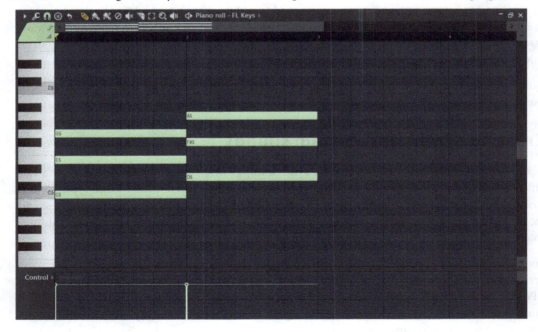

Figure 3.33: FL Keys | Piano Roll | chord progression

The framework I am using involves a similar formula to creating custom drum sounds for me – layering other VSTs over the note midi pattern created using **FL Keys**, experimenting with mixing plugins, and adding layers of additional VSTs.

When it comes to creating records, the general consensus on how you select certain VST preset sounds varies, but at a high level, certain types of synths and sounds work better for certain types of melodic patterns and chords. For chords, it's best to use pads, arpeggios, and keys (including rhodes, synth keys, natural keys, and variations of these). For melody top lines, presets such as leads (synths and natural sounds, including horns, strings, pianos, saws, sines, bells, squares, etc.) work best when creating top-line melody frameworks.

Now that we have a basic chord progression, we are going to load one of FL Studio's stock VST plugins, **Sawer**, into the Channel Rack in replacement of the **FL Keys** VST:

Figure 3.34: FL Keys | right-click | Replace | Sawer

Now, in **Sawer**, we are going to use a pad preset, **FG Classic Mood**, to play the chord progression:

Figure 3.35: Sawer | FG Classic Mood

Now we are going to add a layered VST following the same procedure as we did when creating drum sounds. We are going to add another **Sawer** VST to the Channel Rack and copy and paste the same chord progression into the second **Sawer** VST plugin in the Channel Rack as follows:

Figure 3.36: Channel Rack | Sawer # 2 | Chord progession copied and pasted

Now in the second **Sawer** VST preset selection, we are going to layer it with an additional pad preset, **FG HUGE**, as seen in *Figure 3.37*:

Figure 3.37: Sawer | FG HUGE

This is the basic framework for creating custom synth sounds in an attempt at sound design. From this point, you could follow up by adding additional VST layers with keys, synth sounds, and so on, but we have established the basic framework. A high-level simple point of view is simply layering different sound presets using the same chord progressions to add unique texture.

Now, let's add both **Sawer** VSTs from the Channel Rack to the mixing channel:

Figure 3.38: Mixer | Sawer 1 | Sawer 2

For the first **Sawer** VST, let's add **Fruity Flanger**, using the **Bad Leslie** preset:

Figure 3.39: Mixer | Sawer 1 | Fruity Flanger | Bad Leslie preset

Now, let's add **Fruity Stereo Spacer** to the second-layer VST to give the second VST a wide stereo feel. We can do this by adding this plugin to the channel **Mixer** as follows:

Figure 3.40: Mixer | Sawer 2 | Fruity Stereo Shaper | Delay preset

Viola! We have now created a two-layer custom chord progression. This is a basic framework for how to add plugin effects while using layering for each VST. Each VST has its own input and output effects contained within the VST visual and you can experiment to add attack, delay, soften attack output, and more. I personally do not use these but rather focus more on layering and plugins to create the desired effects.

This basic framework now serves as your design theory when creating synths and sounds to output chords and melodies. Not complicated, and very "duh," but trust me, the greatest secrets in life are usually the simplest – it's not about overdoing it, or pulling your hair out to make something unique, so always follow the rule "keep it simple."

Now that we have walked through the basic framework of how we can leverage FL Studio's stock VSTs and plugins to create unique melodies and chord progressions, let's talk about creating a producer tag and how it relates to your sonic branding as a producer.

Producer tags and sonic branding

It only takes 0.146 seconds to evoke a reaction or response in a listener. We automatically experience an emotional response whenever we hear certain sounds or tones.

When it comes to creating a signature sound, everything we have discussed encompasses your ability to create unique-sounding drums, hi-hats, synths, and arrangement styles. How you create formulas in your own production style and ultimately compose your own productions in FL Studio will define your signature sound in the marketplace. With the nuances associated with productions, this will be noticed typically by super-fans and other creatives who have a musician's ear, but general listeners won't pick up on these nuances. So, how do you let people know you produce a record without telling every single person you come across that you did? This is where a producer tag comes into play. In certain genres, such as rap, hip-hop, and sometimes pop music, producers have what we call "tags." This is a relatively new concept in the general scope of music production that became popular in the late 2000s. When it comes to creating a beat tag, using a third party to record a tag can be beneficial, and you can record your own tagline (with a vocal line such as "DA got that dope!", JR Rotem's "J-J-J-J-R", or Southside's "808 Mafia"). Websites such as Fiverr or hiring a vocalist who specializes in creating vocal tags can do this for you for a small fee.

In addition to having a vocal tagline, let's discuss the concept of sonic logos or what are known as mnemonics. This is a concept that uses a signature or custom sound that represents your unique fingerprint or beat tag in each of your productions. 808 Mafia's "kill bill" siren is a great example of this in recent history. Lex Luger's "riser" also encompasses this framework of sonic branding theory.

To create a sonic logo, you want to ideally have it be neutral in the sense of key or tone. It has to be able to work in every type of production you create. For this reason, I recommend a short stab sound, riser, or transitional sound you can use at the start of your productions.

FL Studio has a good starting point for these types of neutral sounds we can explore to create a sonic logo. Let's look through the **Browser** and identify a few examples:

Figure 3.41: Browser | Packs | Risers | SFX

In order to create a signature sonic logo, you should use the frameworks of layering and adding plugin effects to multiple sounds or a single sound. You can use any type of sound without limitation to make a sonic logo in these two folders, but use them as a framework for how your custom riser or SFX should sound.

I have used both custom sounds and hired vocal tag providers in my production career, and it's a matter of preference. You will run into situations where certain labels or clients may remove your beat tag from the finished master recording, and they do so for a host of reasons. Don't take it personally if this happens. At the end of the day, you are building your discography and leveraging relationships to continue to move forward in your career. A beat tag can be a great way to sonically brand yourself, but it's not a requirement.

Let's now examine some specific methods and equipment that producers might utilize to refine their arranging approach and create a signature sound.

Creating an arrangement style

When it comes to arrangement style, we will discuss how to actually do this in FL Studio in *Chapter 6*, but in this chapter, I will discuss why a producer's approach to arranging records ultimately adds to their own signature sound.

Your arrangement style or formula as a music producer can be extremely important in developing a distinctive sound that is exclusively recognizable as being your own. When it comes to sonic branding, this is especially crucial because it enables listeners to instantly recognize the producer's work and associate it with a specific sound or approach. The use of particular chord progressions, the placement of particular instruments or components in the mix, or the use of particular effects or processing methods can all be examples of a producer's arrangement style.

These components eventually start to blend together to form the producer's sound, giving them a unique sonic identity that distinguishes them from other producers in the field. Producers can develop a strong brand by honing their arrangement techniques and developing a special formula.

In conclusion, a producer's signature approach to arrangements is an intricate fusion of these techniques and other components that come together to produce a distinct sound that is instantly recognizable to fans and peers alike.

Mixing for a creative feel (not the same as mixing for release)

When it comes to how to mix for a creative feel versus mixing for release, we will walk through these steps in *Chapter 7*. For now, I want to highlight to you that this is another component of creating a signature sound that most novice producers don't think about, but that all Power Users do. That is, mixing can be used with a creative approach to build and design a producer's signature, in addition to mixing for commercial release, which is specific to making sure the finished record will sound the same across every type of medium a listener or fan might engage in hearing the final record (e.g., headphones, a car stereo system, a record player, sound systems in a venue, etc.).

A producer's signature sound includes mixing for a creative feel because it gives them the ability to control the final sonic character of their creations. A mix can significantly affect how the listener hears each component of a production and can also be used to bring all of the components of a track together into a single, seamless sound. Producers can differentiate themselves from other producers in the field by developing a distinctive approach to mixing for their productions.

To create a driving, rhythmic feel, for instance, one producer might use a mix that places a lot of emphasis on the bass and drums, while another producer might use a mix that is more subdued and atmospheric to achieve the same effect. Each producer will have their own distinctive approach to using mixing techniques such as reverb, EQ, compression, and automation to alter the sound of a track in different ways. A producer's productions will become more recognizable and distinctive over time as they hone their mixing skills and create a distinctive sound. Listeners will be able to quickly recognize certain sonic elements and traits that are consistent with that producer's earlier work when they hear a new track from them, strengthening their sense of brand identity and fostering the growth of a devoted fan base. The ability to mix for a creative feel is ultimately a crucial component of a producer's toolkit because it enables them to make distinctive and memorable productions that stand out in a crowded market.

Overall, the balance between artistic expression and commercial appeal is what distinguishes mixing to be creative from commercial release. A talented mixing engineer or producer will be able to balance these various priorities to produce a track that is both artistically compelling and commercially viable. Both approaches are significant in their own right.

Summary

To stand out in the crowded music industry, producers must develop their own distinctive sounds. You must put effort into producing unique instrument noises, custom drum kits, and synth sounds in order to accomplish this. This aids in developing a distinctive sound that distinguishes you from other producers and is recognizable to your audience. Custom drum kits are crucial because they support you by giving your tracks a distinguishable rhythm and groove. Stock drum sounds can produce a monotonous, unremarkable sound. Instead, you can achieve a distinctive sound that is particular to your style by making your own drum kits using samples or synthesizers.

Additionally important to developing a producer's signature sound are synth sounds and instrument noises. To make your tracks stand out, experiment with various settings and effects to produce sounds that are distinctive to your style. Even if you are using FL Studio's stock sounds, it's crucial to continuously develop your unique sound as a producer. To do this, experiment with various plugins and presets to produce fresh sounds and textures that match your aesthetic. You can stay relevant and keep your audience interested by consistently improving and evolving your sound.

In conclusion, developing a distinctive sound as a producer is crucial to making a name for yourself in the music business. You can accomplish this by using custom drum kits, synth sounds, and unusual instrument noises. It's also crucial to constantly develop your signature sound, even when using stock sounds. This contributes to developing a distinctive and recognizable sound that distinguishes you from other producers.

Now, let's jump into how we can use FL Studio to leverage your signature sound with drum programming technics that can make or break the overall impact of your tracks!

Exercise

Crafting a custom sound kit in FL Studio: The objective is to develop your own unique sound kit using the stock FL Studio sounds and **Mixer** plugins to enhance your creative sound palette for future productions.

We will follow these steps:

1. **Select a theme or mood**: Choose a specific theme, mood, or genre you want your custom sound kit to cater to. This will help guide your choices and maintain a cohesive sonic identity.

2. **Source stock sounds**: Explore the stock sound library in FL Studio to find suitable base sounds for your sound kit. Look for samples, presets, and loops that resonate with your chosen theme or mood.

3. **Layer and modify**: Use the **Mixer** plugins to layer and modify the selected sounds. Experiment with effects such as EQ, reverb, distortion, and compression to transform the raw sounds into something unique. Remember, the goal is to create variations and textures that align with your desired sonic character.

4. **Synthesize your own elements**: Utilize FL Studio's built-in synthesizers such as 3xOSC, Harmless, or GMS to craft original sound elements. Tweak the oscillators, envelopes, filters, and modulation options to sculpt distinct sounds that can be added to your custom kit.

5. **Create percussive elements**: Dive into FL Studio's percussion and drum samples to generate your own percussive elements. Layer, process, and manipulate these sounds to achieve a dynamic range of percussion that complements your sound kit.

6. **Design synth presets**: Explore the various synthesizer plugins available in FL Studio to design your own synth presets. Adjust parameters such as oscillators, filters, LFOs, and envelopes to fashion unique synth sounds that fit within your chosen theme.

7. **Organize and label**: Assemble your newly created sounds into a well-organized sound kit. Label each sound with descriptive names to easily identify and access them during future productions.

8. **Test and experiment**: Put your custom sound kit to the test by incorporating it into your music productions. Experiment with different combinations and arrangements to see how your kit can elevate your tracks.

9. **Refine and iterate**: As you work with your custom sound kit, take note of what works well and what could be improved. Continuously refine and iterate on your sound kit to ensure it becomes a valuable asset in your production arsenal.

10. **Reflect and expand**: After using your custom sound kit in several projects, reflect on its impact and versatility. Consider expanding the kit by adding more sounds, refining existing ones, or creating variations to keep your sonic palette evolving!

4

Working through Drum Programming and Arrangements

FL Studio, with its user-friendly interface, is regarded by many as one of the best software options for drum programming. Even those who are completely new to music production can easily navigate FL Studio and program drum beats and patterns. One of my favorite parts of producing in FL Studio is the ease of use and flexibility of drum programming in the Channel Rack.

Back in the early days of hip hop and rap production, almost all drum programming was done using a **music production computer** (**MPC**), keyboard, or touchpad hardware. With the advent of FL Studio, this was revolutionized for the sake of being experimental and providing a quick workflow. Now, don't get me wrong, there is a certain feel or vibe to touching pads when creating drum loops; it gives a quasi-live feel to it and it isn't quantized as perfectly as using the Channel Rack, but you would require a ton of practice to properly make use of the hardware.

To that end, we will cover the following topics in this chapter:

- Taking the creation of drum loops to another level
- Creativity versus programming
- Using the Channel Rack to create billboard charting drum loops
- Creating suspense through transitionary ear candy
- Drum programming in FL Studio
- Exploring time-tested drum programming templates

Taking the creation of drum loops to another level

Let's discuss how we can start using the Channel Rack to take your drum programming theory to the next level using foundational principles you can build from.

Two potent FL Studio tools enable thorough and accurate drum programming:

- **Step Sequencer**: Simple beats can be easily programmed using the step sequencer's grid-based interface
- **Piano Roll**: The Piano Roll supports more intricate and nuanced programming

Various built-in drum sounds and samples are available in FL Studio, as well as the option to import your own samples from third-party sources or your own signature sound kit. Creating drum beats and patterns in FL Studio requires utilizing the step sequencer or Piano Roll.

Drum beats may be programmed using the step sequencer's grid-based interface by placing individual steps, or strikes, on the grid. The columns indicate the various beat steps, while each row represents a distinct drum sound. By clicking on the correct cell in the grid, you can change the volume, panning, and other settings for each stage. The Piano Roll is a more conventional user interface where you can create, edit, and remove notes on a grid to program drum beats. Pitch is represented by the vertical axis, while time is represented by the horizontal axis. The Piano Roll can be used to generate more complicated rhythms and patterns and to manipulate MIDI data coming from other sources.

You may either build a new pattern in the step sequencer or a new MIDI clip in the Piano Roll to create a new drum pattern. You can begin adding drum sounds to a new pattern or clip after it has been produced by choosing them from the Channel Rack or the browser, and you can then program the beats using the step sequencer or the Piano Roll.

To improve your drum programming abilities, you can also employ a variety of tools and plugins, including a drum synthesizer, drum samples, and a drum machine.

You can simply arrange, edit, and organize your drum patterns using FL Studio's Playlist window, which you can also utilize to build a full song. This offers countless opportunities for developing distinctive and intriguing drum sounds.

There are a ton of plugins and effects available in FL Studio that can be used to improve and sculpt your drum sounds. Equalization, compression, reverb, distortion, and other effects are part of this.

FL Studio enables you to import audio files or record your own drum sounds to use in your song. You can also use it to edit the existing drum sounds and samples you have by changing the volume, EQ, compression, and other effects. FL Studio has a wide-ranging mixer that enables you to precisely mix and master your drums by allowing you to adjust the levels, panning, and effects of each individual drum sound.

All these features and tools make FL Studio among the most well-liked and widely used programs for drum programming among music producers.

Creativity versus programming

Now, just like everything in music, you can be as creative as you want to be, but here I will share some secrets as they relate to creating billboard charting drum loops and arrangements that have stood the test of time. Drum patterns, loops, or sequences are all about creating an underlying rhythm to your production; they are the foundation for how your song will move and how songwriters will cadence their vocals, and determine whether the song is upbeat, slow, heartfelt, or abstract.

The first point of origin is that, in rap, each coast has its own distinct sound and production style within the genre, and has a specific feel and style of drum programming. Rap music from the East and West Coast typically follows **beats per minute** (**BPM**) range of 80-100, whereas southern music typically follows a BPM range in double time of 130-150. This is important to understand as rap has become the cultural cornerstone of how every other genre now creates productions. Whether it's pop music, country music, or R&B, all of these genres have adapted rap production styles in their drum programming over the last decade. Think about it: country songs can be heard using hi-hat triplets, R&B songs typically feature supporting artists rapping, and pop music has borrowed everything it can from rap production techniques.

From this framework, each genre of rap music has a similar placement of the kicks and snares, but they are slightly different in their placement within the Channel Rack.

Let's talk about how to use the Channel Rack to start implementing programming theory.

Using the Channel Rack to create billboard charting drum loops

Let's first dive into *how* traditional hip hop drum arrangements work in the Channel Rack. There are a few essential stages to creating a hip hop drum arrangement in FL Studio, which are as follows:

1. Create a fresh pattern in the step sequencer or a fresh MIDI clip on the Piano Roll to get things going. This will be the basis for your drum arrangement.

2. Add the various drum sounds that you'll be using in your arrangement after that. To accomplish this, choose them from the Channel Rack or browser, drag them into the pattern or clip, and then drop them into a Channel Rack line. Kick, snare, hi-hat, and clap drums are typical hip hop drum sounds.

3. Start composing your drum beats using the Piano Roll or step sequencer. It's typical for hip hop rhythms to employ a constant kick and snare pattern while changing the hi-hat and clapping rhythms to increase variety and interest. The tools and plugins can also be used to improve the sound of your drums.

4. To arrange your drum patterns and create a full song, you can also use the Playlist window. Here, you can quickly arrange, edit, and organize your drum patterns.

5. Create an original and captivating drum arrangement by experimenting with various rhythms and patterns. Using automation and pattern effects, you can also add variations and create fills on the Piano Roll.

6. Once you have a strong drum arrangement, you can add samples, basslines, and melodies to finish off your hip hop track.

7. Then, mix and master your drums by adjusting the volume, EQ, compression, and other effects.

Using the Channel Rack to create hip hop theory-based drum programming sequences is easy; let's talk about using a simple formula to use as a foundational template. A foundational template is a framework term for describing a base-level template upon which you can expand, specific to a genre or type of music you are composing. I will walk you through the basics of each of these foundational templates, so you have a base foundation for each main driving genre created in FL Studio.

The hip hop Channel Rack framework

Now, let's walk through this framework by opening the Channel Rack and adding a kick and snare sample:

1. Let's set the **Beats Per Minute (BPM)** to 90:

Figure 4.1: In the center of the image, you will see the BPM manipulator at 90 BPM

2. Now, let's set the kick and snare pattern as follows:

Figure 4.2: Channel Rack | Drum sequence pattern 1

3. Now, let's add a hi-hat sound into the Channel Rack, and place it on a basic four-bar loop:

Figure 4.3: Channel Rack | Drum sequence pattern 2

This is the basic hip hop drum loop pattern you will hear in most hip hop records.

The West Coast hip hop Channel Rack framework

West Coast drum programming follows the funk-R&B theory of drum placement. Let's talk about how to use the Channel Rack to identify basic foundational templates you can build from in your productions:

1. Let's set the BPM to `100` and make a West Coast drum pattern that has worked for 3 decades:

Figure 4.4: Channel Rack | 100 BPM | Drum sequence pattern 3

2.   Now, let's place the hi-hat on a two-bar placement loop:

Figure 4.5: Channel Rack | 100 BPM | Drum sequence pattern 3 | Fill each 2 steps

3.   Now, let's give the hi-hat some energy by augmenting the volume of each second hit:

Figure 4.6: Channel Rack | 100 BPM | Drum Sequence Pattern 3 | Velocity | Volume

This makes it sound closer to a live hat, whereas when a drummer hits a cymbal, they don't hit the cymbal with the same intensity as before.

You will see that the kick is sparse; that's because West Coast hip hop relies heavily on bass guitars to create the rhythmic section, whereas in East Coast hip hop, the drums are more driving.

The modern West Coast hip hop Channel Rack framework

Modern West Coast hip hop is a hybrid of southern 808-driven drum programming but keeps the same tempo as its predecessor. Let's show you what that looks like:

1.   Here, we will take a slightly replaced drum pattern but add an additional kick and 808 sound:

Figure 4.7: Channel Rack | Drum sequence pattern 4 | 808 Kick

Now, these two 808 kicks are adding a heavy bottom frequency to the kicks, but 808 sub-kicks typically act as bass notes when composing. They aren't typically kept on middle C or the root note of your track.

2. Open the Piano Roll and place the notes throughout the key sections to create a bass rhythm loop. In this example, I'm following a simple layout:

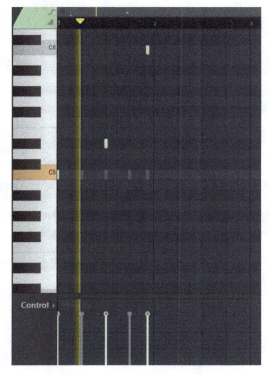

Figure 4.8: Piano Roll | 808 Kick | Note adjustment

3. Now, when it comes to hi-hat patterns in the modern West Coast music style, you can follow a two-bar placement formula like this:

Figure 4.9: Channel Rack | hat closed 3 hard | Hi-hat two-step pattern

You can also follow the modern hi-hat triplet and chop framework in West Coast music when taking a modern approach to creating these types of compositions.

The trap music Channel Rack framework

Now, let's discuss the basic framework for creating hi-hat sequences using the trap framework:

1. Start by opening the Piano Roll and creating a new MIDI clip. This will be the foundation for your hi-hat pattern.

2. Next, add a hi-hat sound to the pattern by selecting it from the Channel Rack or the browser and then dragging and dropping it into the MIDI clip.

    Begin programming your hi-hat pattern using the Piano Roll. In trap music, it's common to use a consistent 16th-note pattern, with the hi-hat being played on every 16th note. However, you can also play with the rhythm and the pattern to add variation and interest.

3. To create the characteristic "rolling" hi-hat effect, you can add a series of 16th-note triplets by adding a series of three 8th-note triplets. This can be achieved by selecting the 8th note, and then using the `Triplet` function.

4.   Once you have the basic hi-hat pattern, you can add variations by inserting ghost notes or open hi-hats. Ghost notes are played with a lower velocity and create a more subtle and smooth flow.

Open hi-hats are played with a velocity of zero and are used to create a break or a build-up in the pattern. You can also add automation and effects to your hi-hat pattern, such as panning, filtering, and reverb, to create a more dynamic and interesting sound.

5.   Finally, don't forget to adjust the volume and the pitch of your hi-hat pattern to make sure that it sits well in the mix with the rest of the elements in your track.

To use this basic framework for creating hi-hat sequences using the trap framework, follow these steps:

1.   Let's open the hi-hat pattern in the Piano Roll:

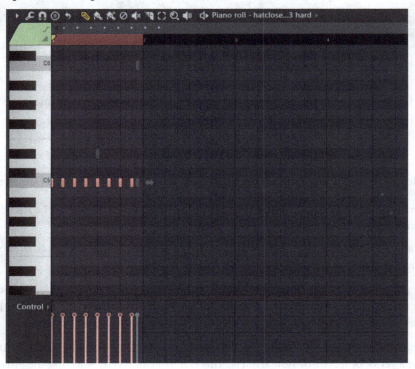

Figure 4.10: Piano Roll | Hi-hat two-step pattern

2. Now, let's stretch the following notes in the Piano Roll so that when we use the Chop tool, we have the runway to add notes:

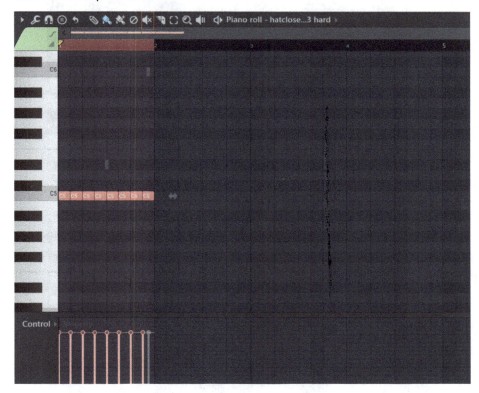

Figure 4.11: Piano Roll | Hi-hat two-step pattern | Note extension

When it comes to adding triplets or chopping hi-hats into the modern hi-hat roles, it's important to note that these types of nuances are best used in transitionary positions within the four-bar loop before the snare, or before the loop end to carry the rhythm section, as in *Figure 4.12*.

3.   Now, let's go to tools and select **Chop** and **4 bar**:

Figure 4.12: Piano Roll | Piano Roll - chopper | Hi-hat triplet

Now, we have a modern hi-hat pattern! You can experiment with how many hi-hat rolls you want to include using the Chop tool, but this describes the basic overview of how to integrate hi-hat rolls in trap music hip hop frameworks. Using this formula and framework, we can also incorporate this hi-hat framework into modern West Coast hip hop templates, as a matter of preference.

Now, let's make a trap or southern loop. In hip hop, *southern music* described the type of sound that was developed in the early 1990s and 2000s, which eventually evolved into modern *trap music*. Southern music, in this instance, refers to the more soulful approach to this genre-specific type of sound. Let's do this now:

1.   Set the BPM to 140. Because we are in double time, we need to add an additional 16 bars in the Channel Rack:

Figure 4.13: Channel Rack

2. Now, place the snare in double time, as follows:

Figure 4.14: Channel Rack | Snare placement

3. Now, let's start adding the kick using a proven trap loop formula:

Figure 4.15: Channel Rack | Kick placement | Snare placement

4. Now, let's add the 808 as follows (we won't tune them in the Piano Roll now; this is to show you where they fit best as far as trap rhythm goes):

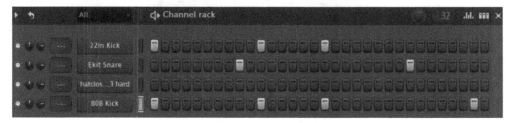

Figure 4.16: Channel Rack | Kick placement | Snare placement | 808 Kick placement

5. Now, let's add a hi-hat on a two-bar placement:

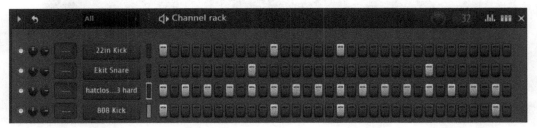

Figure 4.17: Channel Rack | Kick placement | Snare placement | 808 Kick placement | Hi-hat placement

The hi-hat can stay like this, or you can use the modern hi-hat triplet theory as we did in the trap music hi-hat theory. Let's do this now.

6. Open the hi-hat pattern in the Piano Roll and stretch these specific notes to create a rhythm as follows:

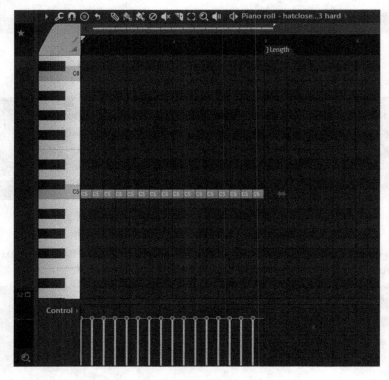

Figure 4.18: Piano Roll | Hi-hat placement | Note extension

7.   Select **Tools** | **Chop** | **4 bar**:

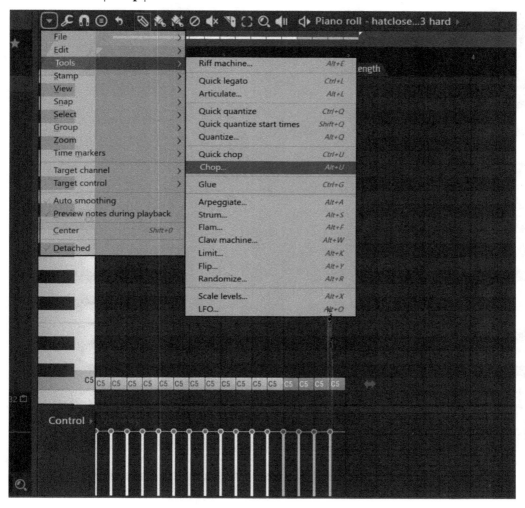

Figure 4.19: Piano Roll | Tools | Chop

8.   Now, let's chop the following hi-hat sections to create a trap hi-hat pattern:

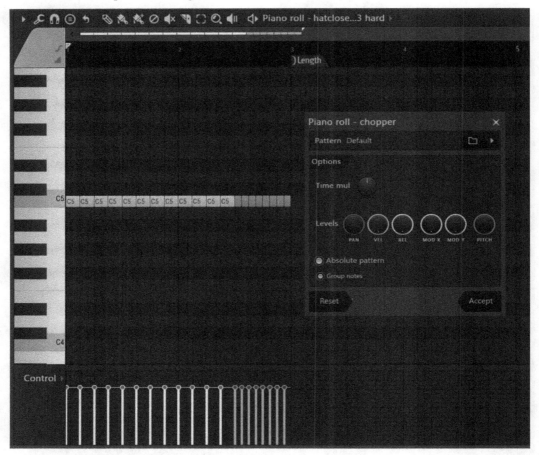

Figure 4.20: Piano Roll | Hi-hat placement | chopper | hi-hat triplets

We can also create another hi-hat triplets pattern as follows:

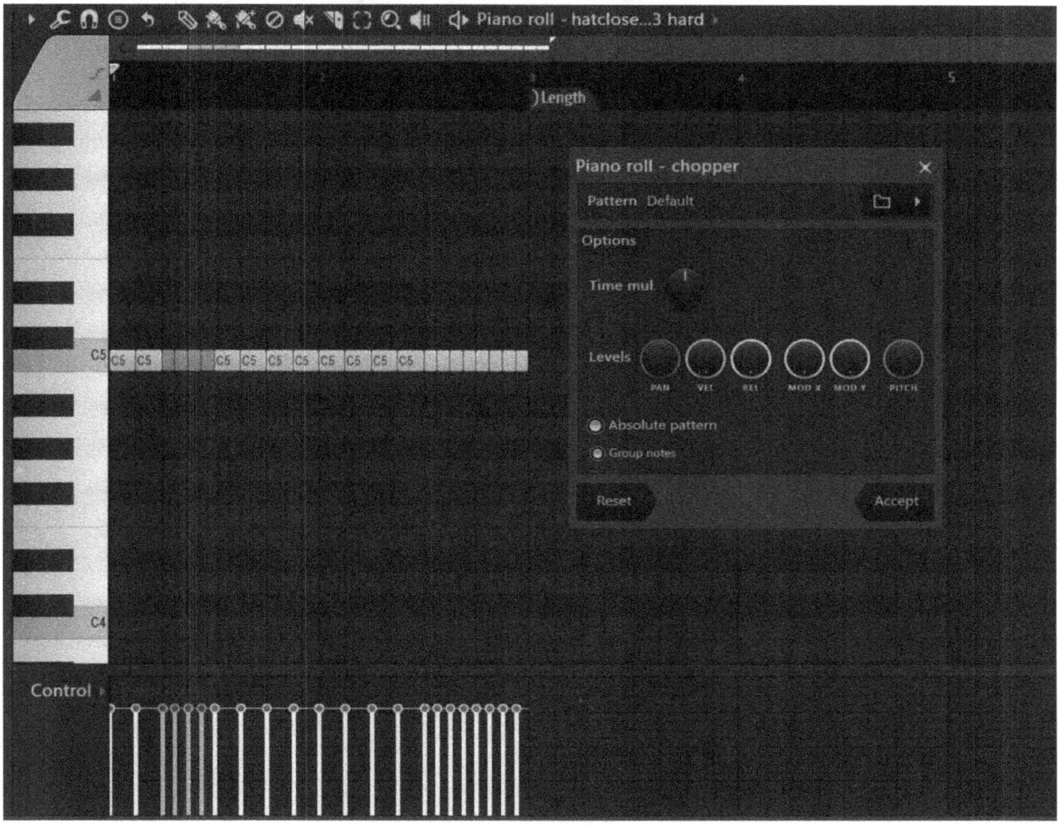

Figure 4.21: Piano Roll | chopper | hi-hat triplets variation two

The examples can be tweaked to fit your personal style and creativity. This example simply shows the framework for using the Chop tool in the Piano Roll to create trap hi-hat roll patterns.

To summarize, the hip hop Channel Rack framework is a structured approach to programming hip hop drum patterns using the Channel Rack in FL Studio. These frameworks involve dividing drum kit sounds into separate channels for each drum sound and exploring different types of drum patterns commonly used in hip hop, including boom bap, trap, and West Coast styles. Throughout the chapter so far, we have emphasized the importance of experimentation and creativity within the framework and provided step-by-step instructions for creating each pattern. By following the guidelines laid out in the chapter so far, you can create authentic and dynamic hip hop drum programming for your tracks.

Now, let's discuss how we can create tension and keep listeners captivated by using transitional ear candy!

Creating suspense through transitionary ear candy

In the context of music production, **ear candy** refers to little elements that you add to a song that grab the listener's attention and keep them engaged. This can include things such as risers, sweeps, vocal chops, drum fills, and other sound effects that are strategically placed throughout a song. Think about things like risers, sweeps, and other sound effects that you can strategically place throughout a track. The whole idea is to add texture and excitement to the song and make it more memorable for the listener. By placing these elements, you can enhance the overall impact of your tracks and create a more engaging listening experience. So, next time you're producing a track, try adding some ear candy and see how it takes your music to the next level!

Ear candy keeps your listeners engaged and wanting more, so let's walk through how to create some suspenseful and smooth transitions between sections in your tracks. One of the key things you should do is use transitionary ear candy such as reverse cymbals, risers, and sweeps to lead the listener from one section to another. This will give your music a sense of progression and keep it interesting.

When you're arranging your drum programming in the Playlist window, you need to pay attention to bar counts and rhythm sections. This means breaking down your track into distinct sections and using different drum patterns for each section. By doing this, you can create a sense of progression and build tension over time. We can also use this framework to add drum fills and breakdowns to create tension and release. Fills at the end of a section can build anticipation for what's coming next, while breakdowns can strip away elements and leave just a sparse drum pattern to build up tension before launching into the next section with full force.

In *Figure 4.22*, I have a basic 8-bar count with a drum fill placed at the end of it to show you how to place ear candy appropriately at the end of 8-bar counts:

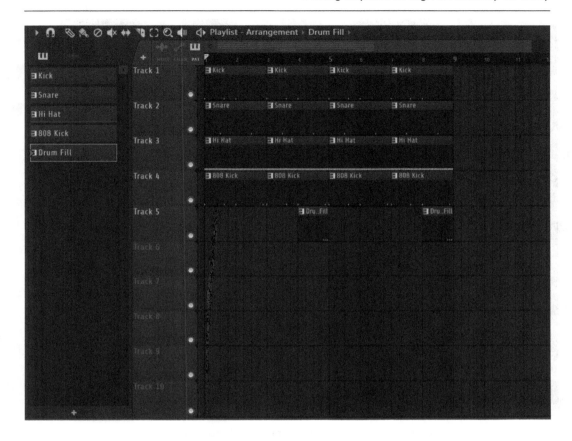

Figure 4.22: Playlist window | Drum arrangement | Drum Fill

As you can see in *Figure 4.22*, the drum fill ends the 8-bar count and leads into the next bar count section.

Now, let's do a simple exercise showing the concept of stripping away elements in the **Playlist** window to create some tension as seen in *Figure 4.23*. Here, we have removed **Kick** and **Hi Hat** in the **Playlist** window as an example:

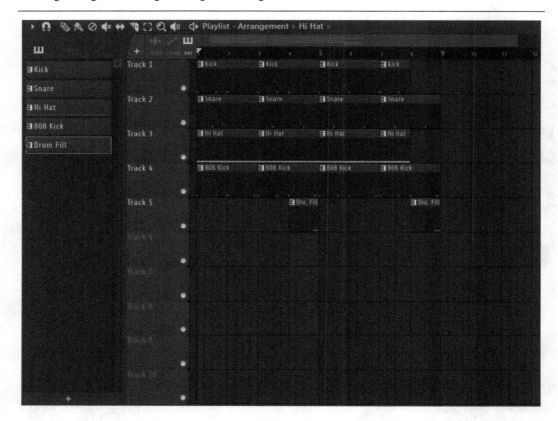

Figure 4.23: Playlist window | Drum arrangement | Drum rearrangement

The key takeaway of using ear candy in section transitions is to keep the listener engaged. When considering ear candy, it can be anything from percussion and effects to musical components that edge into the next bar count section.

In my experience, it is best to keep things simple, but also experiment until you find what works best for you. Certain tracks will sound better with less ear candy, while others that are minimal in nature will benefit more from using it in your transition sections.

Now, let's talk a little about how the structure of a song plays into using ear candy. Songs comprise the following sections:

- **Verse**: This is the section of a song that typically tells a story or sets up the main idea of the song. It usually has the same melody and chord progression each time it's played, but the lyrics change to advance the story or idea. This is known as the **A section**.

- **B section:** The B section is a contrasting section of the song that follows the verse, and is typically the second half of the verse. It can have a different melody, rhythm, or chord progression to create contrast and provide a break from the repetition of the song; however, in modern music, it is simply used to build up to the point of the chorus. I should mention that, in traditional music production before the modern era, B sections would typically be used *after* a chorus, whereas B sections in modern terms come *before* the chorus.

- **Chorus:** The chorus is the section of a song that typically repeats a catchy melody and lyrics. It's usually the most memorable part of the song and so is often what people remember most. It provides a sense of familiarity and ties the different sections of the song together.

- **Bridge:** The bridge is a section of the song that provides contrast to the verse and chorus. It often has a different melody, rhythm, or chord progression and is used to break up the repetition of the song. The bridge can also provide a sense of resolution or lead into the final chorus.

- **Interlude:** The interlude is a section of the song that's used as a musical break between other sections. It can be instrumental or have vocals, but it's often a way to add a new musical idea or texture to the song.

- **Outro:** The outro is the section at the end of the song that provides a sense of closure. It can be a repeat of the chorus or a new melody or chord progression that brings the song to a satisfying conclusion.

Now that we have a general understanding of the song sections, we can discuss how to use ear candy effectively to lead into song sections in a time-tested formula for creating an engaging production.

Here are a couple of key takeaways I've learned in my career that will help you stand out in your productions:

- When it comes to transitionary ear candy placement, the general rule of thumb is to use them at certain song section changes, not every 4 or 8 bars. For example, ear candy should be used to bring a verse into a B section, a B section into a chorus, and so forth. This is a simple tip that will give you a professional-sounding production when used correctly.

- Another tip I have learned over the years is to try using two or three different ear candy components in your overall production. For example, try using a cymbal reverse into the B section, and a sweep into the chorus, while a drum fill at the end of the chorus can be used. This gives your production just that much more of a nuanced sound to it to keep your listeners engaged.

Overall, FL Studio's Playlist window can help you create a track that keeps your listeners engaged and excited from start to finish. With some rhythm sections, transitionary ear candy, and careful attention to bar counts, you can make your drum progressions both captivating and unforgettable.

Now, I'm going to explain high-level drum theory in the upcoming section.

Drum programming in FL Studio

The high-level drum theory relates to each specific subgenre as a working framework of theory. But I will say that when you are creating a production in FL Studio, you should always be open to moving kicks around to best fit the rhythmic top-line melody if you are starting a track with a top line first as opposed to starting a track with a drum arrangement. A good rule of thumb is that a kick should always synchronize with a note change point, or at the start of the next bar.

Let's show you exactly what I mean by using the drum pattern synchronized with a note progression in the Piano Roll:

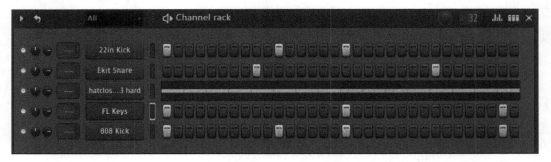

Figure 4.24: Channel Rack | Drum sequence with hi-hat triplets via the Piano Roll

Notice that the FL Keys inputs are on the same pattern block as the kicks; this implies that the keynote has the same block pattern as the kick and follows it succinctly. In most cases, you won't use a VST in this form; it will be composed within the Piano Roll. This is important when using samples in your productions, where the sample hits in line with a kick can create a great cohesive relationship between the two, making the track sound great.

In rap and its subgenres, certain kick and snare placements are applicable as a general rule of thumb. Rap has a specific production style where the kick is more active and drives the rhythm in a section of the track, whereas in country or pop music, the kick drum simply holds the rhythm section as opposed to carrying it fully.

Now that we have the basics, I'm going to share my secret workflow templates, which you can copy and augment as you please.

Drum sequence templates for hacking billboards

The drum sequence templates discussed in this section are just framework suggestions and are not meant to be overly complicated "plug and play" patterns, but rather, starting points to experimentation using BPM ranges and specific pattern points as a frame of reference.

Let's now discuss these drum sequence templates.

East Coast Patterns

So, let's talk about East Coast Patterns, which is a drum programming template for creating hip hop beats in the East Coast style. This style is known for its hard-hitting boom bap drums and sample-based production.

The East Coast Patterns framework is designed for a BPM range of 80-90, and it features a combination of kick, snare, hi-hat, and percussion elements. Here's how it works: the kick drum is placed on the first and third beats of the bar, while the snare is placed on the second and fourth beats, creating that classic boom-bap rhythm. The hi-hat is used to add rhythmic texture and movement, and there are variations in its placement throughout the pattern to keep things interesting. In addition to these core elements, the pattern also includes some percussion elements that are used sparingly to add additional accents and interest to the rhythm. By using the East Coast Pattern framework as a starting point, you can create authentic and dynamic East Coast-style drum programming in your tracks.

Figure 4.25 shows East Coast pattern 1 (BPM range 80-90):

Figure 4.25: Channel Rack | Drum sequence 4

Figure 4.26 shows East Coast pattern 2 (BPM range 80-90):

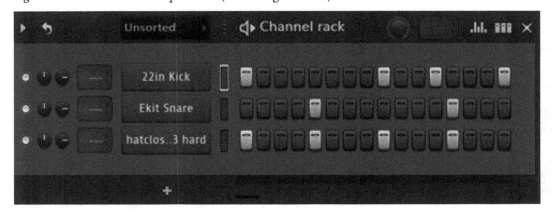

Figure 4.26: Channel Rack | Drum sequence 5

Figure 4.27 shows East Coast pattern 3 (BPM range 80-90):

Figure 4.27: Channel Rack | Drum sequence 6

West Coast Patterns

Let's move on to West Coast Patterns, which is a drum programming template designed for creating hip hop beats in the West Coast style. This style is known for its laid-back, funky grooves and synth-heavy production.

The West Coast Patterns framework is designed for a BPM range of 90-100, and it features a combination of kick, snare, clap, hi-hat, and percussion elements. Here's how it works: the kick drum is placed on the first and third beats of the bar, while the snare and clap are placed on the second and fourth beats, creating a relaxed yet punchy rhythm. The hi-hat is used to add some swing and groove to the pattern, and there are variations in its placement throughout the pattern to keep things interesting.

Similar to East Coast Patterns, West Coast Patterns also include some percussion elements that are used sparingly to add additional accents and interest to the rhythm. By using this template as a starting point, you can create authentic and dynamic West Coast-style drum programming in your tracks. So, give it a try and see what kind of funky grooves you can come up with!

Figure 4.28 shows West Coast pattern 1 (BPM range 90-100):

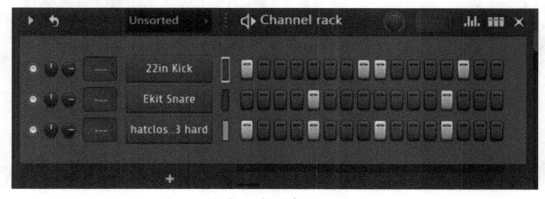

Figure 4.28: Channel Rack | Drum sequence 7

Figure 4.29 shows West Coast pattern 2 (BPM range 90-100):

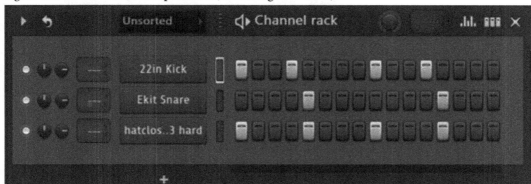

Figure 4.29: Channel Rack | Drum sequence 8

Figure 4.30 shows West Coast pattern 3 (BPM range 90-100):

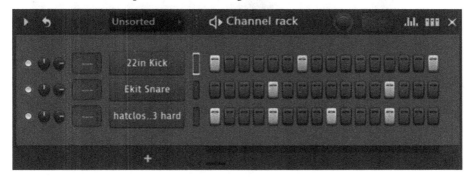

Figure 4.30: Channel Rack | Drum sequence 9

Modern West Coast patterns

In Modern West Coast music production, we use 808 bass hits and a more sped-up BPM as a signature style. Our BPM range is set between 100-105, and we use a unique pattern framework to create our beats. We start with a kick drum placed on the first and third beats of each bar, giving us that solid foundation. Next, we add in the snare and clap on the second and fourth beats, creating that classic West Coast rhythm, which is both relaxed and punchy.

To keep things fresh, we use a variety of hi-hat placements throughout the pattern, adding some swing and groove to keep our listeners moving. And of course, we incorporate some percussion elements to add some extra flavor and texture. With this combination of elements and our unique production style, you can start creating some of the hottest Modern West Coast-sounding tracks in the game.

Figure 4.31 shows Modern West Coast pattern 1 (BPM range 100-105):

Figure 4.31: Channel Rack | Drum sequence 10 | Piano Roll Hi Hat placement

Figure 4.32 shows Modern West Coast pattern 2 (BPM range 100-105):

Figure 4.32: Channel Rack | Drum sequence 11

Figure 4.33 shows Modern West Coast pattern 3 (BPM range 100-105):

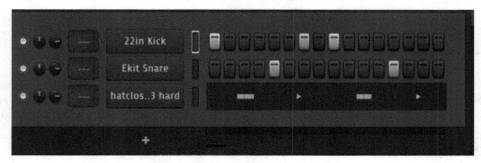

Figure 4.33: Channel Rack | Drum sequence 12

Trap Patterns

Now, let's look at Trap Patterns, which are drum programming templates designed for creating hip hop beats in the trap style. This style is known for its heavy use of 808s, hi-hats, and snares, and its slow tempo, with a heavy emphasis on the downbeat.

Trap Patterns are designed for a BPM range of 130-145, and they feature a combination of kick, snare, 808, hi-hat, and percussion elements. Here's how they work: the kick drum is placed on the first and third beats of the bar, while the snare is placed on the second and fourth beats, creating the basic rhythm. The 808 is used to add weight and depth to the pattern, and it's typically placed on the first beat of each bar. The hi-hat is used to add rhythm and energy, with fast, stuttering patterns being a common feature of trap music.

In addition to these core elements, Trap Patterns also include some percussion elements that are used to add additional accents and interest to the rhythm. These could include things such as shakers, claps, and other percussive sounds. By using these templates as a starting point, you can create authentic and dynamic trap-style drum programming in your tracks. So, give it a try and see what kind of hard-hitting beats you can come up with!

Figure 4.34 shows Trap pattern 1 (BPM range 130-145):

Figure 4.34: Channel Rack | Drum sequence 13

Figure 4.35 shows Trap pattern 2 (BPM range 130-145):

Figure 4.35: Channel Rack | Drum sequence 14 | Piano Roll Hi Hat placement

Figure 4.36 shows Trap pattern 3 (BPM range `130-145`):

Figure 4.36: Channel Rack | Drum sequence 15| Piano Roll Hi Hat placement

Club Patterns

Let's move on to Club Patterns, which are drum programming templates designed for creating hip hop beats in the club style. This style is known for its upbeat and energetic rhythms, often featuring electronic elements and a faster tempo.

The Club Patterns framework is designed for a BPM range of `100-116`, and it features a combination of kick, snare, clap, hi-hat, and percussion elements. Here's how it works: the kick drum is placed on the first and third beats of the bar, while the snare and clap are placed on the second and fourth beats, creating a driving rhythm. The hi-hat is used to add some rhythm and energy to the pattern, and there are variations in its placement throughout the pattern to keep things interesting.

Similar to the other patterns we've discussed, the Club Pattern templates also include some percussion elements that are used sparingly to add additional accents and interest to the rhythm. These could include things such as cowbells, claves, and other percussive sounds. By using this template as a starting point, you can create authentic and dynamic club-style drum programming in your tracks.

Figure 4.37 shows Club pattern 1 (BPM range `100-116`):

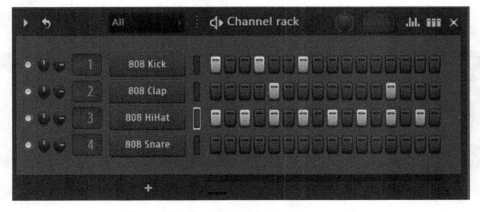

Figure 4.37: Channel Rack | Drum sequence 16

Figure 4.38 shows Club pattern 2 (BPM range `100-116`):

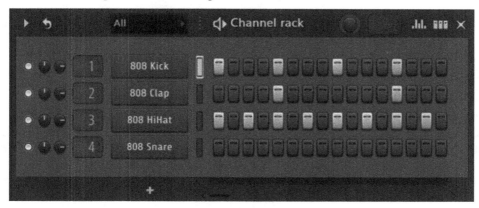

Figure 4.38: Channel Rack | Drum sequence 17

Figure 4.39 shows Club pattern 3 (BPM range `100-116`):

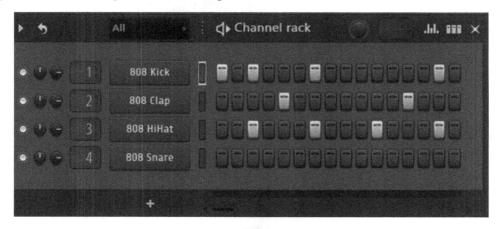

Figure 4.39: Channel Rack | Drum sequence 18

Now, start by creating these patterns in your Channel Rack and save them as templates in your FLP file folder!

When it comes to creating drum loops and patterns that work for billboard charts, use these basic frameworks to build from – don't overcomplicate it, keep it simple, but use your own creativity to play around with placement within the Channel Rack and Piano Roll. This chapter gave you a high-level overview of how to create these sequences, so start making those drum patterns!

Summary

In this chapter, we explored how to use the Channel Rack in FL Studio to create different drum programming templates for hip hop beats. As a producer, it's important to have a solid understanding of how different elements (such as kick, snare, hi-hat, and percussion) work together to create the rhythms that drive the genre. So, I wanted to share four different templates that are commonly used in different styles of hip hop music.

First, we discussed East Coast Patterns, which is a classic template used in the East Coast style. We talked about how they have a BPM range of 80-90 and feature swing rhythms and layered percussion elements. Next up, we explored West Coast Patterns, which have a BPM range of 90-100 and feature a more stripped-down approach with emphasis on the snare and clap. We also talked about the unique 808 bass elements that are commonly used in West Coast hip hop. Moving on to trap music, we talked about Trap Patterns, which have a BPM range of 130-145 and are known for their hard-hitting 808s and aggressive percussion. We talked about how to layer different elements to create a dynamic and powerful sound. Finally, we discussed Club Patterns, which are drum programming templates designed for creating hip hop beats in the club style. This style is known for its upbeat and energetic rhythms, often featuring electronic elements and a faster tempo.

Throughout the chapter, we talked about how each template works and how to use them as a starting point to create your own unique beats. We also highlighted some of the common features and techniques used in each style, such as swing rhythms and layered percussion. By learning about these templates and techniques, you can create professional-sounding hip hop beats that stand out from the crowd.

Next, we will focus on the theory behind melody and composition in music production, particularly within the context of FL Studio. We'll explore different approaches to creating melodies, including using scales and chord progressions, as well as techniques for creating interesting and dynamic compositions. We will begin by exploring specific techniques used in the industry for creating chart-topping hits. We'll look at common chord progressions, song structures, and other compositional elements used in popular music genres such as pop, R&B, and hip hop.

By learning and applying these techniques, you can increase your chances of creating music that resonates with audiences and has the potential to top the charts.

Now, let's explore melody and composition theory!

Exercise

As an exercise, I challenge you to use the Channel Rack to create your own hip hop, trap, and club drum programming templates, which you can use and save as FLP files to increase your workflow.

5
Approaching Melody and Composition Theory

Now that we have a framework for programming and arranging drums, let's talk about how to approach melody and composition theory as a whole. The framework I'll outline in this chapter will provide you with a high-level perspective on how to use the tools I've employed throughout my career, giving you the ability to create patterns to improve your workflow.

One of the most crucial steps in the music production process is coming up with catchy melodies and chords. You have a plethora of tools and features at your disposal when using FL Studio to create captivating musical concepts. Whether you're starting with a simple idea or developing a complex harmonic structure, FL Studio offers a variety of options for creating melodies and chords, from the Piano Roll to the Step Sequencer and beyond. For any producer looking to produce music of a professional caliber that connects with their audience, understanding the various methods and tools available for composing melodies and chords in FL Studio is essential. This chapter will examine these methods.

As you progress in your career, it is crucial to comprehend the fundamental ideas behind music theory, including scales, chords, and harmony, as you grow your expertise using FL Studio and Piano Roll. FL Studio is an intuitive software program that fills in the gaps between the composer's lack of experience with music theory and their ability to create great productions. Therefore, FL Studio can be used to strengthen your weaknesses in this area and gives you the ability to simply use your ears, without a deep understanding of music theory. At this point in my career, I can tell you all about music theory, its different approaches, styles, and genres. But when I started, I didn't know what middle C was! I relied heavily on FL Studio to compose my ideas using the Piano Roll as a crutch (as it was designed to be).

So, in this chapter, we will cover the following topics:

- The basics of composing music and studying icons
- How to effortlessly compose a melody using proven methods
- How to compose like a power user in FL Studio

- Creating billboard-fitting melodies
- Understanding chord progression frameworks

Basics of music composition theory

Let's review some fundamentals before moving on to how to develop compositions and melodies from a framework that records on Billboard charts use. You will be familiar with them if you are studying music theory, but if you're like me, you didn't discover these fundamentals until much later in your professional life. Up until I started learning music theory, I used FL Studio to create the majority of my work by ear. The classically trained pianists I've collaborated with in the studio have told me that although my approach to music is very unconventional, it still functions just as well as the classic approach. At the end of the day, good-sounding music is the goal.

Fundamentals of music theory

The study of music theory encompasses the language and notations used to create and communicate music, as well as the principles and practices of music. The fundamentals of music theory are as follows:

- **Pitch**: A sound's pitch determines how high or low it is. An **interval** is a space between two pitches.

- **Scale**: A scale is a group of pitches that are arranged in ascending or descending order. There are many different types of scales, but the **major** and **minor** scales are the most widely used.

- **Notes**: Nothing new under the sun. There are only 12 notes used in Western or modern music production; the first 7 letters of the alphabet (A, B, C, D, E, F, and G) and the corresponding sharps (#) and flats (Bb and b) are used to name the 12 notes in Western music. These notes repeat in **octaves**, with the frequency of the notes in the previous octave being doubled in each succeeding octave. Keep in mind that some traditional Middle Eastern and Indian musical styles use microtonal systems that use more than 12 notes per octave. The majority of the music theory and compositions in Western music, however, are based on 12 notes.

- **Chord**: A chord is a set of three or more notes played simultaneously. The notes of a particular scale are frequently used to construct chords.

- **Key**: A key is a group of pitches used as the foundation of a musical composition. It is frequently determined by the piece's opening and closing notes, as well as the chords that have been utilized.

- **Rhythm**: Rhythm is the term used to describe how music is timed. The length of notes, the placement of accents, and the overall tempo or speed of the music are all factored in.

- **Harmony**: Harmony is the term used to describe the arrangement of chords and how they relate to one another.

- **Notation**: The system of writing music using symbols to represent pitch, rhythm, and other musical elements is known as musical notation. The most popular type of notation is sheet music, which represents musical information using a staff and different symbols.

I want you to become familiar with the idea of *pulling from experience*. This idea refers to your capacity to advance from *perfect practice makes perfect* to the point of unconscious competence, at which point you can use everything I've taught you so far to draw on your experience to make records on the spot.

Studying the icons

I have learned everything I know about music composition and theory by studying the masters. Over the course of my career, I've had the privilege of working in studios with some of the world's brightest and best minds, and I've discovered commonalities in all of their approaches. To be clear, you can be ghost-mentored by the greats by listening to their music. I did this before I was good enough to work with any of them in the studio. I advise you to do the same, even when you are good enough to be in the room; mastery is a journey that never ends. In the modern world, there are a ton of popular producers who upload content to their **YouTube** channels, social media accounts, and other platforms, giving you the chance to learn how they create music. Take advantage of the enormous assistance that your generation enjoys that I didn't have access to.

When it comes to music production, trends are constantly changing, even if they sound similar for an 18-month period; this is because record labels are attempting to squeeze every last bit of profit out of a popular sound before the trend shifts, and independent artists are doing the same to try and catch trend waves in the hopes of making it big! It's important to keep learning from other successful producers on how they approach their own production palette if you want your career to last a long time and keep evolving.

Finding your icons and studying them thoroughly will help you gather information and gain experience for your own production styles in your particular situation, depending on your age, when you were born, and the type of music you are producing.

Let's explore some key takeaways from successful producers that I've had the opportunity to work with in my career. While I won't be able to cover everything in this book, let's look at some essential elements:

- First, the popular producers are known for their inventive and non-traditional sampling methods, using samples from unusual sources such as animal noises, everyday objects, and video game sound effects to create fresh sounds and rhythms.

- They also pay meticulous attention to detail during the recording process, spending significant time fine-tuning and perfecting their productions. They are known for being perfectionists and may work on a single project for months or even years at a time.

- Innovative rhythms are a hallmark of their productions, often incorporating layered and syncopated beats. They use rhythmic variation and timing to build tension and interest in their music.

- Vocals play a crucial role in their productions, with strong vocal performances supported and enhanced by the music. Vocal processing techniques such as doubling and pitch shifting are often used to create a unique sound.

- Sound quality is emphasized, using top-notch tools and methods such as **equalization** (**EQ**), which plays a fundamental role in the process of mixing audio, and compression, which is an audio processing technique used in mixing and mastering to control the dynamic range of a sound signal to achieve crystal-clear and powerful productions.

- Collaboration is a key aspect of their approach; they work with a wide range of musicians and producers to bring out the best in their team members and create music with a consistent and unified sound.

- They also frequently incorporate live instruments such as drums, guitars, and bass into their productions to add warmth, depth, and an organic feel to their music. With FL Studio, you can leverage its stock VSTs to mimic or copy live instrumentation with a little bit of mixing.

- Sampling is a common technique used by these producers, who are often locating and modifying obscure and unusual samples to create fresh and intriguing sounds. Some producers may replay or *interpolate* samples rather than use traditional chopping and borrowing methods, which can be a powerful way to start a fresh production.

- A strong sense of melody is a hallmark of their productions, often starting with a simple melody or chord progression and layering it to create intricate arrangements.

- Groove and rhythm are also emphasized, using syncopated and off-beat rhythms to give their music a distinctive and contagious feel.

In summary, top producers share common traits such as imagination, perfectionism, meticulousness, focus on audio quality, collaboration, and authenticity. These are fundamental building blocks for creating compositions that have the potential to top the billboard charts and create a long career as a top producer in the music business.

Creating on the fly from experience

As a producer, when you reach the big studios in significant music markets, you will be required to either play music from your back catalog or immediately produce something new for the A&R, artists, or songwriters. For the avoidance of doubt, "A&R" means Artist and Repertoire. In the music industry, A&R refers to the division or department of a record label, music publishing company, or entertainment agency that is responsible for scouting, signing, and developing new talent, as well as overseeing the artistic and creative aspects of a recording artist's career. The capacity to draw inspiration from prior experiences is what distinguishes professional producers from others (even if they are still trying to establish themselves as known producers). What am I alluding to here?

Pulling ideas from past experiences is a phrase I coined on my journey, which represents a producer's ability through consistent use of FL Studio and its tools to know what melodies, drum patterns, VSTs, and plugins work for a specific situation or opportunity you are placed in at a given moment. Think of it this way: you need to be able to perform when you're put in any situation (and impress those around you). The best way to achieve this is to pool your 10,000 FL Studio hours and concentrate on using those frameworks as opposed to purely experimenting.

Now, I don't want to bamboozle you or the situation, but there will be studio sessions where you have time to get really experimental; these are usually the sessions where the studio clock isn't ticking at $500 per hour. You have unlimited time to experiment with various plugins, VSTs, and melody patterns when you are at your home studio or your own studio that you built out in a commercial space that you have leased.

When you're on the spot, it's important to work from a template-based framework so you can produce a production quickly and effectively that the other people in the room will want to use.

One of these elements is your approach to melody and composition structure. Working with rap artists, pop singers, or songwriters doesn't matter; you need to be able to confidently approach each scenario with the appropriate framework – that's where this chapter comes into play. I'm going to give you the frameworks you will need to start plugging and playing.

Working off the cuff

So, you have been invited to a studio session with an A&R at a major record label. They have the studio booked out for 3 hours, so you open your laptop and start playing tracks from your back catalog. They pick two but tell you they need something more upbeat and poppy. You know how to approach a pop record because you have practiced 10,000 times in your home studio space working on tracks within this framework. So, you open up FL Studio and immediately start loading your templates and approach the melody from this viewpoint using your go-to VSTs, plugins, drum kits, and pattern templates. In 20 minutes, you have a bare idea and the A&R really likes it. They tell you to bounce that idea to a .wav file, and they send it to a songwriter to pen an idea over.

A few days go by, and you get a reference track back with vocals over your idea, and the A&R asks you to finalize the track. You are now back home in your own studio so you have time to get experimental. Once you add your additional flare to it, you send it back and, before you know it, a major artist has cut the record and you just got a placement.

This happened over and over again with me. Even if you're a remote producer, all professionals in the music industry value the ability to deliver tracks and ideas at short notice.

As always, practice makes perfect! Like any other skill, FL Studio's melodic and musical composition workflows benefit from practice. Never stop experimenting with new approaches, sounds, and aesthetics,and don't be afraid to make mistakes. The more you use the program, the more at ease you'll feel, and the more unique your music will sound. Fail quickly and severely! For those who fall and quickly get back up after doing so, the Promised Land is just around the corner.

So, let's talk about the basic frameworks for composing melodies in FL Studio.

Composing in FL Studio – the basics

FL Studio is a powerful and effective **digital audio workstation** (**DAW**) that enables you to write music in a variety of genres and create melodies. To approach melody and composition theory in FL Studio, follow the guidelines in this section.

Conventional wisdom will tell you to learn the fundamentals of melody. This is definitely something you should invest time and energy into throughout your career. However, FL Studio's tools allow you to hack the music composing system by giving you a clear set of tools that can be used in simplicity to create melody and chord progressions by ear, without knowing the exact names of the chords and keys from the outset.

Rather, while you build your own knowledge bank of the music theory, understand that melody is the central element of musical composition and is composed of a series of notes played in a specific order. When you begin to understand the fundamentals of music theory, such as scales, chords, and intervals, you will improve your workflow as you create a melody. The Piano Roll can be used to write and edit melodies and will be where you spend the majority of your time in FL Studio.

Now that we understand what makes a melody, let's talk about how to approach creating a new one from a basic framework.

Selecting a key

Before you can start writing a melody, you must decide on a key. A key is a collection of notes that blend well. By utilizing the **Scale Highlighting** feature in the Piano Roll in FL Studio, you can set the key. This will make the notes in the chosen key stand out, making it simpler to compose a melody.

When it comes to scratching ideas in the Piano Roll, you can always start on middle C and move the keys around to find a better fit later, or you can choose a different key from the outset. I suggest this because FL Studio allows you to use your typing keyboard as a MIDI piano if you aren't using a traditional MIDI keyboard (most of my productions have been done on the typing keyboard!). This allows you the space to start jotting ideas down, with the thought that you can alter and change the key line later if you so desire.

The location of middle C in the Piano Roll is shown in *Figure 5.1*:

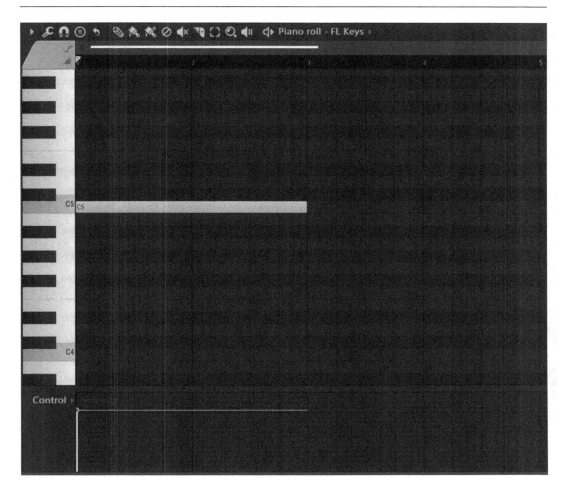

Figure 5.1: Piano Roll – middle C

In *Figure 5.1*, we see the middle C key placed within the Piano Roll. On a standard 88-key piano, middle C is located roughly in the center of the keyboard. It is the C note that is closest to the middle of the keyboard (hence its name), sitting just to the left of a grouping of two black keys. Middle C holds significance in music theory and notation because it is often used as a reference point for identifying other notes on the keyboard and understanding the relationship between different pitches in written music.

Using rhythms in composition

The rhythm is a crucial component of a melody and can aid in generating excitement and really forming the *vibe*. Depending on the type of track you are producing, you may find that it makes sense to approach the melody from a simplistic straight line, or if you are composing an upbeat pop or dance record, spacing and introducing rhythm points sparsely may make more sense.

An example of a straight-line melody progression using the Piano Roll is shown in *Figure 5.2*:

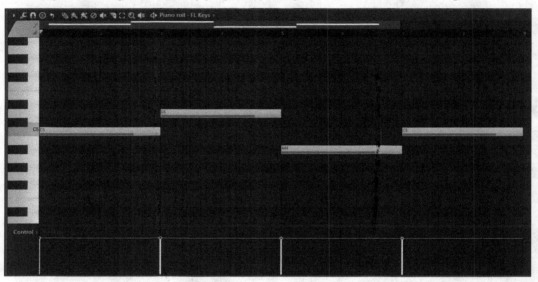

Figure 5.2: Piano Roll – straight-line melody progression

Now, another example of rhythmic line melody progression using the Piano Roll is shown in *Figure 5.3*:

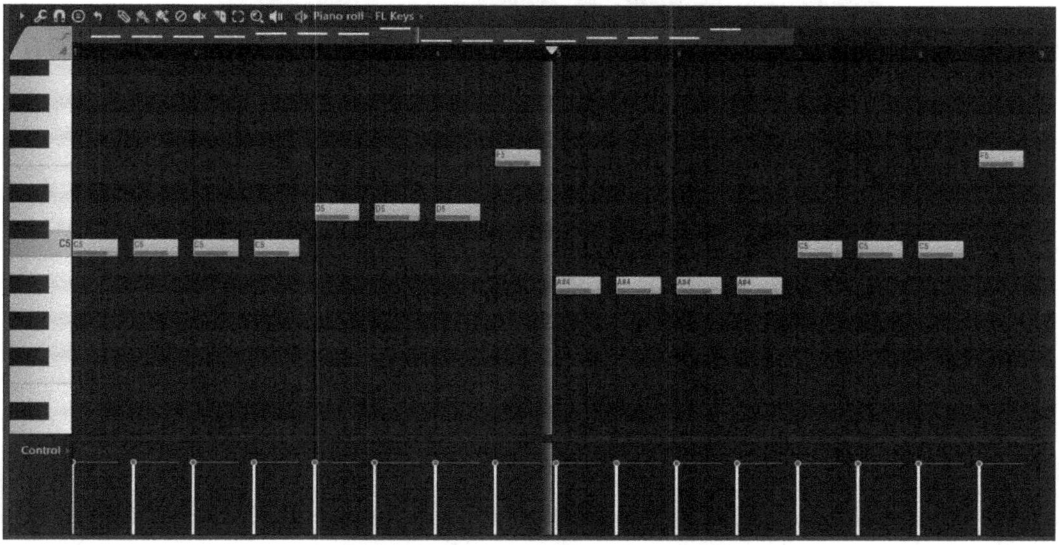

Figure 5.3: Piano Roll – rhythmic line melody progression

In *Figure 5.3*, the melody line has a repeating rhythmic pattern that establishes a particular groove or feel. This pattern can be straightforward and consistent or more complex, with syncopated rhythms or offbeat accents. The rhythm helps drive the energy and flow of the melody. The example is shown in *Figure 5.3*.

Picking your sound palette

As we know, FL Studio includes a range of virtual instruments and samples that you can use to produce a variety of sounds and textures for your music. When building a workflow framework, as it relates to *pulling from experience*, it's important to have go-to sounds and plugins that you will use. These can always be switched out when it's time to get experimental or augment your own sound design. I'm going to show you the stock FL Studio VSTs that I use regularly to produce distinctive and captivating melodies.

Bass

FL Studio's **BooBass** is a virtual instrument included in the software that is specifically designed for creating deep and punchy bass sounds. It is a subtractive synthesizer that allows producers and musicians to generate a wide range of bass tones suitable for various genres, including electronic, hip hop, and pop music.

Figure 5.4 shows the **BooBass** instrument:

Figure 5.4: Channel Rack | right-click | Insert | Misc | BooBass

Pads

Sytrus is a commonly used plugin in FL Studio for sound synthesis and adding spatial effects to audio. The **Ambience** preset is a type of synthesizer sound that is primarily used to create sustained, atmospheric, and evolving textures in music. Pads are commonly used in genres such as ambient, electronic, and cinematic music to add depth, warmth, and a sense of space to the mix, and this preset is my favorite one to create soundscapes and add texture to chord progressions and melody support.

Figure 5.5 shows the Sytrus VST with the Ambience preset:

Figure 5.5: Channel Rack | right-click | Insert | Synth Classic | Sytrus | Ambience

Bassy lead

Sawer is a virtual analog synthesizer plugin included in FL Studio. It is designed to emulate the sound and behavior of classic analog synthesizers, specifically focusing on recreating the capabilities of the famous Roland JP-8000. **MC Chains** is a preset that is known for its energetic and cutting-edge sound, often used in electronic and dance music genres. The MC Chains preset in Sawer is characterized by its bright and aggressive tone, suitable for creating powerful synth lines or layers in a mix.

Figure 5.6 shows the **MC Chains** preset:

Figure 5.6: Channel Rack | right-click | Insert | Synth Classic | Sawer | MC Chains

Rhodes keys

FL Keys is a virtual instrument included in FL Studio that aims to emulate the sound of classic electric pianos, such as the Rhodes and Wurlitzer. It provides a range of presets that mimic the distinctive tonal characteristics and playing feel of these vintage instruments. The Rhodes preset in FL Keys is designed to replicate the warm and mellow sound of the Fender Rhodes electric piano, which gained popularity in various genres, including jazz, soul, and funk.

Figure 5.7 shows the **Rhodes** preset:

Figure 5.7: Channel Rack | right-click | Insert | Misc | FL Keys | Rhodes

Piano

In FL Keys, the **Piano** preset in FL Keys is designed to replicate the sound of a grand piano and can be used to create amazing-sounding piano compositions within FL Studio.

Figure 5.8 shows the **Piano** preset:

Figure 5.8: Channel Rack | right-click | Insert | Misc | FL Keys | Piano

The key here is to use these tools to scratch a rough idea down, which you can augment later or as you go when creating a track.

Layering and stylistic rules

Composition theory also takes into account harmony, rhythm, form, and texture. To create a well-rounded composition, you can arrange your composition and add additional components to create a finished musical piece in FL Studio by using the **Playlist** tool.

We have discussed how to create sound design for melody and chord progressions. Layering sounds and instruments can create a unique and exciting end sound that will add an additional vibe to your melody and composition.

Remember, we want to keep it simple. Layering should be used to add elements to your melody or chord progression or add a little transitional flare to the end of a loop. We don't want to add too many additional layers to modern pop or rap music.

Let's walk through an example of how to layer using the Piano Roll, as shown in *Figure 5.9*:

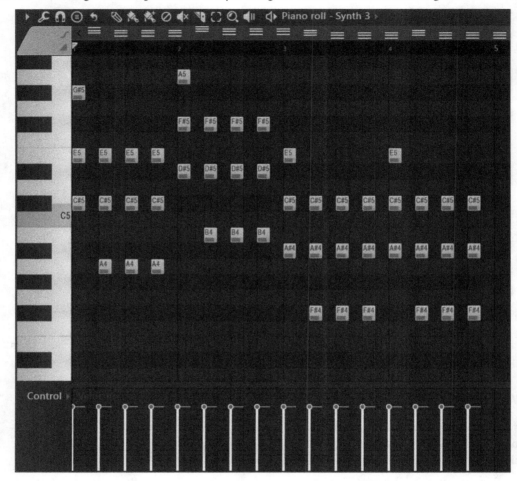

Figure 5.9: Channel Rack | Sytrus | Synth 3| Piano Roll | Chord progression

In *Figure 5.9*, I have created a chord progression framework using FL Studio's stock **Sytrus** VST plugin, and chosen a simple synth sound, **Synth 3**, to establish the concept of how we can use a single sound to add layers of additional texture to create a more exciting sound design.

Now, let's add another Sytrus VST and we will use an ambient sound, copying and pasting the chord progression into the Channel Rack to give the chord progression sound more texture, as shown in *Figure 5.10*:

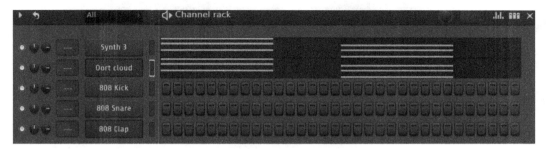

Figure 5.10: Channel Rack | Sytrus | Oort cloud

As you can see in *Figure 5.10*, within the Channel Rack, we have inserted another stack of Sytrus and used the **Oort cloud** synth sample with the same chord progression to follow the first layer of the sound design. This is a simple yet effective framework for creating and adding additional texture to stock sounds and third-party VST sounds that you may indulge in later in your production career.

Crafting melodies in FL Studio

Now, let's walk through how to create melodies step by step. Then, I will give you frameworks that have helped me in my own career to create workflows efficiently.

FL Studio offers a full range of tools and features to aid the quick and effective creation of melodies. The FL Studio **Piano Roll editor**, a graphical representation of a piano keyboard that lets you see and edit the notes of your melody, is where melodies are created and edited.

For this example framework, let's start by creating a new project in FL Studio and setting the **beats per minute** (**BPM**) to 95, as indicated in the **Transport** window. Now, in the Channel Rack, let's add the **Sytrus** VST and drag it into the Channel Rack. Click on the **Piano Roll** button on the toolbar or press *F7* on your keyboard to create a new project. Using the Piano Roll editor's **Scale Highlighting** feature, we will select the middle C key to work with. This will make it simpler for you to visualize the notes of the chosen key and to compose a melody that fits within it, as shown in *Figure 5.11*:

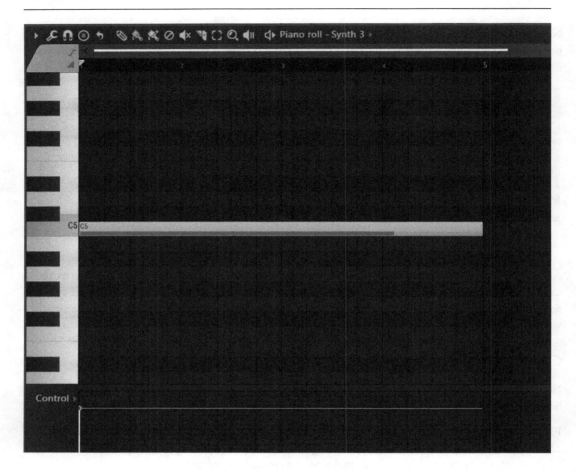

Figure 5.11: FL Studio | Piano Roll | middle C

In the Piano Roll editor, you can add notes by using your mouse. By clicking and dragging the corresponding parameters, you can change the length, pitch, and velocity of each note.

This is how you can start composing a melody within the Piano Roll. You can use the Piano Roll editor to edit and perfect the melody by adding or removing notes and changing each note's timing, pitch, and velocity until the melody sounds just the way you want it to. Overall, FL Studio's melody creation process is simple, allowing you to quickly and easily test out various melodies until you find the one that best suits your musical composition. When experimenting in the Piano Roll, you can make melodies that are memorable and compelling and that encapsulate the essence of your music with a little practice and experimentation. As we discussed how to use the Piano Roll in *Chapter 2*, this brief refresher is to establish a point of continuation. Now, I will share with you my exact frameworks for approaching melody from a billboard chart perspective.

Creating billboard chart melodies in FL Studio

Have you ever wondered how hit songs on the radio are created? Well, in modern times, they often use a bit of science and a lot of creativity to come up with catchy tunes that grab your attention. Here is a key secret to composing charting records: producers use specific formulas for chord progressions and melodies. In this chapter, I will share those specific formulas with you; this is a key framework for creating hits!

First, let's differentiate between making music for yourself and making music for the general public. The difference is mainly in what the outcome of a specific piece of music can be, specifically related to commercial success versus creative admiration. Many contemporary pop songs have successfully used specific melodic structures and patterns for hit records in modern times and continue to do so. Pop music, which includes any type of music that is consumed by the mainstream public, follows these formulas. There is a formulaic approach to writing hit melodies and chord progressions that all major producers and writers follow. The key is getting creative in how you approach these basic frameworks. Let's look at these frameworks in the Piano Roll to start getting familiar with the formulas used to make billboard chart records used frequently in contemporary pop music.

Composition theory

When approaching music composition, there are several key components any producer should be aware of, as they relate to structuring notes and chords. This includes types of approaches and the utilization of certain scales:

- **Pentatonic scale**: This is a five-note scale that is frequently used in pop, rock, and blues music. This scale is simple to sing and offers a melodic hook that is frequently used in choruses, as shown in *Figure 5.12*:

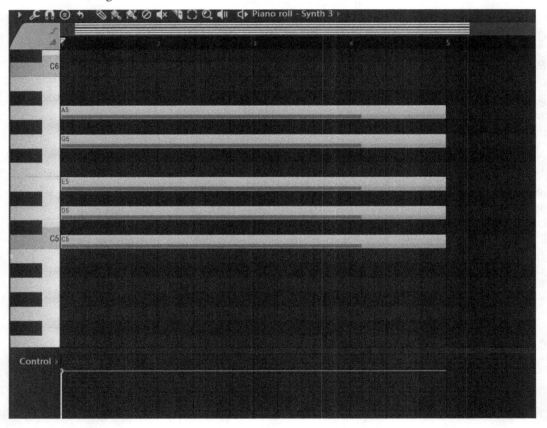

Figure 5.12: Piano Roll – pentatonic scale

- **Arpeggiated chord progressions**: To create this melody, a chord's notes are sequentially played one after the other. This produces a melody that flows well and is simple to remember and can be used in verses or choruses.

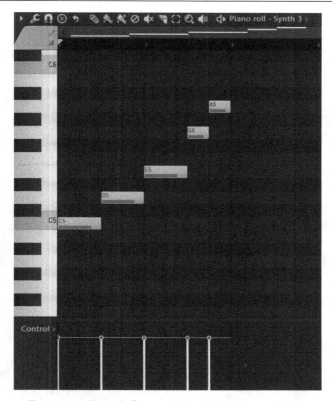

Figure 5.13: Piano Roll – arpeggiated chord progressions

- **Repeating melodic phrases**: This melody makes use of a brief phrase that is repeated throughout the song several times. This produces a melodic piece that is memorable and catchy and can be used in choruses or verses. For example, let's say we're in the key of C major. We can create a repeating melodic phrase by using a simple two-note pattern. We'll start with the C note, which is the root note of the scale, and then add the E note, which is the third note in the scale. To input this pattern into the Piano Roll, you'll need to start by selecting the C note on the Piano Roll and then input the E note. You can then repeat this pattern by copying and pasting it several times on the Piano Roll, as shown in *Figure 5.14*:

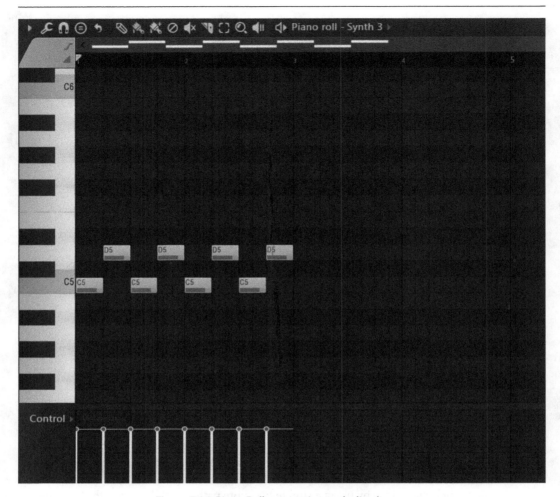

Figure 5.14: Piano Roll – repeating melodic phrases

- **Call-and-response melody**: In this melody, one section *calls* and another *responds* in a question-and-answer format. As a result, a captivating and exciting melody that can be used in verses or choruses is produced. To create a call-and-response melody in FL Studio's Piano Roll, you'll need to start by selecting a key and creating a simple melody. Let's say we're in the key of G major. First, we'll create the *call* section of the melody. We'll start with a simple three-note pattern: G, A, and A#. We'll use these notes to create a short phrase that will serve as the *call*. We can input this phrase into the Piano Roll as shown in *Figure 5.15*:

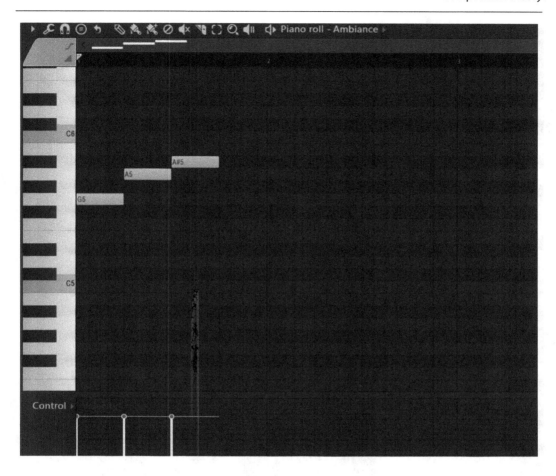

Figure 5.15: Piano Roll call-and-response melody – the call section

This creates a simple ascending pattern that serves as the *call* section of the melody.

Next, we'll create the *response* section of the melody. We'll use a similar pattern, but we'll change the starting note to D, which is the fifth note in the G major scale. This would create a descending pattern that serves as the *response* section of the melody. We can input this pattern into the Piano Roll as shown in *Figure 5.16*:

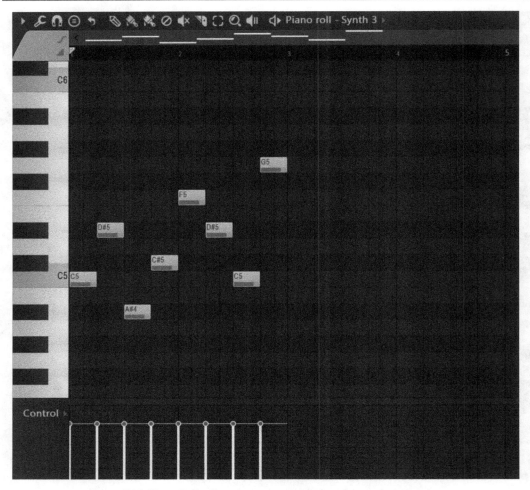

Figure 5.16: Piano Roll call-and-response melody – the response section

This creates a simple descending pattern that responds to the *call* section of the melody.

To create a call-and-response melody, you can alternate between the *call* and *response* sections of the melody. For example, you could start with the *call* section and then follow it with the *response* section. You can then repeat this pattern throughout the melody to create a captivating and exciting melody that can be used in verses or choruses.

- **Simple melodic interval patterns**: This melody employs straightforward interval structures, such as thirds, fifths, or octaves, that repeat. This produces a simple melody that is easy to remember and can be used in verses or choruses. To create a simple melodic interval pattern in FL Studio's Piano Roll, you'll need to start by selecting a key and creating a simple melody using interval structures such as thirds, fifths, or octaves. Let's say we're in the key of A minor. We'll start with a simple two-note pattern using fifths. We'll use the notes A and F to create a short phrase that will serve as the foundation for our melody. We can input this phrase into the Piano Roll as shown in *Figure 5.17*:

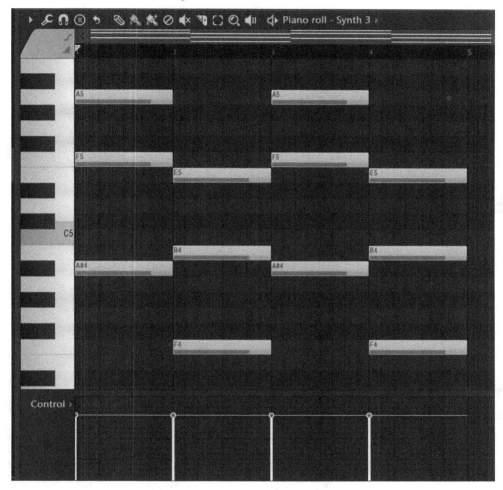

Figure 5.17: Piano Roll – simple melodic interval patterns

This would create a simple pattern that uses fifths to create a straightforward melody. Next, we can repeat this pattern to create a melody that is easy to remember. We can use octaves to add variation and interest to the melody. For example, we can create a four-note pattern that repeats. This would create a simple melodic interval pattern that uses fifths and octaves to create a straightforward melody that is easy to remember. To use this melody in verses or choruses, you can repeat the pattern throughout the section. You can also experiment with different interval structures and patterns to create more complex and interesting melodies.

- **Melodic leap**: This melody makes dramatic, stand-out leaps between two or more notes that are far apart in pitch. To add excitement and impact, this can be used in choruses or other crucial sections of a song. To create a melody with melodic leaps in FL Studio's Piano Roll, you'll need to start by selecting a key and creating a simple melody that includes large intervals between notes. Let's say we're in the key of C major. We'll start with a simple four-note pattern that includes a large leap. We'll use the notes C, E, G, and C to create a short phrase that will serve as the foundation for our melody. We can input this phrase into the Piano Roll as shown in *Figure 5.18*:

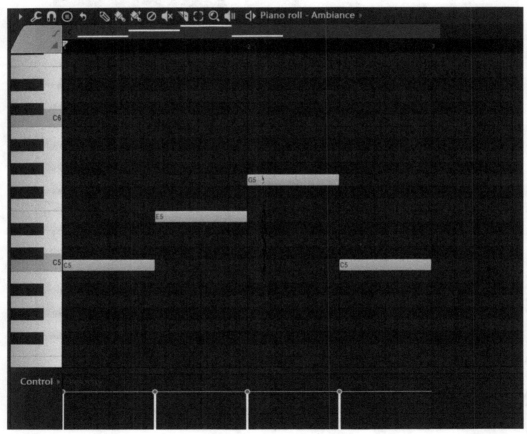

Figure 5.18: Piano Roll – melodic leap

This would create a simple pattern that includes a large interval leap from E4 to G4.

To add excitement and impact to the melody, we can use this pattern in a chorus or other crucial sections of the song. We can also experiment with different intervals and patterns to create more complex and interesting melodies with dramatic, stand-out leaps between notes. For example, we could use a larger leap, such as a sixth or an octave, to create an even more impactful melody.

> **Note to remember**
> While melodic leaps can be exciting and attention-grabbing, they can also be challenging to sing or play. Be sure to consider the range and abilities of your vocalist or instrumentalist when creating a melody with large intervals.

We have now learned about a few classic examples of melodic patterns and structures that have supported the expansion into numerous modern pop songs. Studying these patterns and experimenting with them in your own music can help you come up with memorable and captivating melodies that stand the test of time, even though there is no surefire formula for writing a hit melody.

Now, let's talk about chords. Chords are the backbone of the composition of your underlying melodic leads.

Billboard charting pop chord progression frameworks

Now, let's explore some time-tested chord sequences that have been used on records that have charted on billboards since the dawn of modern pop music. These progressions are simple, and they can be used in a variety of combinations and with different sound designs to create unique and appealing productions using middle C as the root note. However, note that each of the actual songs uses a different key, and the progressions I'll describe in this section are just starting points to show you what chord progressions that have already worked look like in FL Studio's Piano Roll. These progressions work; you just need to *make* them work. These are songs that span generations and are just as useful today as they were 30 years ago. Modern pop music borrows composition frameworks and reintroduces them under the guise of trap drums and generation-trending BPMs, which is a unit of measurement used to describe the tempo or speed of the music. For clarity, I'm going to give you examples of how these progressions manifest within the Piano Roll, and it will be up to you to learn the notes and get creative with them in your own time. Now, let's dive in! The following chord progressions have been used frequently in pop music, and I'll show you how you can incorporate them into your FL Studio workflow frameworks.

Let It Be chords

One of the most well-liked chord progressions in popular music is **I-V-vi-IV**. It can be heard in many well-known songs, such as Coldplay's *Viva la Vida*, Adele's *Someone Like You*, and The Beatles' *Let It Be*. To input this chord progression into FL Studio's Piano Roll, you'll need to select a key and choose the corresponding chords that fit into this progression.

Let's say we're in the key of C major. The following are the chords that correspond to the I-V-vi-IV progression:

- I = C major
- V = G major
- vi = A minor
- IV = F major

Following a simple straight formula, these chords would appear in the Piano Roll as shown in *Figure 5.19*:

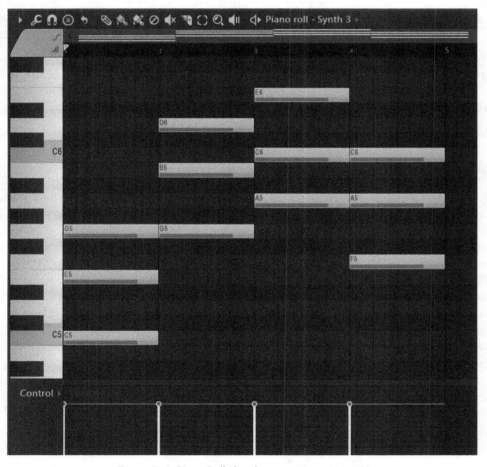

Figure 5.19: Piano Roll chord progression – I-V-vi-IV

You can repeat this progression as many times as you like to create a chord sequence for your song. Be sure to experiment with different rhythms and voicings to create a unique sound for your progression.

Wild Thing chords

Next, **I-IV-V** is a traditional rock and roll chord progression that has been incorporated into a number of songs, including *Louie Louie* by The Kingsmen, *Wild Thing* by The Troggs, and *Rock Around the Clock* by Bill Haley and the Comets. To create the I-IV-V chord progression in FL Studio's Piano Roll, you'll need to choose a key and select the chords that fit into this progression. In this case, we'll use the key of C major.

The following are the chords that correspond to the I-IV-V progression in the key of C major:

- I = C major
- IV = F major
- V = G major

This chord progression in the Piano Roll is shown in *Figure 5.20*:

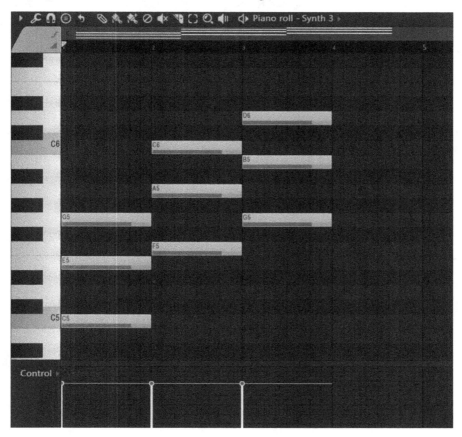

Figure 5.20: Piano Roll chord progression – I-IV-V

As we aren't composing the chords to a specific rhythm, you will notice that they appear incomplete to the fifth bar in the Piano Roll. That's because *Figure 5.20* is simply showcasing the three notes and how they appear in the Piano Roll. To input this progression into the Piano Roll, you'll need to create a new pattern, select the appropriate length, and then add the chords.

You can repeat this progression as many times as you like to create a chord sequence for your song. You can also experiment with different rhythms and voicings to create a unique sound for your progression.

Don't Stop Believing chords

Many pop ballads and slow songs use the chord progression **vi-IV-I-V**. Examples include Whitney Houston's *I Will Always Love You*, Journey's *Don't Stop Believin'*, and Train's *Drops of Jupiter*.

To create the vi-IV-I-V chord progression in FL Studio's Piano Roll, you'll need to choose a key and select the chords that fit into this progression. Let's use the key of C major for this example.

The following are the chords that correspond to the vi-IV-I-V progression in the key of C major:

- vi = A minor
- IV = F major
- I = C major
- V = G major

To input this progression in the Piano Roll, you'll need to create a new pattern, select the appropriate length, and then add the chords:

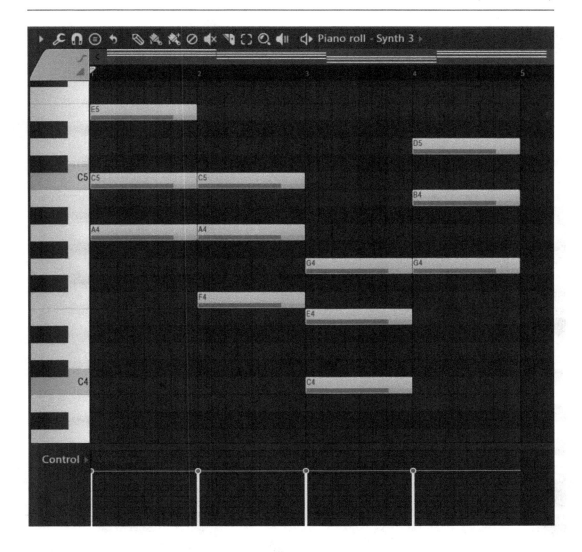

Figure 5.21: Piano Roll chord progression – vi-IV-I-V

Sweet Child o' Mine chords

Compared to the I-V-vi-IV progression of the *Let It Be* chords, the progression of the *Sweet Child o' Mine* chords (**vi-V-IV-III**) uses the vi and V chords in the opposite order. Numerous pop songs have used it, such as U2's *With or Without You*, Guns N' Roses' *Sweet Child o' Mine*, and One Direction's *What Makes You Beautiful*. To create this progression in FL Studio's Piano Roll, let's again use the key of C major for this example.

The following are the chords that correspond to the vi-V-IV-III progression in the key of C major:

- vi = A minor
- V = G major
- IV = F major
- III = E minor

To input this progression in the Piano Roll, you'll need to create a new pattern, select the appropriate length, and then add the chords, as shown in *Figure 5.22*:

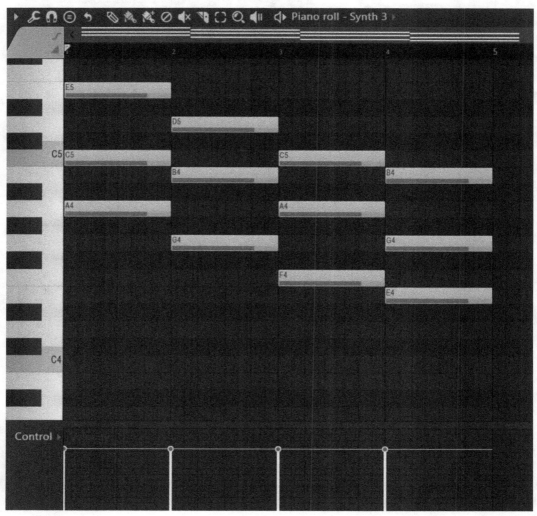

Figure 5.22: Piano Roll chord progression – vi-V-IV-III

Shape of You chords

Shape of You by Ed Sheeran uses a chord progression that can be described as **I-VI-IV-V**. In the key of C major, the chords are C major, A minor, F major, and G major. This chord progression has been used in many popular songs across various genres. In *Shape of You*, the chords are used in a repeating pattern throughout the song. This simple and catchy chord progression is one of the key elements that helped make the song a huge hit. In FL Studio's Piano Roll, you can input this progression by creating a new pattern and adding the chords in the order of C major, A minor, F major, and G major. To create this progression in FL Studio's Piano Roll, let's again use the key of C major for this example.

The following are the chords that correspond to the I-VI-IV-V progression in the key of C major:

- I = C major
- VI = A minor
- IV = F major
- V = G major

To input this progression in the Piano Roll, you'll need to create a new pattern, select the appropriate length, and then add the chords, as shown in *Figure 5.23*:

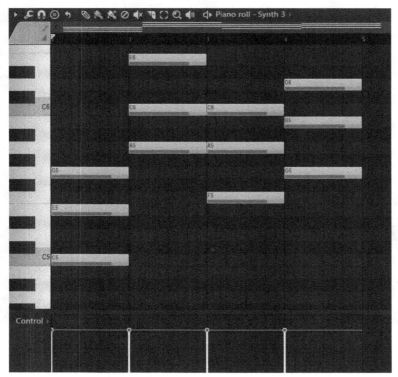

Figure 5.23: Piano Roll chord progression – I-VI-IV-V

Uptown Funk chords

The chord progression of Mark Ronson's *Uptown Funk* song is a variation of the I-vi-IV-V progression, which is commonly used in pop music. In the key of D minor, the chords are Dm (I), Bb (VI), F (IV), and C (VI). The progression is repeated throughout the song, with slight variations to create different sections and build dynamics. To create the chord progression of Uptown Funk in FL Studio's Piano Roll, we can use the key of D Dorian. The chords that correspond to the progression are as follows:

- I (Dm) = Dm7 (D minor seventh chord)
- VI (Bb) = BbMaj7 (B-flat major seventh chord)
- IV (F) = Fmaj7 (F major seventh chord)
- VI (C) = CMaj7 (C major seventh chord)

To input this progression in the Piano Roll, see *Figure 5.24*:

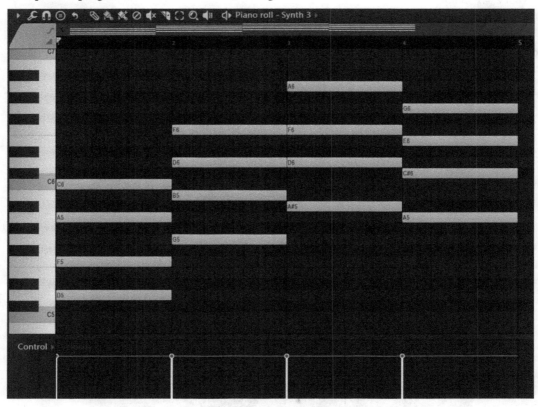

Figure 5.24: Piano Roll chord progression – I-vi-IV-V

Apologize chords

Apologize by One Republic uses the chord progression **I-IV-V-vi**. It has been used in many hit songs over the decades and is a great chord template to work from. To create the chord progression of *Apologize* in FL Studio's Piano Roll, let's use the key of A minor for this example. The following are the chords that correspond to the chorus progression in the key of A minor:

- I = C# minor
- IV = A major
- V = B major
- vi = F# minor

To input this progression in the Piano Roll, you'll need to create a new pattern, select the appropriate length, and then add the chords, as shown in *Figure 5.25*:

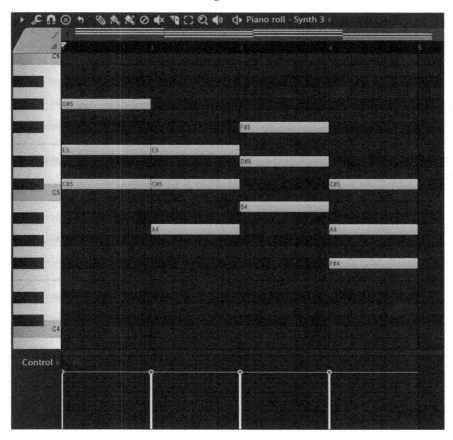

Figure 5.25: Piano Roll chord progression – I-IV-V-vi

These are a few classic examples of popular chord progressions that have been adopted in pop music. Although there aren't any objective standards for using these progressions, being aware of them and experimenting with them can help you write songs that are impressive and memorable.

Now, let's discuss chord frameworks that are used in rap and hip hop productions that have stood out in each era and genre. These frameworks will provide you with the template and foundation to start creating rap and hip hop tracks that will grab listeners' attention.

Rap chord progression frameworks

Rap music is best known for its wide variety of chord progressions, frequently combining jazz, soul, and funk music influences. The following are some well-liked rap chord progressions that have appeared in songs that work on billboard charts:

- **I-VII-VI**: I-VII-VI is a popular chord progression in trap music that can be heard in a number of well-known songs, including *XO Tour Llif3* by Lil Uzi Vert and *Look Alive* by BlocBoy JB ft. Drake. To create this progression in FL Studio's Piano Roll, let's use the key of C# minor for this example.

  The following are the chords that correspond to the progression in the key of C# minor:

  - I = C# minor

  - VII = B major

  - VI = A# minor

  To input this progression in the Piano Roll, you'll need to create a new pattern and select the appropriate length, as shown in *Figure 5.26*:

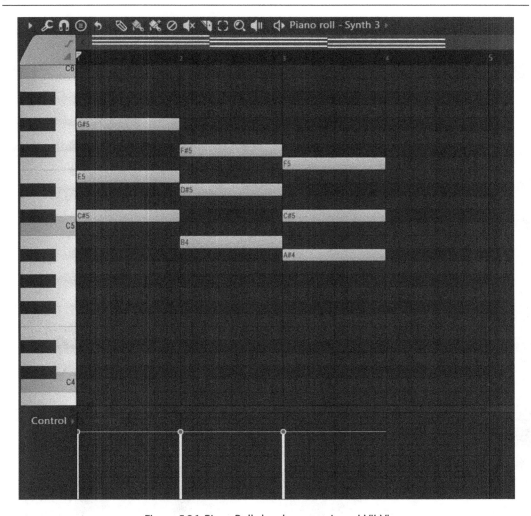

Figure 5.26: Piano Roll chord progression – I-VII-VI

- **i-VI-III-V**: Rap songs that are emotional and introspective frequently use the chord progression i-VI-III-V, like in Juice WRLD's *Lucid Dreams* and *All Girls Are the Same*. To create this progression in FL Studio's Piano Roll, let's use the key of C for this example.

  The following are the chords that correspond to the progression in the key of C:

  - i = C Eb G

  - VI = Ab C Eb

  - III = E G Bb

  - V = G Bb D

To input this progression in the Piano Roll, you'll need to create a new pattern and select the appropriate length, as shown in *Figure 5.27*:

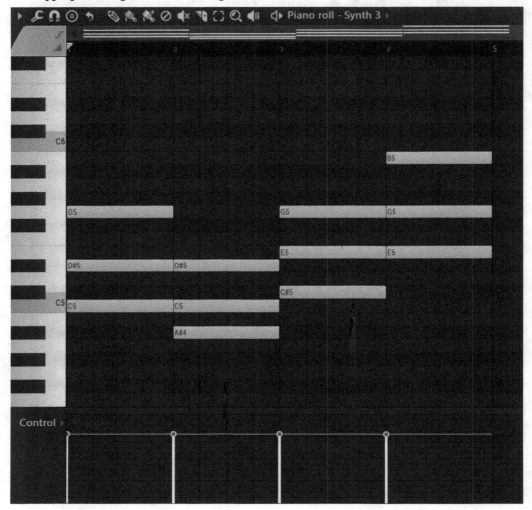

Figure 5.27: Piano Roll chord progression – i-VI-III-V

- **I-V-vi-IV**: I-V-vi-IV is a popular chord progression in pop music, but it has also been used in a few rap songs, such as Post Malone's *Circles* and Halsey's *Without Me*. To create this progression in FL Studio's Piano Roll, let's use the key of C for this example.

The following are the chords that correspond to the progression in the key of C:

- I = C E G
- V = G B D
- vi = A C E
- IV = F A C

To input this progression in the Piano Roll, you'll need to create a new pattern and select the appropriate length, as shown in *Figure 5.28*:

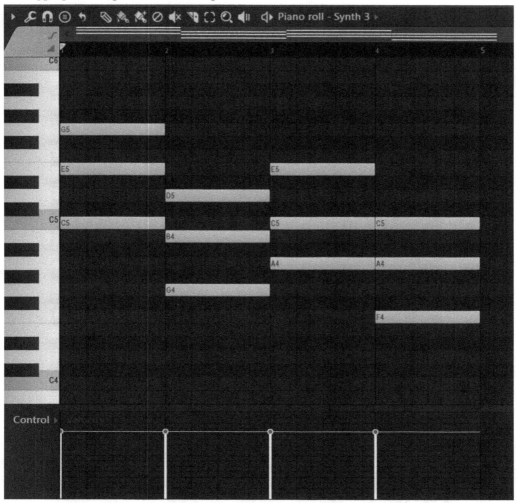

Figure 5.28: Piano Roll chord progression – I-V-vi-IV

- **i-VII-III-VI**: This chord progression can be heard in numerous drill and trap songs, including the hits *What's Poppin* by Jack Harlow and *Don't Stop* by Megan Thee Stallion ft. Young Thug. To create this progression in FL Studio's Piano Roll, let's use the key of C for this example.

The following are the chords that correspond to the progression in the key of C:

- i (C, Eb, G) = Cm (C minor chord)
- VII (Bb, D, F) = BbMaj (B-flat major chord)
- III (E, G, B) = Em (E minor chord)
- VI (A, C, E) = Am (A minor chord)

To input this progression in the Piano Roll, you'll need to create a new pattern and select the appropriate length. Then, add the notes for each chord in the progression, as previously listed. Adjust the timing, duration, and velocity of the notes as needed to create your desired sound, as shown in *Figure 5.29*:

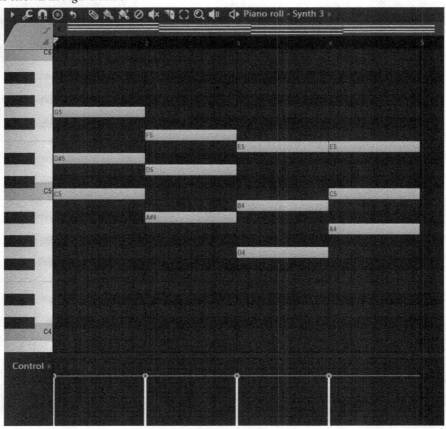

Figure 5.29: Piano Roll chord progression – i-VII-III-VI

We have now seen a few illustrations of common rap chord progressions that have appeared in songs that have been charted on billboards. Although these progressions are not unique to rap music, they have been successfully used in many well-known rap songs, and you can incorporate them into your composing frameworks as the foundation for building your own billboard charting songs.

Chord progression frameworks in modern music

Let's now discuss basic chord theory and concepts that have been used in music composition and production since the inception of music theory. Chord theory is the study of how chords are constructed and how they function within music, encompassing concepts such as major chords, minor chords, and more. Major chords generally create a bright and happy sound, while minor chords tend to evoke a darker and more melancholic mood. Let's explore these now:

- **Minor chords**: Rap songs frequently use minor chords, which have a depressing or melancholic sound. These chords are frequently used to express emotion or infuse an environment with mood. To create a minor chord progression in FL Studio's Piano Roll, let's use the key of C for this example. The notes for this chord progression in the Piano Roll are as follows:

  - C#m = C#3, E3, G#3

  - E = E3, G#3, B3

  - G#m = G#3, B3, D#4

  - Fm = A#2, C#3, F3

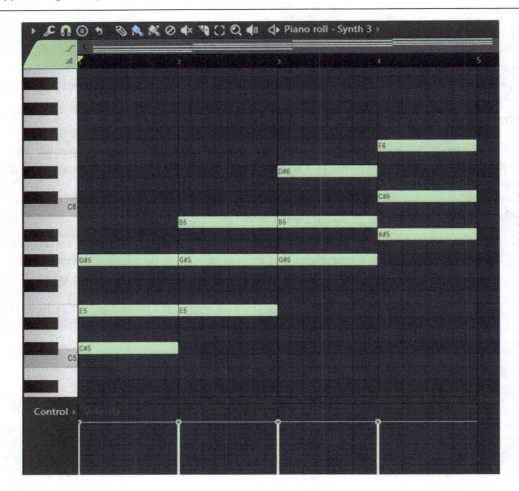

Figure 5.30: Piano Roll chord progression – minor chords

- **Power chords**: Rock and metal music frequently employs power chords, but rap songs have also begun to use them. These chords produce an intense sound that can be used to emphasize the beat or give a song more intensity. The following is an example of a power chord progression:

  - E5 = E power chord (E and B notes)

  - D5 = D power chord (D and A notes)

  - A5 = A power chord (A and E notes)

  - C5 = C power chord (C and G notes)

In this progression, the chord names indicate that we are playing power chords, and the number *5* refers to the fact that we are only playing the root note and the fifth note of each chord:

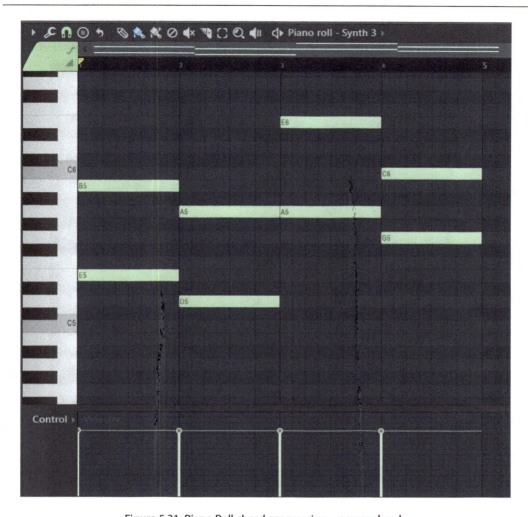

Figure 5.31: Piano Roll chord progression – power chords

- **Dominant seventh chords**: These are frequently used in jazz and blues music, but they have also been incorporated into many rap songs. These bluesy chords are frequently used to evoke feelings of tension or expectation. The following is an example of a dominant seventh chord progression:

    - G7 = G dominant seventh (G, B, D, F)

    - C7 = C dominant seventh (C, E, G, Bb)

    - D7 = D dominant seventh (D, F#, A, C)

    - G7 = G dominant seventh (G, B, D, F)

In this progression, each chord is a dominant seventh chord, and the number *7* in the chord symbol indicates that the seventh note of the corresponding scale is included in the chord:

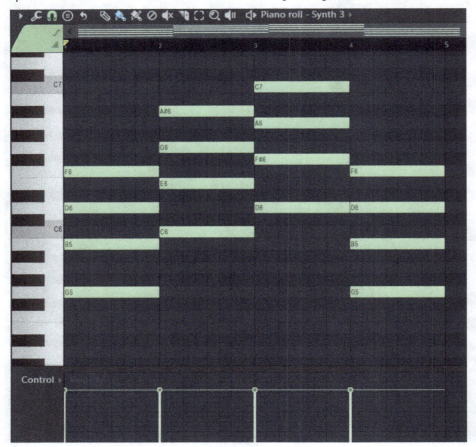

Figure 5.32: Piano Roll chord progression – dominant seventh chords

- **Suspended chords**: Rap songs have occasionally used suspended chords, which are commonly used in pop and rock music. These chords have a distinctive sound that can give the song an air of intrigue or mystery. The following is an example of a suspended chord progression:

  - Asus4 = A suspended fourth (A, D, E)

  - Dsus4 = D suspended fourth (D, G, A)

  - Esus4 = E suspended fourth (E, A, B)

  - Asus4 = A suspended fourth (A, D, E)

In this progression, each chord is a suspended fourth chord, and *sus4* indicates that the third note of the chord has been replaced with the fourth note of the corresponding scale:

Figure 5.33: Piano Roll chord progression – suspended chords

- **Augmented chords**: Songs can be made more dramatic and tense by using augmented chords, which have a dissonant sound. Some rap songs have employed these chords to evoke unease or uncertainty.

The following is an example of an augmented chord progression:

- Caug = C augmented (C, E, G#)

- Eaug = E augmented (E, G#, B#)

- Gaug = G augmented (G, B, D#)

- Caug = C augmented (C, E, G#)

In this progression, each chord is an augmented chord, and *aug* indicates that the fifth note of the corresponding scale has been raised by half a step. To play these chords on a guitar or piano, you can simply play the root note, the major third, and the augmented fifth together:

Figure 5.34: Piano Roll chord progression – augmented chords

We have now seen some examples of how chords can be produced using the Piano Roll and the corresponding notes. Ultimately, it will be up to you and your own creativity to utilize these frameworks to create ear-catching progressions and make them unique. Don't copy hit songs but, instead, follow their unique imprint as the baseline foundation to build from – every hit producer does this. In the same breath, don't limit yourself to following technical frameworks only; create records that chart on billboards and follow a formula but also have their own creative stamp for the composer and producer.

Now that we have discussed some common frameworks, this should give you the technical knowledge base of how rap and modern music are composed using specific time-tested chord theories in FL Studio. Remember, music is subjective; practice, experiment, and work on your skill set every day to get the most out of FL Studio.

Summary

In conclusion, the melody is a crucial part of music structure that has the power to enhance or undermine a song's impact. Having a solid understanding of melody theory and how to apply it in FL Studio will greatly enhance your ability to produce catchy and memorable music. You can find your own sound and write songs that connect with your audience by experimenting with various melodies, chord progressions, and rhythms. Do not be afraid to experiment and try new things when composing melodies, as there are no absolute rules. You can master melody with time, effort, and practice, and your music will soar to new heights.

By taking the time to compose your tracks with intention and creativity using the frameworks in this chapter, you'll be able to create a musical journey that will captivate your listeners from beginning to end. Whether you want to build tension and excitement or create a sense of calm and introspection, FL Studio's Piano Roll gives you the power to shape your music in any way you see fit. So, now that we are ready, let's dive into some tips and techniques for using the Playlist tool to arrange your tracks and bring your musical vision to life.

Exercise

Use two of the chord templates to create a **Fruity Loops Project** (**FLP**) template as a workflow hack and start creating, using these theories of music to get ahead.

6

A Billboard-Ready Production Arrangement

In this chapter, we'll talk about one of the most important parts of creating productions that can resonate with fans globally – the arrangement. You can think of an arrangement as the blueprint of how your track plays out while the singer or artist sings or raps over it. A solid arrangement will keep the listener focused, create emotion, take it away, and keep the listener in suspense. When we talk about arranging, we aren't just talking about using a verse and chorus framework; we are talking about *how* we can leverage formulaic approaches to create tension and emotion within a simple chord or melody loop that sounds interesting and exciting. A good arrangement gives the listener a ride, a ride into a fantastical world of sound and emotion. So, arranging your tracks to create a compelling composition is one of the most crucial tasks you will perform as a music producer.

The **Playlist** tool in FL Studio is a crucial tool in your toolbox when it comes to organizing your music. The **Playlist** tool's user-friendly interface and robust features make it simple to manipulate and arrange your patterns, automate your effects, and turn your track into a seamless and dynamic musical journey. Whether you're a novice or a seasoned pro, mastering FL Studio's **Playlist** tool is essential to elevate your music production skills. A good arrangement should take the listener on a rollercoaster ride, taking them through a journey, from start to finish.

In this chapter, you will learn *how* to leverage FL Studio's powerful features to enhance your workflow and create compelling arrangements. We will explore the evolution of arrangement throughout history and delve into modern-day techniques for crafting dynamic musical journeys. You'll discover *how* to create your own billboard charting arrangement template, and we'll also cover essential skills such as transitions to keep your listeners engaged from start to finish.

In the chapter, we will cover the following topics:

- Introduction to arrangement
- Using FL Studio to increase your workflow arrangement

- Creating billboard charting arrangement templates
- Arrangement transitions

Whether you're a beginner or a seasoned producer, this chapter will equip you with the knowledge and tools you need to take your arrangements to the next level.

Introduction to arrangement

For the sake of understanding what arranging is, let's talk about music arrangements from a historical standpoint so we understand it in detail, following the principle that *perfect practice makes perfect*!

History of arrangement

The history of music arrangement or arranging spans many centuries and involves a range of genres and styles. From a basic view, arranging is the science of putting your music pieces together to create a full song or instrumental piece. As a meta point, arranging can also be described as *how* you arrange your individual sounds into cohesive loops or progressions. This includes everything from your drum arrangements and your chord arrangements to the entire song in the end. By examining the arrangements of influential artists and composers from various eras, we can learn more about the methods and approaches used to compose memorable and powerful musical compositions. This historical analysis can also reveal the cultural and social factors that influenced the evolution of various musical styles and genres, giving context to arrangements that various artists have chosen.

Knowing *how* various musical genres and styles have evolved over time can be a fascinating journey, and studying music arrangement from a historical perspective is an excellent way to explore this. By examining the arrangements of influential artists and composers from different eras, we can gain insights into the methods and approaches used to compose memorable and powerful musical compositions. We can also uncover the cultural and social factors that influenced the evolution of various musical styles and genres, providing valuable context for the arrangements that different artists have chosen.

Looking back through history, we see that music arrangements have a rich and varied history. In medieval times, for example, it was common for musicians to add harmonies or embellishments to plainchant melodies, which is one of the earliest examples of music arrangement. In the Renaissance period, composers such as William Byrd and Giovanni Pierluigi da Palestrina frequently arranged existing sacred texts in polyphony. Meanwhile, during the Baroque era, renowned composers such as Johann Sebastian Bach and George Frideric Handel built intricate variations on existing melodies using the technique of *figured bass* or *continuo*.

As music evolved into the classical era, the consistency of arrangements became more pronounced. Composers would write symphonies or concertos with particular instrumentation, and arrangements continued to be significant, especially in the world of opera, where arias were often transposed into different keys or arranged for different voice types. In the 20th century, as popular music genres such as jazz and rock and roll emerged, arrangements gained even more significance. Jazz musicians, for example, were particularly known for rearranging pre-existing melodies with new rhythms, harmonies, and instrumental solos. During the big band era, ensembles such as Duke Ellington's orchestra would craft intricate arrangements of well-known songs, and this practice was especially prevalent.

Today, arrangements continue to play an essential role in music production, creating a soundscape that captivates listeners and keeps their attention focused on the piece of music. Whether it's a classical composer creating a new version of an old piece, a jazz musician improvising over a familiar melody, or a pop artist reimagining a classic song, the art of arranging music remains an integral part of musical creativity, and ultimately the production process. Music arrangements give musicians a way to showcase their creativity, experiment with new musical concepts, and give well-known songs a fresh spin, all while adding their unique touch to the musical landscape.

Modern-day arranging

Pop music, as we call it today, is the evolution of cultural reflection of an era and generation. Arrangements have evolved to reflect what the current generation is attuned to, and *how* music operates in pop culture at that moment in time. Pop music aims to appeal to and be understandable by a large audience, hence the term *popular music*. Genres are interchanged in the definition of pop music, as it relates to what is current at the time of its creation. What was once pop music 30 years ago is different from today's standards. Pop music's main objective is to entertain and captivate listeners with catchy melodies, enduring lyrics, and straightforward but effective song structures. Pop music frequently has positive, upbeat lyrics with messages about love, relationships, and self-empowerment (among a wide range of other topics). Pop music not only provides entertainment but also acts as a means of cultural expression. Pop music is a reflection of the social issues, trends, and attitudes of the time in which it was made. Pop music has been used to advance social and political causes, express disapproval and protest, and question social norms and conventions, and is frequently connected to youth culture.

In the 1990s, hip hop as a subgenre emerged within the commercial music scene and eventually became the dominant genre of consumption among Western cultures in the mid-2000s. Today, this still rings true. Rap generally follows a similar framework. As I have said, pop music is simply a term that reflects what is popular at any given time in history. In modern times, pop music is created using a plethora of software and hardware tools, such as FL Studio. Using FL Studio, we want to lay out the foundation of *how* we can leverage its **Playlist** tool to create formulaic arrangement templates to optimize our workflow under the guise of time-tested approaches. As time goes on, these may be augmented as pop culture shifts, and it's up to you as an FL Studio Power User to set these trends, inject your own creative spin into it, and continue to evolve music in a direction that reflects the current landscape of pop culture.

So, let's really dig into *how* we can leverage the past and present to direct the future of pop culture using FL Studio. Let's talk about *how* pop music is structured from an arrangement standpoint now.

Pop music frameworks

Pop songs typically follow a fairly standard structure known as the verse-chorus form. Other names for this structure include the A-B form and the ABABCB form. Here is a breakdown of the typical song structure in pop music:

- **Intro**: Many pop songs begin with an introduction, which can include instrumental music, sound effects, or a brief musical statement that sets the tone for the song.

- **Verse**: The song's main section, the verse presents the main idea or tells the story. With each repetition, the verse's melody and lyrics typically change, but the music may stay largely the same. The chorus usually comes after the verse.

- **Chorus**: The chorus of a song contains the primary hook or catchphrase that listeners are most likely to remember. Typically, the chorus is easier to sing along to than the verse because it is more repetitive and simplistic musically. With each repetition, the chorus's melody and lyrics stay the same.

- **Pre-chorus** or **bridge**: To connect the verse and chorus, some pop songs have a pre-chorus or bridge section. This part usually provides a sense of tension and release before the chorus.

- **Interlude**: A section of instrumental music or a brief musical statement that breaks up the song and serves as a transition between various sections may be present in some pop songs.

- **Outro**: A section of music that concludes a song, an outro is a common feature of pop songs. A fade-out, in which the music gets progressively quieter, or a definitive ending, in which the music abruptly stops, can be used as the outro.

As a high-level sketch, without using any patterns or notes, this is what a pop formula framework looks like in FL Studio's **Playlist** tool:

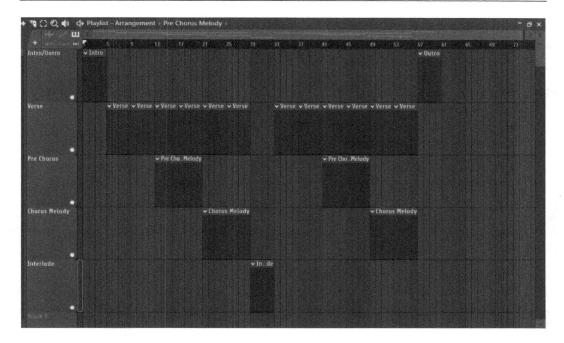

Figure 6.1: Playlist tool | song arrangement

Using FL Studio to increase your workflow arrangement

When it comes to using FL Studio to arrange your productions, the main tool of focus is the **Playlist** tool.

The FL Studio's **Playlist** tool is where we sketch out our arrangements. The **Playlist** tool enables you to quickly and effectively arrange your patterns and create dynamic musical structures, thanks to its drag-and-drop interface and simple controls. Getting familiar with the **Playlist** tool will assist you to better understand the organization of songs and *how* the various components of a track work together to form a coherent track. The **Playlist** tool also gives you more creative freedom and enables you to experiment with new concepts and sounds by making it simple to automate your effects and create intricate arrangements. Mastering FL Studio's **Playlist** tool is crucial for developing your skill set and music production abilities.

As we have discussed in *Chapter 1*, the Channel Rack in FL Studio is used to arrange and program musical instruments, patterns, and sounds. When writing and arranging music in FL Studio, you will devote a significant amount of time to it. It is a crucial part of the FL Studio workflow, and *how* you use it will affect *how* quickly you can organize music in the **Playlist** tool. As a key element of the **Playlist** tool in FL Studio, mastering your workflow when using the Channel Rack is necessary to create professional arrangements. In the Channel Rack, you can create, edit, and manage your various MIDI and audio channels, instrument, and effects. This makes it quick and easy to add and switch out different sounds, instruments, and effects.

You can create complex arrangements with a variety of instrument layers quickly by assigning patterns to different channels using the Channel Rack. Learning about FL Studio's Channel Rack is essential for honing your musical composition skills and creating songs that are compelling and dynamic, whether you're a beginning or seasoned producer. Now, let's discuss *how* we should approach using the Channel Rack from my point of view to maximize and give flexibility to your ability to arrange your full songs in the **Playlist** tool.

One way is to make all of the drum sounds in one Channel Rack channel when making drum patterns, which is fine when you are composing ideas. However, I advise you to separate each loop pattern into a different channel so that you can arrange them in the **Playlist** tool separately, which will give you an easier option to add and remove sounds as needed to build tension in your arrangement.

When we separate each drum sound and drag it into the **Playlist** tool, it will appear as shown in *Figure 6.2*:

Figure 6.2: Playlist | drum sequences

Let's see how we can separate each drum sound:

1. Go to the **Playlist** window by clicking on the **Playlist** button on the toolbar or by pressing the *F5* key on your keyboard, as shown in the red highlighted box in *Figure 6.3*:

Figure 6.3: Playlist

2. In the **Playlist** window, a new pattern identified as **Pattern 1** will populate. To create a new pattern, simply right-click on **Pattern 1** in the playlist and select **Insert one** from the context menu, as shown in *Figure 6.4*:

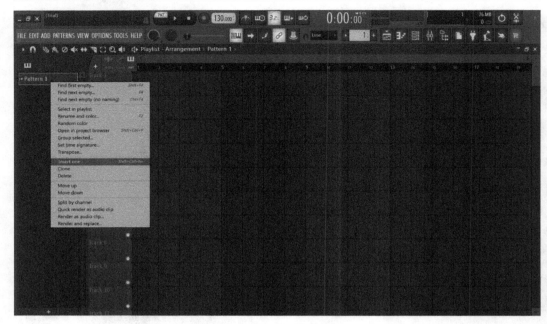

Figure 6.4: Playlist | Insert one

3. Create a drum pattern for your kick, naming it Drum Kick. Then, add another pattern for your snare or clap and then a pattern for your hi-hat, naming it Clap (as I have done in this instance). Select the drum pattern you created earlier from the list of available patterns, as shown in *Figure 6.5*:

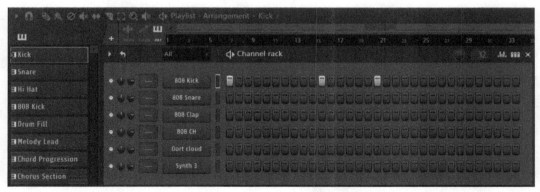

Figure 6.5: Playlist | Channel Rack | Drum Kick

4.   Drag each pattern to the desired location in the playlist using your mouse, as shown in *Figure 6.6*:

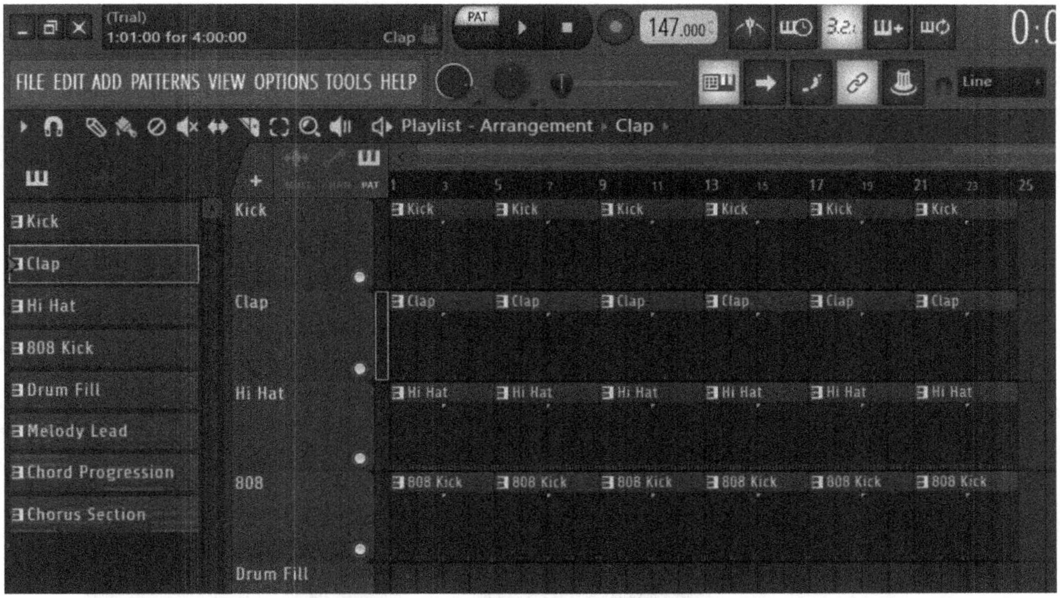

Figure 6.6: Playlist | Drum arrangement

This framework of separating each pattern by individual layer is an important concept that you should follow with every instrument, as it will give you the flexibility to properly arrange layers and augment your production throughout.

Let's look at how to separate patterns with a two-layer keyboard loop. Using the Piano Roll, I have created a basic chord progression. We will follow the same steps as described for the drum pattern layers:

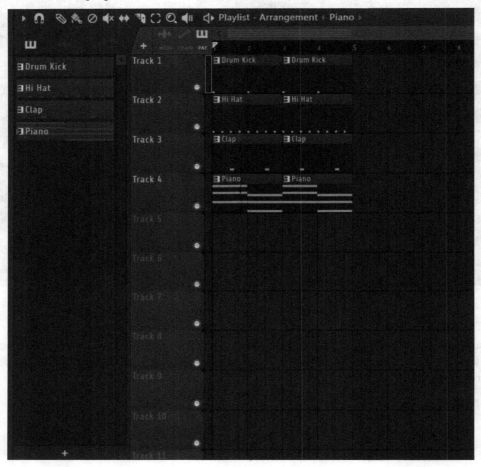

Figure 6.7: Playlist | Arrangement

Now, let's add the second keyboard layer to the **Playlist** tool:

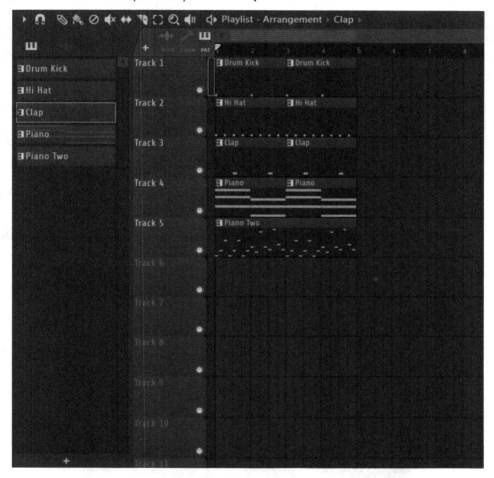

Figure 6.8: Playlist | Arrangement | Piano 2

Voila!

Now let's talk about *how* to follow the billboard charting formula when arranging productions in FL Studio, which you can use as a template and start making records that work for charts!

Creating the billboard charting arrangement templates

We'll begin by structuring an A-B framework in FL Studio. Once we have this basic framework template created, we can dive into what makes arrangements stand out by using my Power User strategies:

1. Create a new project in FL Studio.

2. Begin by coming up with unique patterns for the various verse, chorus, and bridge sections of the song. We will create the melody, chord, and drum patterns using **Step Sequencer** or the Piano Roll.

3. When you have finished creating all of your patterns, open the **Playlist** window. You can arrange the various patterns there to produce the song's overall structure.

For the sake of this example, we won't dive into creating a mind-blowing composition, just something we can use to fill each step of building the A-B pop framework:

1. So, let's start by creating the intro of the song. I have chosen the **FL Keys** VST to make the melody shown in *Figure 6.9*:

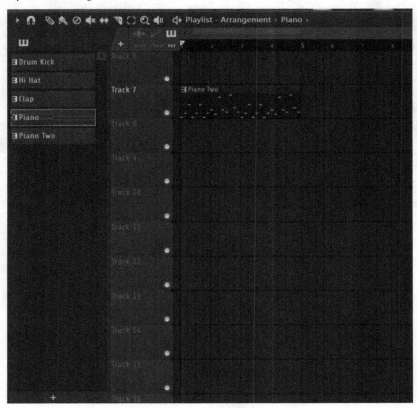

Figure 6.9: Playlist | Piano pattern | intro

2. Now, let's create the first verse of the song. Using the **FL Keys** VST, I have composed a basic chord progression using the *Billboard Charting Chord* framework as the foundation for my verses (you can use any instrument or combination of instruments to create the melody and harmony for the verse). Keep in mind that the melody and lyrics of the verse usually change with each repetition. Drag the patterns into the **Playlist** window using the mouse from the **Browser** or the Channel Rack. To do this, we will use the chord progression as the basis of the verses, and the intro notes as the pre-chorus, as shown in *Figure 6.10*:

Figure 6.10: Playlist | intro-verse structure

3. Now, let's create the first chorus of the song. In this example, I have added a layer of the *Billboard Charting Chord Progression* framework to make the chorus stand out. The chorus section should feature the main hook or catchphrase that listeners are likely to remember. Keep the melody and lyrics of the chorus the same with each repetition. Drag the patterns into the **Playlist** window using the mouse from the **Browser** or the Channel Rack.

4.   Following the chord progression, we will use the intro to create a pre-chorus section. This section should connect the verse and chorus and provide a sense of tension and release. You can use a different melody or chord progression to create a sense of anticipation leading up to the chorus.

Here's what the intro-verse-chorus structure would look like:

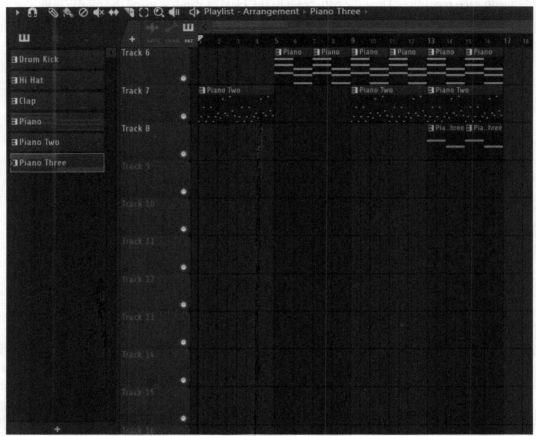

Figure 6.11: Intro-verse-chorus structure

5. Now, create the second verse. Follow the same steps as shown in *Figure 6.11* and place the second verse in the bar structure section. Place the **Piano** pattern four times, and then add **Piano 2** under the last two **Piano** patterns, as shown in *Figure 6.12*:

Figure 6.12: Intro-verse-chorus-second-verse structure

6. Now, let's add the second chorus and an interlude following it. This section can include instrumental music or a brief musical statement that breaks up the song and provides a transition between different sections. Here's what an interlude section would look like:

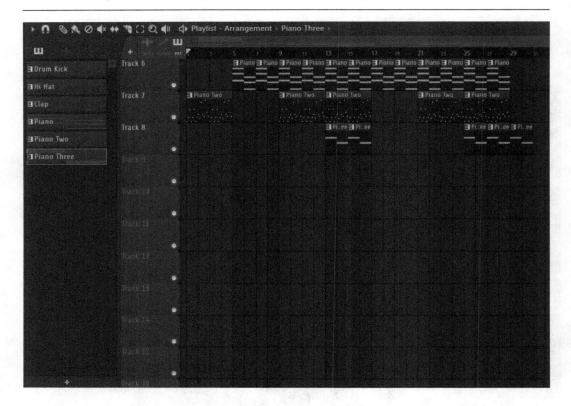

Figure 6.13: Interlude structure

Here, I have created a pattern variation using the **FL Keys** VST to change the note pattern of the verse and chorus to create the interlude for reference.

7. Now, let's add the third chorus of the song. We'll use the same melody and lyrics as the first and second choruses.

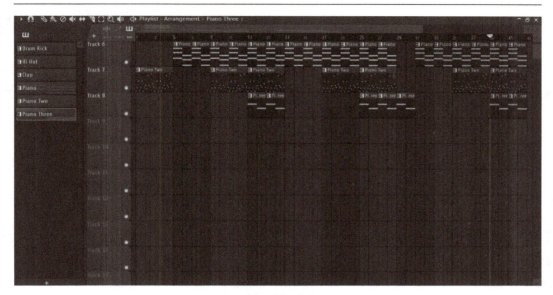

Figure 6.14: Third chorus

8. Next, we'll create an outro for the song. This section should bring the song to a close. You can use a fade-out or a definitive ending where the music comes to a sudden stop, or you can use the intro pattern to relay it back, which I have done in this example:

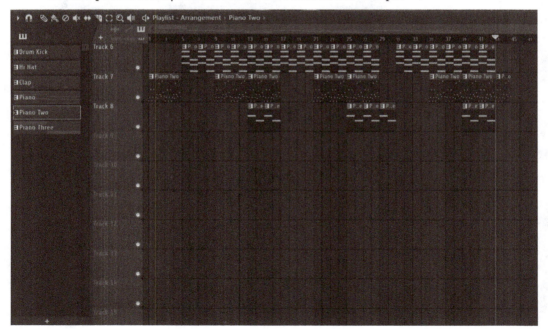

Figure 6.15: Outro

9. Finally, let's save this as a template framework so you can use this arrangement as a workflow template. Exporting the song to a file will let you know when the arrangement is perfect. The song can be exported in many different formats, including MP3, WAV, and MIDI.

By following the formula described in this section, you can create the basic foundational framework of *how* to create a pop song in FL Studio that follows the standard A-B form or verse-chorus structure. You should keep in mind that you can use any instruments, sound effects, or samples you like to produce an original song that reflects your own sense of style.

Now that we have a general billboard charting arrangement framework, let's discuss the small differences in what a rap arrangement looks like in the **Playlist** tool and then *how* we can add our own signature sound to our arrangements, which gives the subtle effect of a sonic signature.

The rap arrangement formula

Rap music (in its current commercial format) follows a similar arrangement style to pop music but simplifies itself with the removal of the interlude following the first chorus and typically only has two choruses. It follows a simple framework that in the **Playlist** tool looks as it does in *Figure 6.16*:

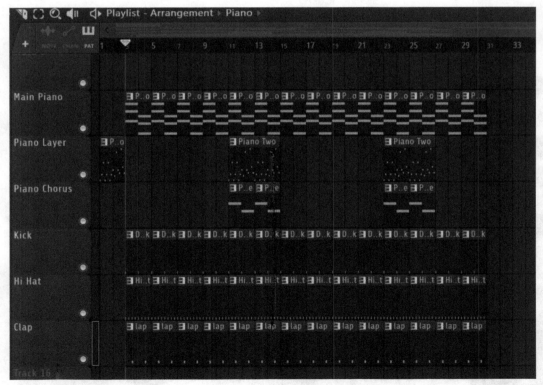

Figure 6.16: The rap arrangement formula

The rap arrangement formula has the following structure:

- **Intro**: The introduction establishes the mood of the song and draws the listener in. This could be a vocal intro, an instrumental break, or a catchy hook.

- **Verse 1**: 12-16 bars. The rapper usually introduces themselves and their viewpoint in the first verse. Personal narratives, political commentary, or any other subject the artist chooses to explore can be included in this.

- **Chorus 1**: 8 bars. Also known as the **hook**, it is a catchy, enduring passage that appears repeatedly in the song. It frequently has a memorable melody or vocal riff that aids in the song's retention by the listener.

- **Verse 2**: 12-16 bars. The second verse frequently expands on the themes introduced in the first verse and may offer more in-depth examples or observations.

- **Chorus 2**: 8 bars. The second chorus follows the second verse.

- **Bridge**: 4-8 bars. Most rap songs don't have a bridge unless there is a featured melodic singer on the song. This can be added at your discretion. For context, the song's bridge offers a contrast to the rest of the song. A different melody, chord progression, or rhythm can be used in this. It is frequently used to switch between the song's various sections.

- **Verse 3**: 12-16 bars. This verse continues the commentary of the concept of the song at the conclusion of the first verse.

- **Outro**: This ends the song and is usually a short 4- to 8-bar instrumental component.

In modern music, songs have become shorter (less than 2 minutes 30 seconds long) and rappers have started to record verses using the 12-bar formula, rather than the full 16-bar formula used in the 1990s and 2000s. This has a lot to do with pop culture shifts and the way we consume music due to disruptive technologies, which have increased the variety of consumable music. A 12-bar rap arrangement formula in the **Playlist** tool looks like what is shown in *Figure 6.17*:

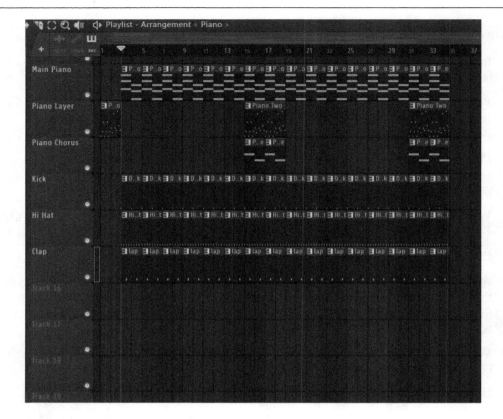

Figure 6.17: 12-bar rap arrangement formula

You can create a rap formula in FL Studio using the same framework I described in this chapter, so we have a framework template we can save for our workflow arsenal. To create a rap formula framework template, we will follow the same steps as we followed when creating the pop formula.

Sonic signature in arrangements

When it comes to arranging music using a sonic signature arrangement framework, we have everything we need to properly create a full song. But *how* do we make it our own? Think about it like this – you have a house and all houses are built structurally in the same way, but it's the unique, finished inside and outside of the house that make it exclusive to each individual builder. Music works the same way.

Let's talk about *how* we can use FL Studio to add our own unique finishes to the arrangement structure to add to our sonic signature.

In the *Studying the icons* section of *Chapter 5*, we discussed certain characteristics that make great producers. Using FL Studio and its tools, we can start to implement our own workflow habits that will make your arrangements stand out to listeners.

Arrangement transitions

Knowing *how* to build the tension using transitionary frameworks creates exciting moments in each song section. It is a massive skill hack you need to start practicing and is something that all successful producers do. This will bring your productions to the next level when you are arranging your productions. The excitement and impact of a song can be greatly increased by incorporating transition effects into the song arrangement. Whether moving from the verse to the chorus or from one chorus to the next, a transition effect is employed to make the transition seamless. You can create a smooth transition between the song's various sections by including transition effects, which will make the song sound more cohesive and interesting. Transitional effects can take the form of musical elements such as drum fills or breakdowns, or they can take the form of sound effects such as risers, impacts, or swells. These effects build tension and suspense, which can be released with the addition of a new section or melody, making the song arrangement more dynamic and exciting. A song's ability to captivate and move the listener can be determined by *how* well the transition effects are used. Songs that feel flat often lack these effects.

Let's explore *how* we can use transitional effects from a macro standpoint to build and add tension to your arrangement:

Let's look at an example of a fully arranged song using the billboard charting framework and *how* we can implement transitional effects at each section change. For this example, let's use a **Riser** sound clip. The FL Studio includes stock riser sounds in the **Browser** under **Packs | SFX**:

Figure 6.18: Browser | Packs | SFX

We will use the riser sound **Riser Piano** for this example to see *how* to create tension in an arrangement and indicate a bar change from verses to pre-chorus and from pre-chorus to chorus. To use the sound, we will drag it directly into the **Playlist** tool. You may also insert it into the Channel Rack and create a pattern block if you wish. However, I prefer to drag transition sounds directly into the **Playlist** window so we can edit and manipulate these types of sounds to fit the time sequencing:

1. Let's drag the **Riser** sound into the **Playlist** tool at each of these section changes:

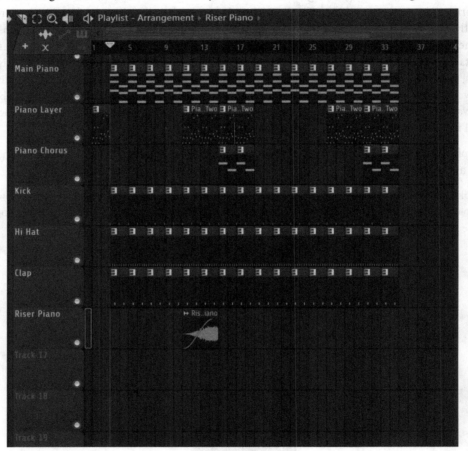

Figure 6.19: Playlist | Piano Riser | pre-chorus transition

Now, let's drag the riser at the end of the **Piano Chorus** section to introduce the second verse:

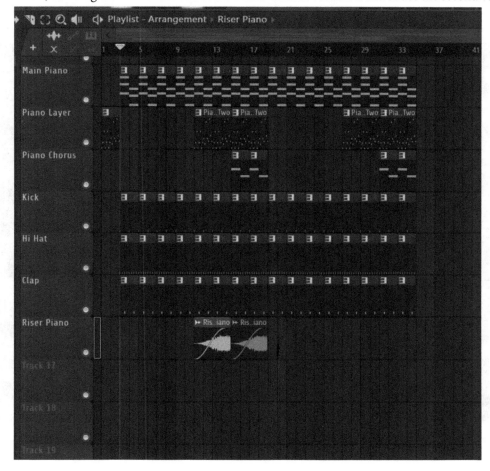

Figure 6.20: Playlist | Piano Riser | chorus transition

2. Next, let's drag the riser to the end of the second pre-chorus and second chorus to get a view of what your **Playlist** view will look like when the riser is inserted consistently into the arrangement:

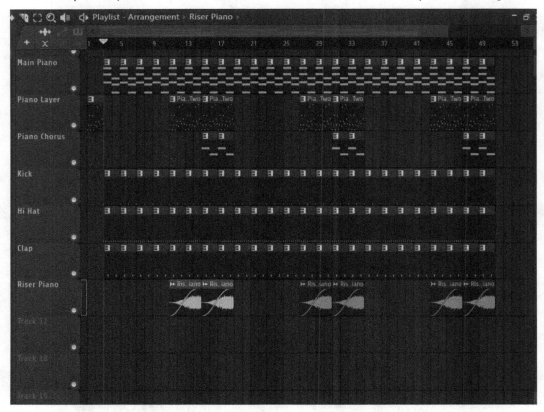

Figure 6.21: Playlist | Piano Riser | riser pattern throughout

3. Now, let's augment this **Riser** sound clip so we make it a little more personalized and fit the arrangement. To do this, we will bend the front end of the riser sound to create a higher rise than the stock sound as is. This will give the riser sound a better rising feeling and a little bit of nuance and changeability. Double-click the riser sound to bring up the **Master** interface of the sound:

Figure 6.22: Piano Riser | Master Interface

4. Now, let's augment the **IN** button on the **Master** interface to lessen the front end of the riser sound to make it more transitional:

Figure 6.23: Piano Riser | Master interface | IN raised 25%

In *Figure 6.23*, you will see a red circle highlighting the **IN** button and *how* I have moved it 25% up to shorten the front end of the WAV sample to give it a better *rising* feeling. This is a tip you can use for any type of FX to increase how it rises to create a transitional sound.

In *Figure 6.24*, you can see *how* the **Piano Riser** WAV image in **Playlist** has been adjusted:

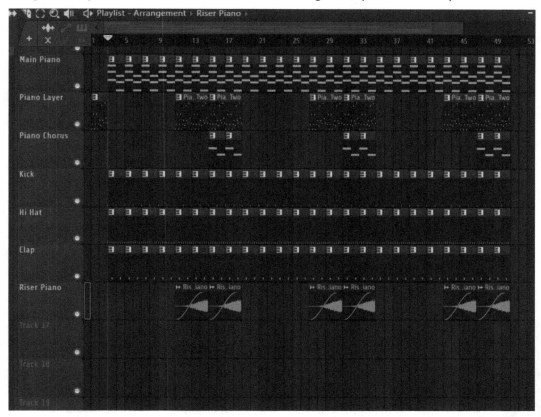

Figure 6.24: Playlist | augmented Piano Riser

This FL Studio framework offers a comprehensive set of tools and techniques for harnessing the power of risers in order to create seamless and impactful transitional effects in music production. Risers, with their ability to build anticipation and tension, serve as invaluable assets in enhancing the overall dynamics and energy of a track. Within this framework, producers gain access to a wide array of pre-designed riser samples, meticulously crafted to cover various musical genres and moods. Additionally, FL Studio provides a user-friendly interface that allows for effortless manipulation and customization of these riser elements. With intuitive controls, producers can adjust parameters such as pitch, length, and intensity, ensuring a perfect fit for their desired sound. Furthermore, the framework offers a range of built-in effects and plugins, enabling producers to further shape and refine the riser's sonic characteristics. Whether it's a subtle transition between sections or an explosive build-up to a drop, the FL Studio framework empowers music creators to achieve professional-grade transitional effects using risers with ease and precision.

Transitional effects

Now, let's explore using transitional effects in FL Studio and *how* they can add even more tension and excitement to your arrangement in the **Playlist** tool. FL Studio has a number of integrated instruments and sound effects. You can design distinctive and captivating arrangements that stand out from the crowd by experimenting with sound waves. To create new textures and tones, try layering audio clips or using effects such as reverb, delay, and distortion. About 80 mixing and effect plugins are available in FL Studio, with a great selection of plugin tools that can be used both methodically and illuminatingly to improve section transitions in our arrangements.

One of my favorites for creating and building tension is **Gross Beat**, however. As we discussed in *Chapter 1*, Gross Beat is a real-time tempo and volume manipulation effect plugin in FL Studio. It is a stock plugin that is included in the **Signature Bundle**, which is the version of FL Studio that includes all of the software's additional plugins and sounds. I like Gross Beat because it gives you the ability to gate, slow down, and speed up the master track from your channel mixer, among other things. Now, I'll show you *how* I use Gross Beat to add tension to transitional sections in my arrangements:

1. You can add Gross Beat to any single VST or WAV sound. For the following example, I want to add the **Gross Beat** VST plugin to the mixer channel on the master channel. You can do this by clicking on the + button on a mixer channel, then selecting **More plugins**, and navigating to your VST folder:

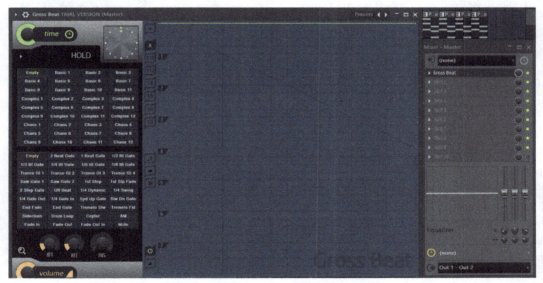

Figure 6.25: Mixer | master channel | Gross Beat

2. In Gross Beat, choose a preset or create your own effect pattern by adjusting the various parameters. For this example, we will choose the **1/2 Speed** effect:

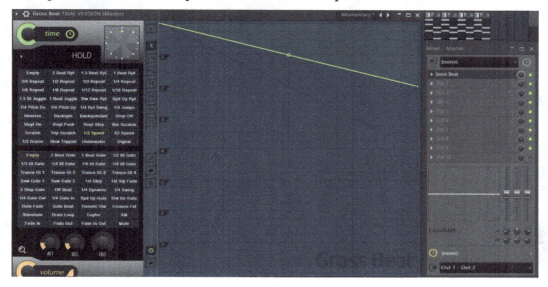

Figure 6.26: Gross Beat | preset | ½ Speed

The **1/2 Speed** preset is a well-used preset in trap music productions that in effect slows down the selected channel (in this case, the entire master) to alter the sound wave in a way that creates a distinct and unique ending, section, or intro.

3. Click on the button in the top-left corner of the Gross Beat interface to show the automation parameters and click **Browse parameters**:

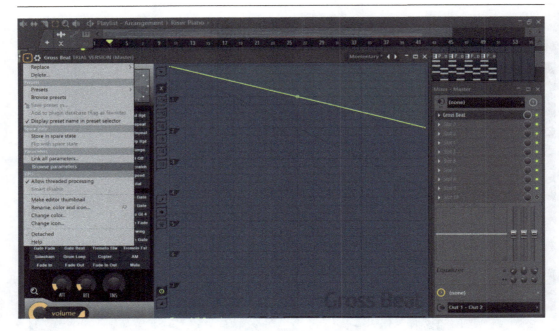

Figure 6.27: Gross Beat | Preset | Param

4. Right-click on the parameter you want to automate and choose **Create automation clip** from the context menu, in this case, **Time Slot**:

Figure 6.28: Gross Beat | Create automation clip

This will create a new automation clip for the selected parameter, which you can then edit and adjust as needed.

5.   To use the automation clip, simply drag it into **Playlist** where you want the effect to occur, and adjust the clip's start and end points as needed:

Figure 6.29: Gross Beat | automated clip

Voila! Now you have automated a Gross Beat effect on the outro to our arrangement to give it a unique sound and feel. You can do the same process at any section change, get experimental with your melodic patterns, or even experiment with other VST effect plugins and presets.

When arranging drums in general, I typically don't include any drum sounds in my intros. This is self-explanatory and doesn't require you to place any of your drum sounds in the intro section, as shown in *Figure 6.30*:

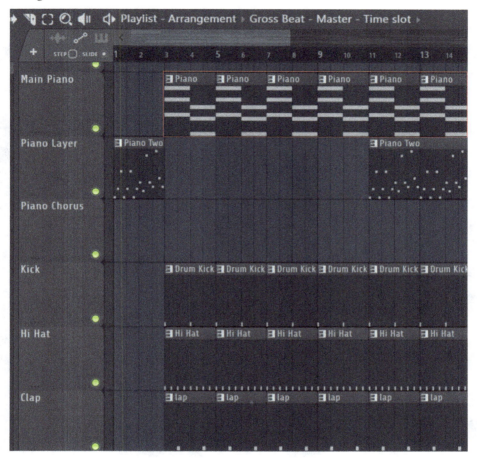

Figure 6.30: Arrangement | drum sequence after intro pattern

In *Figure 6.30*, the drums are shown starting after the third bar and are highlighted in the red box. Now let's let look at *how* we can drop certain drum sounds out of the last two bars of the pre-chorus section to add a bit of climax to the chorus section. First, let's do this with the clap sound. For reference, whether you are using a snare, clap, or snap, this framework is universal. In the **Playlist** tool, remove the following patterns to create the framework shown in *Figure 6.31*:

Figure 6.31: Playlist | Arrangement | clap removed at 13

The same framework can be used for the kick and hi-hat, as follows:

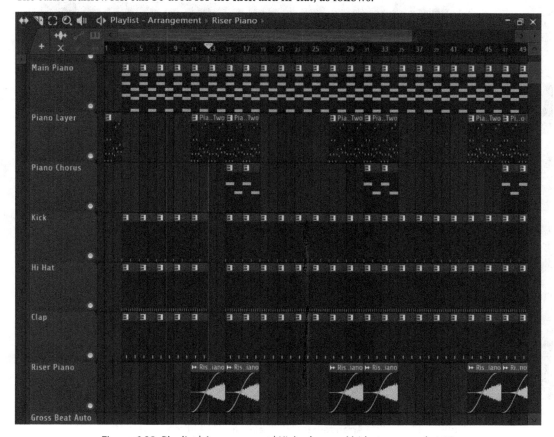

Figure 6.32: Playlist | Arrangement | Kick, clap, and hi-hat removed at 13

Now, when it comes to dropping drum sounds out at the second verse, the theory is we want to bring the climax down from the chorus, but not totally remove the rhythmic section as the second verse continues to carry the track forward for the listener. In my experience, taking out one of the elements works best. This can manifest as removing just the hi-hat (like I have done in *Figure 6.33*) or removing the kick or snare. *Figure 6.33* shows *how* this framework looks in the **Playlist** tool at the beginning of the second verse:

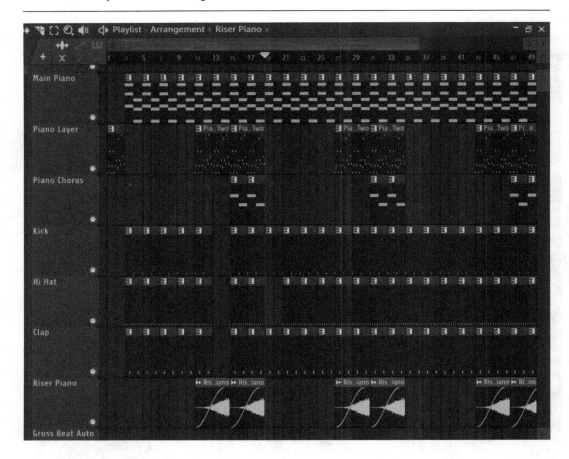

Figure 6.33: Playlist | Arrangement | Kick, clap, and hi-hat removed at 19

This simple framework adds massive compelling nuance to your arrangements, and I recommend you experiment with this within your own productions. It's the simple things that keep your arrangement interesting!

Now, as this is related to creating a sonic signature, certain producers create a framework of using the drop-in and dropout theory in specific places within an arrangement, where the listener can tell a certain producer made the production based upon *how* those drum patterns interact with the arrangement. This is in essence the foundation of giving your arrangements a consistent sonic signature. For example, in my productions, as seen in *Figure 6.33*, this is where I like to drop rhythmic sections in and out, and it adds to my own sonic signature. For you, you can copy this framework, or add nuance based on your own creativity. The key is using an established drop-in and dropout framework in all of your tracks to create a consistent production style that can become recognizable to listeners.

Now that you have the general concept of dropping drums in and out, experiment with your own arrangements!

Summary

So, in this chapter, we looked at the fundamental ideas of arrangement, including patterns, playlist tracks, and template formulas. Producers and musicians can create intricate and dynamic arrangements that hold listeners' attention throughout by using the strategies discussed in this chapter. The possibilities for arranging in FL Studio are essentially limitless with practice and experimentation, so I encourage readers to keep learning and honing their arranging techniques. Everything in this chapter should be expanded upon from a framework of foundation!

Now that we have covered the fundamentals of music production, it's time to delve into the realm of mixing techniques. Mixing is the art of balancing and enhancing individual elements within a track to create a cohesive and polished sound. In this next chapter, we will explore a wide range of tools, tips, and strategies that will help you achieve a professional mix. We will discuss the importance of proper gain staging and *how* to create a well-balanced mix using techniques such as EQ, compression, panning, and reverb. Additionally, we will explore advanced mixing concepts such as automation and parallel processing, which can add depth, dimension, and movement to your tracks. By the end of the next chapter, you will have a solid understanding of the principles behind effective mixing and be equipped with the knowledge to elevate your productions to the next level. So, let's dive in and uncover the secrets of creating a stellar mix!

Exercise

In this exercise, you will apply the knowledge gained from this chapter to formulate a billboard charting arrangement using the **Playlist** tool. By arranging the deliverables discussed throughout the chapter, you will create a solid foundation for your project and set the stage for the production process. Here are the steps we will follow:

1. **Setting up your project**: Begin by launching FL Studio and creating a new project. Set the project tempo, key signature, and time signature according to the style and feel you want to achieve with your record production. Ensure that you have all the necessary audio files and plugins ready for use.

2. **Organizing your audio assets**: Take a moment to gather and organize the audio assets you intend to use in your record production. These assets may include recorded vocals, instrumentals, drum samples, and any other audio elements you plan to incorporate. Create dedicated folders within your project directory to keep everything well organized.

3. **Creating the billboard charting arrangement**: Implement the rap arrangement formula and sketch out the structure by creating patterns or arranging audio clips in the **Playlist** tool. Experiment with different drop-ins, dropouts, and transition effects until you are satisfied with the flow and progression of your song. Once completed, save the .FLP file and add it to your FL Studio workflow templates!

Drop-ins and dropouts of drum patterns

When it comes to drum patterns in the **Playlist** tool, we can take several approaches that give rise to tension and climatic build-up heading toward the chorus section of the arrangement. In my experience, drums carry the rhythmic experience of the track and should also act as the underlying foundation of the production's groove. Let's talk about a few template frameworks for arranging your drum pattern loops that work.

Dropping in and out

This framework concept revolves around the idea of taking drum patterns out of certain sections to build a climatic event toward the height of a chorus section or verse. There may be a time when keeping the drum pattern running throughout the track makes sense. For instance, in a trap or rap track, this can be useful to carry the rhythm for the artist, and even in some pop variations (such as dance music). However, you should experiment when you are building your arrangements to find what works best for each specific song situation.

Dropping drums in and out is the concept of either taking out or removing certain drum sounds such as the kick or snare from a certain section and bringing them back once the section concludes. An example would be taking the kick out of the first half of the verse section and dropping it back into the second half of the verse section to create tension in the verse. In the following section, let's walk through some template frameworks you can use to make your arrangement stand out and create the build-up and climax of each section.

Maximizing your kick arrangement in the Playlist tool

Kick drums carry the rhythmic feel of a record and can be arranged in the **Playlist** tool to take away and add rythmic low end to a composition. In my experience, there are a few key areas of an arrangement where kick drums sound the best when dropped out. These are as follows:

- In the intro
- At the end of the pre-chorus
- At the beginning of the second verse

Part 3:
Best Techniques and How to Appear on the Billboard Charts

In this part, we will delve into the art of mixing using FL Studio's stock plugins, empowering you to create professional-sounding records that meet radio airwave standards. Moreover, you will discover how to leverage these mixing techniques to enhance your sound design and creative compositions, unlocking the full potential of your music. Building on that, we will take an in-depth walk-through of how to produce music to the caliber of Billboard chart-topping hits, providing invaluable insights and strategies to guide your success in the music industry. You will learn how to effectively use networking platforms such as social media and cold email to secure placements with major artists, companies, and record labels. Lastly, we will focus on what comes next after you've created your masterpiece in FL Studio and explore the best practices for promoting, distributing, and navigating the music industry to propel your music career to new heights.

In this part, we have the following chapters:

- *Chapter 7, Chart-Topping Mixing Techniques*
- *Chapter 8, How to Get Records Placed So They Land on Billboard Charts*

7

Chart-Topping Mixing Techniques

In *Chapter 7*, we will delve into the world of mixing and mastering within FL Studio, exploring various tips and frameworks that I have developed through years of experience. The ultimate goal is to equip you with the necessary knowledge and techniques to maximize the potential of your productions and prepare them for the market. Mixing is a crucial step in the music production process where all individual elements of a track are balanced, polished, and blended to create a cohesive and professional sound. Within FL Studio, we will explore techniques such as **equalization (EQ)** to shape the tonal balance of different instruments, compression to control dynamics and add punch, and spatial effects such as reverb and delay to create depth and space.

We will cover the importance of proper gain staging to ensure optimal audio levels and prevent distortion or clipping. Understanding the concept of panning and stereo imaging will enable you to position elements within the stereo field, creating a sense of width and separation. Once the mixing process is complete, we move on to mastering, which involves fine-tuning the final mix to achieve a commercially competitive and polished sound. In this stage, we will explore the use of dynamic processing tools such as multiband compression and limiting to enhance the overall loudness and clarity of the track. EQ and stereo enhancement techniques will be employed to further refine the tonal balance and width. Moreover, we will discuss the importance of referencing your track against professional productions to ensure it holds up to industry standards. By utilizing various meters and analyzers available in FL Studio, we can objectively assess the frequency response, dynamics, and stereo field of our mix, making necessary adjustments as needed. By implementing these mixing and mastering techniques, you will gain the skills to elevate your productions to a professional level, ready for the market.

FL Studio is a fantastic mixing and mastering program in addition to being a powerful and effective music production tool. In order to help you perfect your music tracks, it offers a variety of tools and features. FL Studio makes it simple to produce mixes and masters that sound professional, regardless of your level of experience as a producer. You can easily change the levels, EQ, and compression of your tracks as well as add effects thanks to its user-friendly interface and flexible routing options. Additionally, FL Studio provides cutting-edge features such as mastering plugins, multiband compression, and stereo widening, which assist you in producing a more professional sound. In this chapter, we'll look at the various mixing and mastering strategies you can use in FL Studio to give your music that chart-topping professional sound!

In this chapter, we will cover the following topics:

- What are the differences between mixing and mastering?
- Creative mixing versus technical mixing
- The key FL Studio toolbox plugins for mixing and mastering
- What I use for creative mixing and signature sound nuances
- How you can leverage mixing and mastering to create Billboard-charting quality records

By the end of this chapter, you will have a solid understanding of the difference between mixing and mastering, the importance of creative and technical approaches, and what I use and how I use it, as well as a comprehensive grasp of FL Studio's powerful tools for achieving professional mixes and masters. This knowledge will equip you with the necessary skills to take your productions to the next level and ensure that your mixes sound polished, balanced, and are ready for the commercial music market.

Now, let's dive into why we use mixing and mastering, and how we can leverage them to create professional-sounding records!

Why we mix, and why we master

Mixing and mastering are two crucial steps in the process of creating a polished and professional-sounding record. Understanding the differences between mixing and mastering is crucial because both are essential parts of music production. The process of balancing and combining the various components of a song into a cohesive mix is called mixing, while mastering is the last step that makes sure the mix is ready for all playback devices. It takes talent, experience, and a great ear to do them well, but good mixing and mastering can make the difference between a passable track and an outstanding one. However, anyone can learn *how* to mix and master their music to a professional standard if they have the right tools and knowledge.

To help you achieve the best results, we will examine the various methods and tools available in FL Studio and the frameworks I developed over the course of my career, which will give you the foundational know-how to leverage your productions to get on the Billboard charts.

Mixing from a technical standpoint versus a creative standpoint

FL Studio is my favorite DAW because of its easily accessible and learnable software UI. If you work with it for a long enough time, it becomes second nature, or an extension of your creative mind when making records. I was never professionally trained on all of the specific frequency ranges, plugins, or rules of mixing like some of the greatest producers in the industry, but after using FL Studio for a while, I was able to get a grasp on a lot of these skills by trial and error. Later in my career, I was able to actually watch some of the masters in the industry work, and soaked up a lot of knowledge of *how* they approach mixing. I'm going to share those secrets with you in this section.

There are two purposes for mixing:

- Mixing for technical reasons
- Mixing for creative purposes

Mixing for technical reasons entails making sure that each component of a mix is well balanced and distinct and fits comfortably in the frequency spectrum. On the other hand, mixing for creativity entails using mixing as a tool for artistic expression, experimentation, and taking chances.

Although technical mixing abilities are necessary to produce a clear and polished sound, mixing for creativity enables a producer to push the envelope and produce singular sonic experiences that stand out from the competition. A mix that is too technical may sound sterile and uninspiring, while a mix that is too creative may lack clarity and cohesiveness. Finding the right balance between technical and creative mixing is essential.

The best mixes ultimately strike a balance between technical mastery and creative expression, producing a polished and dynamic sound that best showcases the unique sound of the creator. A mix can be improved by mixing for both technical and creative reasons, which can ultimately mean the difference between a forgettable track and a number-one hit.

Even if you don't know anything about mixing from a technical standpoint, FL Studio can still be used to get a commercially viable and professional mix done for your records. Also, despite the availability of advanced features and options, a great mix can be made with only a few simple tricks and a little imagination. FL Studio's user-friendly interface and straightforward workflow make it simple to experiment with various effects and processing options. You can quickly add, remove, and rearrange elements in your mix using its drag-and-drop functionality, allowing you to approach mixing from a creative rather than a technical perspective. You can use FL Studio to make mixes and masters that are both technically sound and creatively inspiring by concentrating on the overall feel and emotion of the music.

Creative mixing

Creative mixing is my world. Truthfully, when I'm working with established artists, or even strong indie artists, I know that our record will be passed onto a professional engineer to finish or do a pass of a mix on the record before it's released. So, it's my job to give that engineer a mix that is as close to perfect as it can be for the sake of my own sonic signature. Modern music producers tend to focus more on the creative aspects of music production, such as writing and producing music, rather than on the technical details of mixing and mastering. While the mixing engineer uses their technical skills to achieve the desired sound, the producer offers feedback and guidance on the mix's creative direction and sound. The producer and mixing engineer ultimately collaborate to realize the artist's vision in the finished mix.

This is crucial because if you don't add a baseline mix to your tracks before submitting them to a third-party engineer, you run the risk of that person completely altering the feel of the record with a purely technical approach. The majority of us producers, however, want our kicks to hit as hard as they do when we bounce them from FL Studio, our snares to pop, and our baselines to fit perfectly, even though these aspects may be overlooked by others. This is one reason, among others, why it's important for producers to develop their mixing skills.

In *Chapter 3*, I discussed *how* to make a kick stand out in a mix. This is a form of creative mixing versus technical mixing because it breaks the rules of technical mixing, but it works from a sonic standpoint. This is exactly what I mean when I say *creative mixing*; we are in fact developing the basic mixing framework that an engineer will work from to blend into a technical radio-ready record when we create our signature sound, whether it comes from our drum kits, our layered synths and keys, or the type of transitional effects we use to carry and build tension in our arrangements.

Now, let's do a deep dive into some technical mixing theory you can start using in FL Studio today!

Technical mixing

To produce music with a polished and professional sound, exploring technical mixing abilities is a necessary first step. In order to produce a consistent and dynamic sound, mixing requires a variety of technical skills and techniques in addition to balancing the levels of the various tracks in a mix. Anyone can learn to master the technical aspects of mixing and produce a mix that sounds great on any playback system with the right information and equipment. In the sections that follow, we'll look at a few of the technical abilities and methods used by pro mixing engineers to produce a great-sounding mix in FL Studio.

In the trajectory of my career, a strategic choice I have often made is to entrust engineers with the final stages of mixing for my tracks. After meticulously tending to the creative intricacies of the mix, I've come to appreciate that the essence of harnessing FL Studio's plugins lies in achieving a harmonious equilibrium in your track. This equilibrium serves as a crucial foundation, ensuring that when the time arrives for a composition to find its place alongside a talented artist, their dedicated engineer can seamlessly refine levels and polish imperfections and prepare the opus for widespread radio play. As we delve into this section, our focus will sharpen on each of the plugins that facilitate the meticulous preparation of your composition for the expert touch of an engineer. We will embark on a journey into the realm of terminology, unraveling the lexicon of audio engineering and unveiling the pivotal plugins that will empower you to convey with precision the areas that necessitate refinement. Furthermore, we will venture into the art of playful experimentation, arming you with the skills to artfully manipulate these plugins to attain a preliminary mastery over your sound.

Let it be known, however, that the art of mixing engineering exists as an entity distinct from the creative act of music production. Not every producer is innately endowed with mastery over the intricacies of mixing, just as not every mixer possesses the innate flair for original music creation. While there may exist exceptional individuals who defy these trends, it remains prudent for producers to channel their energies toward honing their creative mixing prowess. When you are starting in your career, you will need to learn how to get the basics down to get a track ready for pitching (more on this in *Chapter 8*). This provides producers with the opportunity to collaborate with, or seek out, a seasoned engineer whose expertise can harmonize and elevate their sonic journey. In this symphony of sound, the collaborative synergy between producer and engineer harmoniously coalesces to create audio magic that resonates far and wide.

These methods—which range from EQ and compression to stereo widening and automation—are crucial for producing a polished and expert mix. The advice and methods in this section will enable you to advance your mixes and speak the language of engineers, regardless of your level of experience.

Let's go over a detailed list of the types of technical mixing tools and terms you should get familiar with and what they correspond to in FL Studio. Then, we will discuss *how* to leverage the tools for creating tracks in FL Studio's powerful software.

Here is the list of the types of technical mixing tools and terms in FL Studio:

- **EQ**: Adjusts the frequency balance of individual tracks to create a cohesive mix. In FL Studio, I recommend **Fruity Parametric EQ 2**:

Figure 7.1: Fruity Parametric EQ 2

- **Compression**: Controls the dynamic range of individual tracks to create a more consistent overall sound. In FL Studio, I recommend **Fruity Compressor**:

Figure 7.2: Fruity Compressor

- **Reverb**: Adds a sense of space and depth to the mix by simulating natural acoustic environments. In FL Studio, I recommend **Fruity Reeverb 2**:

Figure 7.3: Fruity Reeverb 2

- **Delay**: Creates rhythmic interest and depth by adding echoes and repeats to individual tracks. In FL Studio, I recommend **Fruity Delay 3**:

Figure 7.4: Fruity Delay 3

- **Panning**: Positions individual tracks in the stereo field to create a balanced and immersive mix. In FL Studio, I recommend **Fruity Stereo Shaper**:

Figure 7.5: Fruity Stereo Shaper

- **Level balancing**: Adjusts the volume of individual tracks to create a balanced and cohesive mix. In FL Studio, I recommend **Fruity Balance**:

Figure 7.6: Fruity Balance

- **Saturation**: Adds harmonic distortion to individual tracks to create warmth and character. In FL Studio, I recommend **Fruity soft clipper**:

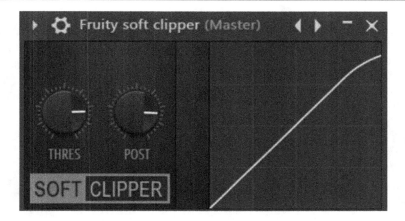

Figure 7.7: Fruity soft clipper

- **Parallel processing**: Creates parallel signal chains to process individual tracks, allowing for greater control and flexibility in the mix. In FL Studio, I recommend **Fruity send**:

Figure 7.8: Fruity send

- **High-pass and low-pass filtering**: Removes unwanted frequencies from individual tracks to create a cleaner and more focused mix. **Fruity Parametric EQ 2** (see *Figure 7.1*) gives you the ability to set up a high-pass filter. You can adjust the **Frequency** knob to determine the cutoff point below which frequencies will be accentuated. Similarly, for a low-pass filter, you can adjust the **Frequency** knob to set the cutoff point above which frequencies will be accentuated.

For more advanced high-pass/low-pass filtering, I prefer to use **Fruity Love Philter**. You can tweak things such as low-pass, high-pass, band-pass, and notch filters to control how your audio sounds. It's like having your own DJ mixer. **Fruity Love Philter** has this awesome feature called "advanced modulation capabilities." Basically, it means you can add some serious flair to your music by making the filters move and groove. You can set up automation and modulation options such as **Low-Frequency Oscillator** (**LFO**) modulation, envelope following, and step sequencing. It's like giving your music a life of its own with evolving and rhythmic filter patterns:

Figure 7.9: Fruity Love Philter

- **Stereo widening**: Uses stereo imaging tools to create a wider and more spacious mix. In FL Studio, I recommend **Fruity Stereo Enhancer**:

Figure 7.10: Fruity Stereo Enhancer

- **De-essing**: De-essing is a technique used to reduce sibilance and harshness in vocal recordings. In this process, selective frequency compression is applied to target specific problem areas. The **Maximus** plugin in FL Studio is an excellent tool for accomplishing this because it allows you to precisely pinpoint and control the range of sibilant frequencies.

With the **Maximus** plugin, you can set up a specialized compression band that specifically targets the sibilant frequencies in the vocal performance. This enables you to tame those annoying "s" and "sh" sounds without affecting the rest of the vocal's natural tone. By adjusting the compression threshold and ratio settings, you can dial in the perfect amount of reduction, ensuring that the vocals remain clear and smooth:

Figure 7.11: Maximus

- **Sidechain compression**: Controls the level of one track based on the level of another track to create a more cohesive mix. In FL Studio, I recommend **Fruity peak controller**:

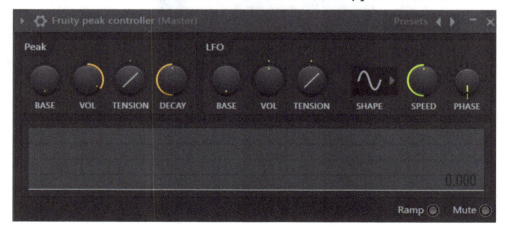

Figure 7.12: Fruity peak controller

- **Multiband compression:** Applies different levels of compression to different frequency bands to create a more balanced and controlled mix. In FL Studio, I recommend **Fruity Multiband Compressor**:

Figure 7.13: Fruity Multiband Compressor

- **Mid-side processing**: Separates the center (mono) and side (stereo) information of a mix to allow for more precise control over the stereo image. In FL Studio, I recommend **Fruity Stereo Shaper** (see *Figure 7.5*).

- **Frequency ducking**: Lowers the level of certain frequency bands in one track to create space for other elements in the mix. In FL Studio, I recommend **Fruity peak controller** (see *Figure 7.12*).

- **Exciters**: Adds harmonic distortion and high-frequency detail to individual tracks to create a more exciting and dynamic mix. In FL Studio, I recommend **Fruity WaveShaper**:

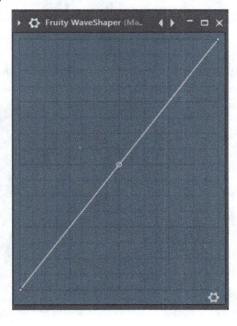

Figure 7.14: Fruity WaveShaper

- **Stem mastering**: Creates submixes (stems) of individual groups of tracks to allow for more targeted processing during mastering. In FL Studio, I recommend **Fruity Parametric EQ 2** (see *Figure 7.1*) and **Maximus** (see *Figure 7.11*).

- **Phase alignment**: Adjusts the phase relationships between individual tracks to prevent phase cancellation and create a more focused mix. In FL Studio, I recommend **Fruity Stereo Shaper** (see *Figure 7.5*).

- **Tape saturation**: Applies tape emulation plugins to individual tracks or the entire mix to add warmth and character. In FL Studio, I recommend **Fruity WaveShaper** (see *Figure 7.14*) and **Fruity soft clipper** (see *Figure 7.7*).

- **Parallel distortion**: Creates parallel signal chains to add distortion to individual tracks, allowing for more control and flexibility in the mix. In FL Studio, we use **Fruity send** (see *Figure 7.8*) and **Fruity WaveShaper** (see *Figure 7.14*).

- **Volume shaping**: Applies dynamic processing, such as volume fades and automation, to create more dynamic and interesting arrangements. In FL Studio, I recommend **Fruity X-Y controller**:

Figure 7.15: Fruity X-Y controller

- **Transient shaping**: Adjusts the attack and decay characteristics of individual tracks to create more punch and impact. In FL Studio, I recommend **Maximus** (see *Figure 7.11*) and **Fruity WaveShaper** (see *Figure 7.14*).

- **M/S EQ**: Applies EQ to the mid and side information of a mix separately to create more precise control over the stereo image. In FL Studio, I recommend **Fruity Parametric EQ 2** (see *Figure 7.1*) and **Fruity Stereo Shaper** (see *Figure 7.5*).

- **Stereo width control**: Adjusts the stereo width of individual tracks to create a more immersive and dynamic mix. In FL Studio, I recommend **Fruity Stereo Shaper** (see *Figure 7.5*).

- **Dynamic EQ**: Applies EQ based on the level of the signal to create more dynamic and responsive tonal control. In FL Studio, I recommend **Fruity Parametric EQ 2** (see *Figure 7.1*).

- **Distortion blending**: Blends multiple types of distortion on individual tracks to create a unique and textured sound. In FL Studio, I recommend **Fruity WaveShaper** (see *Figure 7.14*) and **Fruity soft clipper** (see *Figure 7.7*).

Now that we have covered a wide range of plugins available in FL Studio for various aspects of mixing and mastering, we will now move on to the next section, which focuses on chart-topping mixing techniques. In this section, we will dive into advanced mixing strategies and insights aimed at achieving professional-level mixes that stand out and compete in the charts. Let's go!

Plugins for chart-topping mixing techniques

When it comes to leveraging plugin tools in FL Studio, from my personal experience, the following plugins are ones that you are likely to use on every track:

- EQ: **Fruity Parametric EQ 2**
- Compression: **Fruity Compressor**
- Reverb: **Fruity Reeverb 2**
- Delay: **Fruity Delay 3**
- Panning: **Fruity Stereo Shaper**

These are at the heart of every track I've ever composed in FL Studio. While the other plugins are great tools, they tend to be what real engineers use when mixing the finished product. I want to give you, as a producer, the framework for the plugins you will use in almost every track you produce, while having a base foundation knowledge of the other plugins and what they do in FL Studio.

It is important to note that in the music business, the interaction between a producer and a mixing engineer is essential to the process of making music. The producer is in charge of overseeing the project's creative direction, collaborating with the artist to create the music's sound and vision, and managing the entire production process. On the other hand, the mixing engineer is in charge of taking the various tracks and combining them into a polished and seamless mix. Although the roles of the producer and mixing engineer are distinct, they work together, and communication is crucial to the project's success.

Let's dive into each of these plugins and explore how we can utilize them to leverage chart-topping mixing techniques, both creatively and technically within a structured framework.

Parametric EQ 2

Utilizing EQ Parametric 2 to produce distinctive tonal effects on specific tracks is one instance of creative mixing. For instance, a producer may decide to creatively boost or cut specific frequencies to give a sound more personality and character. This might entail altering the high-end frequencies of a vocal to add warmth and depth or boosting the low-end frequencies of a kick drum to produce a more potent and punchy sound. In *Chapter 3*, I gave you the exact framework for how we can leverage this plugin to maximize our kick bottoms and thicken our snare sounds.

Let's dive deeper into what else we can use this plugin for.

Using Parametric EQ 2 for automation theory

The use of automation to produce dynamic tonal changes throughout a track is another illustration of *how* creatively EQ can be used. To create tension and a sense of anticipation, a producer might use EQ automation to gradually increase the high frequencies of a lead instrument during a buildup section or cut the low frequencies of a track during a breakdown. In *Chapter 6*, we discussed how you can use FL Studio automation from the **Gross Beat** plugin (which follows the same framework for each plugin within FL Studio).

Let's discuss some examples of how to use Parametric EQ 2 for automation theory:

- Buildup and anticipation:

  - Gradually boost the presence of a vocal track to make it stand out more as the intensity of the song increases

  - Increase the high frequencies gradually on a lead instrument during a buildup section to create a sense of brightness and energy

  - Automate a narrow frequency band to sweep across the stereo field, creating a sense of movement and excitement

- Breakdown and impact:

  - Cut the low frequencies of a track abruptly during a breakdown to create a dramatic effect and emphasize certain elements

  - Use a notch filter to create a "telephone" or lo-fi effect during a breakdown, giving the track a nostalgic or vintage vibe

  - Automate a resonant peak to sweep through the frequency spectrum, adding tension and impact to specific sections of the track

- Transitions and effects:

  - Create a filter sweep effect by automating a low-pass or high-pass filter to open up or close off certain frequency ranges

  - Automate the Q (bandwidth) parameter to create a dynamic and evolving resonance effect

  - Use EQ automation to create rhythmic effects by cutting or boosting specific frequencies in sync with the beat

- Sound design and texture:

  - Automate a parametric band to create a "wah-wah" effect on a guitar or synth line. Modulate the frequency of a band to simulate the movement of a source in a virtual space, adding depth and realism to the mix.

  - Automate the gain or frequency of a band to emphasize or de-emphasize certain harmonics in a sound, altering its character.

These are just a few examples, and the possibilities are virtually endless. The key is to experiment and let your creativity guide you in using Parametric EQ 2's automation capabilities to shape and transform your sounds in unique and interesting ways.

The ability to use EQ in a way that increases the overall emotional impact of the music is necessary for creative EQ use. This requires a thorough understanding of the sonic characteristics of each component in a mix. When used skillfully, creative EQ can elevate a mix from average to extraordinary and make the difference between a passable track and one that stands out.

Using Parametric EQ 2 from a technical standpoint

Let's now explore *how* we can use this plugin from a technical standpoint:

- **Carving out space:** By using **Fruity Parametric EQ 2**, a producer can carve out space by removing frequencies that conflict or interfere with other tracks. For instance, the producer may use **Fruity Parametric EQ 2** to reduce some of the low frequencies from the bass guitar in order to give the kick drum more space if it is competing with the bass guitar for the same frequencies.

- **Increasing the character of individual sounds:** A producer may use **Fruity Parametric EQ 2** to boost or cut specific frequencies in order to increase the personality of specific sounds. For instance, the producer might use **Fruity Parametric EQ 2** to boost the high frequencies of a vocal track if it sounds flat or muffled in order to make it sound brighter and more present.

- **Balancing the overall mix:** A producer may use **Fruity Parametric EQ 2** to adjust the mix's overall frequency balance. For instance, the producer may use **Fruity Parametric EQ 2** to boost some high frequencies and cut some low frequencies if the mix sounds too boomy or lacks clarity. This will help the mix sound more balanced.

Having established a general understanding of the possibilities offered by FL Studio's powerful EQ 2 plugin and how it can be utilized to elevate your creative and technical mixing, let's now turn our attention to another essential tool: **Fruity Compressor**.

Fruity Compressor

The **Fruity Compressor** plugin holds immense potential to shape the dynamics of your audio and achieve a polished and professional sound. **Fruity Compressor** allows you to exert precise control over the dynamic range of your tracks, enabling you to even out inconsistencies in volume and add punch and clarity to your mix. With its extensive range of parameters and versatile functionality, this compressor becomes an indispensable asset in your audio processing toolkit.

Utilizing **Fruity Compressor** to achieve a more dynamic and punchy sound involves duplicating a track, heavily compressing the duplicate, and blending the compressed signal with the original signal. This method is frequently used to give bass, vocals, and drums more impact and presence.

Instead of just using **Fruity Compressor** to control dynamics, creative users can also use it to shape sounds. As an illustration, a producer may decide to use the sidechain input to instruct the compressor to pump in time with the beat of the track, resulting in a pumping effect that improves the groove and vigor of the music. **Fruity Compressor** is a versatile and powerful compressor plugin that allows you to control the dynamics of your audio signals. It helps you achieve a more balanced and controlled mix by reducing the dynamic range of individual tracks or the overall mix.

Using Fruity Compressor creatively

Here are some key points to consider:

- Dynamic control:

  - **Fruity Compressor** allows you to adjust the threshold, ratio, attack, release, and other parameters to control the dynamics of your audio signals

  - You can use it to tame peaks, reduce the dynamic range, and create a more consistent and polished sound

- Leveling and balancing:

  - Use **Fruity Compressor** to level out the volume of different elements in your mix.

  - For example, you can compress a dynamic vocal track to ensure it stays at a consistent level throughout the performance.

  - Balance the levels of individual tracks in a mix by applying compression to control the dynamic range of each element. This helps create a more cohesive and professional-sounding mix.

- Enhancing sustain and presence:

  - With **Fruity Compressor**, you can increase the sustain of instruments such as guitars or pianos

  - By using a longer release time, you allow the compressor to keep the audio signal level for a longer duration, enhancing the sustain and presence of the instrument

  - By applying gentle compression, you can bring forward subtle details and nuances in the audio signal, making it more prominent in the mix

- Creative shaping and sound design:

  - **Fruity Compressor** can be used as a creative tool to shape the sound of your tracks

  - By pushing the compressor's settings beyond traditional dynamic control, you can achieve unique and artistic effects

  - Experiment with extreme compression settings, such as high ratios and fast attack times, to create exaggerated pumping or breathing effects

  - This technique is often used in genres such as EDM to add energy and movement to the mix

- Parallel compression:

  - **Fruity Compressor** can be used for parallel compression, also known as New York compression or parallel drum compression.

  - This technique involves blending a heavily compressed version of a track with the original uncompressed signal to retain the dynamics while adding weight and sustain. Set up a parallel compression chain by duplicating the track, applying heavy compression to the duplicate, and then mixing it in with the original track to achieve a desirable balance of dynamics and impact.

- Sidechain compression:

  - **Fruity Compressor** offers sidechain functionality, allowing you to use one audio source to control the compression of another.

  - This technique is commonly used in electronic music to create rhythmic pumping effects or to make the kick drum stand out in a mix.

  - Route a trigger signal (such as a kick drum) to the sidechain input of **Fruity Compressor** and set the appropriate settings to control the compression of another track or instrument. This results in the desired rhythmic pumping effect.

By leveraging the features and capabilities of **Fruity Compressor** in FL Studio, you can achieve greater control over the dynamics, balance, and overall sound of your mix. Experiment with different settings and techniques to explore the wide range of possibilities and unleash your creativity in both technical and artistic mixing.

Using Fruity Compressor from a technical standpoint

Let's now explore *how* we can use this plugin from a technical standpoint:

- **Controlling dynamic range**: One common use of compression is to even out the levels of a track by reducing the dynamic range

- **Sidechain compression**: Another popular use of compression is sidechain compression, which allows one track to duck or be reduced in level when another track is playing

Having explored the capabilities of FL Studio's powerful **Fruity Compressor** plugin, let us now shift our focus to another exceptional tool in the FL Studio arsenal: **Fruity Reeverb 2**.

Reverb – Fruity Reeverb 2

Fruity Reeverb 2 is a versatile plugin, which offers a myriad of possibilities to transform your audio with immersive and realistic reverberation effects. **Fruity Reeverb 2** opens up a world of sonic possibilities, allowing you to infuse your tracks with depth, space, and a sense of realism. With its array of adjustable parameters and controls, you have the freedom to sculpt the ambiance and tonal characteristics of your audio recordings.

Fruity Reeverb 2 can be used ingeniously to give a mix a sense of depth and space. A producer might decide to use the plugin on a lead vocal, for example, to give the sound a lush, atmospheric quality and the appearance that the singer is singing in a big, open space. The producer can control the size and shape of the virtual room and create an atmosphere that adds emotion and depth to the music by adjusting the decay time, pre-delay, and other reverberation parameter settings. **Fruity Reeverb 2** can also be creatively used as a sound design tool. A producer might also decide to use the plugin, for example, in order to produce ethereal, otherworldly sounds that can be used as pads or textures in a mix. The producer can produce distinctive and evocative sounds that add interest and excitement to the music by experimenting with different settings and automation techniques. **Fruity Reeverb 2** is an effective tool for adding atmosphere and depth to a mix, as well as for producing distinctive and interesting sounds that can make a track stand out. A producer can use this plugin to elevate a mix by carefully experimenting with it and being open to new ideas.

Here are some key points to consider for using **Fruity Reeverb 2** creatively:

- Ambiance and space:

  - **Fruity Reeverb 2** provides various parameters to control the size and character of the virtual space

  - You can adjust parameters such as room size, decay time, early reflections, and diffusion to create a sense of ambiance and depth in your audio

  - Increase the room size and decay time for a more spacious and immersive reverb effect, ideal for creating a sense of realism or for enhancing the atmosphere in your mix

- Tone and color:

  - The plugin offers controls to shape the tonal characteristics of the reverb. You can adjust parameters such as high-frequency damping, low-frequency damping, and high-frequency roll-off to tailor the reverb's tone and color.

  - Use high-frequency damping to reduce the brightness of the reverb, simulating the absorption of high frequencies in a real-world environment. Low-frequency damping can help control the buildup of low-frequency energy in the reverb, avoiding muddiness or excessive boominess.

- Pre-delay and early reflections:

  - **Fruity Reeverb 2** allows you to set a pre-delay time, which introduces a delay before the reverb tail begins. This parameter is useful for separating the dry signal from the initial reflections, giving a clearer sense of space and distance.

  - Adjust the early reflections to control the initial reflections of the reverb. Increasing the early reflection level can add realism and simulate the reflections bouncing off the walls in a specific space.

- Reverb types and algorithms:

  - **Fruity Reeverb 2** offers different reverb algorithms, including **Room, Hall**, and **Plate**. Each algorithm simulates a specific type of acoustic environment and provides its own unique characteristics.

  - Experiment with different reverb types to find the one that suits your audio material. For example, a **Room** reverb might be suitable for adding subtle ambiance to a vocal track, while a **Hall** reverb could be ideal for creating a larger-than-life sound on orchestral instruments.

- Modulation and automation:

  - **Fruity Reeverb 2** allows you to modulate certain parameters using internal modulation sources, such as LFOs or external automation. This adds movement and variation to the reverb effect over time.

  - Automate parameters such as room size, decay time, or modulation depth to create evolving and dynamic reverb effects. This can be particularly useful for creating transitions or adding interest to specific sections of your track.

- Wet/dry mix and send/return:

  - **Fruity Reeverb 2** offers control over the wet/dry mix, allowing you to blend the processed reverb signal with the dry (unprocessed) signal. Adjusting this mix parameter lets you find the perfect balance between the original sound and the reverb effect.

- You can also use **Fruity Reeverb 2** as a send/return effect by routing multiple tracks or instruments to a single instance of the plugin. This allows you to apply the same reverb settings to multiple elements in your mix, creating a cohesive and unified sonic space.

Fruity Reeverb 2 in FL Studio provides a wide range of controls and parameters to shape the reverberation characteristics in your audio productions. Whether you're looking to add a subtle sense of space or create lush, ethereal environments, this plugin can elevate the depth and realism of your mix. Experiment with its settings, explore different algorithms, and don't hesitate to automate parameters to unlock the full potential of **Fruity Reeverb 2**.

Now, let's talk about leveraging FL Studio's delay plugin—**Fruity Delay 3**.

Delay – Fruity Delay 3

Fruity Delay 3 can be used ingeniously to add rhythmic movement and patterns to a mix. For example, a producer might decide to apply the plugin to a percussion track to produce an echo effect that highlights the song's rhythm. The producer can design intricate patterns that add interest and excitement to the music by adjusting the feedback, delay time, and other delay parameters.

Fruity Delay 3 can also be used to create special effects. A producer might decide to apply the plugin to a lead vocal, for example, to produce a stutter effect in which the sound is repeated and chopped up in time with the music. This can energize and tense up the vocal performance and make it easier for the singer's words to be heard above the background noise.

Fruity Delay 3 is a flexible tool that can be used to add movement and interest to a mix as well as to produce unusual and unexpected sounds that can make a track stand out. A producer can use this plugin to increase the impact and emotional resonance of a track with careful experimentation and a willingness to think outside the box. Here are some key points to consider:

- Delay time and feedback:

  - **Fruity Delay 3** allows you to adjust the delay time, controlling the length of the delay effect. Shorter delay times create tighter and more immediate echoes, while longer delay times result in more pronounced and spacious echoes.

  - The feedback parameter controls the number of repetitions or echoes. Increasing the feedback value produces more repetitions, creating a dense and sustained delay effect.

- Delay types and modes:

  - **Fruity Delay 3** offers different delay types and modes, each with its own unique characteristics. These include mono, stereo, and ping-pong.

  - Experiment with different delay types to achieve the desired spatial effect. Ping-pong delay, for example, creates a bouncing effect between the left and right channels, while stereo delay adds width and movement to the sound.

- Filtering and EQ:

  - **Fruity Delay 3** provides filtering and EQ controls to shape the tonal characteristics of the delayed signal. You can apply low-pass, high-pass, or band-pass filters to control the frequency range of the echoes.

  - Use the **EQ** section to boost or cut specific frequencies in the delayed signal, allowing you to highlight certain elements or shape the overall tonality of the delay effect.

- Modulation and LFO:

  - **Fruity Delay 3** includes modulation options, such as LFO modulation. This allows you to modulate parameters such as delay time, feedback, or filter cutoff, adding movement and variation to the delay effect.

  - Apply modulation to introduce subtle pitch fluctuations, create tape-like wow and flutter effects, or achieve rhythmic variations in the delay pattern.

- Tempo sync and time division:

  - **Fruity Delay 3** offers tempo sync functionality, allowing you to synchronize the delay time to the project's tempo. This ensures that the delay effect stays in sync with the rhythm of your track.

  - Use the time division feature to set the delay time in musical subdivisions, such as quarter notes, eighth notes, or triplets. This makes it easy to create rhythmic delays that match the groove of your music.

- Creative applications:

  - **Fruity Delay 3** can be used for various creative applications. You can create spacious and atmospheric effects by combining longer delay times, feedback, and filtering. Experiment with rhythmic delay patterns to add movement and complexity to your tracks.

  - Try setting shorter delay times and syncing them with the tempo to create rhythmic echoes that sync up with the beat.

  - Use **Fruity Delay 3** as a creative tool by automating parameters such as delay time or feedback to introduce dynamic variations and build tension in your music.

- Creating rhythmic interest:

  Delay can also be used to create rhythmic interest in a mix, either by creating simple echoes or more complex patterns. You can use automation to create evolving delay effects that add interest and variation to the mix.

Fruity Delay 3 in FL Studio offers a wide range of controls and features to shape and manipulate delay effects. Whether you're looking for subtle echoes, rhythmic patterns, or atmospheric textures, this plugin can add depth and dimension to your audio productions. Explore its settings, experiment with different delay types and modulation options, and let your creativity run wild.

Now, let's explore how we can use FL Studio's stock plugin—**Fruity Stereo Shaper**—for volume panning.

Panning – Fruity Stereo Shaper

Fruity Stereo Shaper can be used cleverly to create stereo effects that give a mix depth and width. To add depth and space to the mix, a producer might, for example, use the plugin on a guitar or keyboard track. The producer can make an instrument's sound appear to move from left to right or back and forth by adjusting the stereo width and other plugin parameters, adding movement and interest to the mix.

Fruity Stereo Shaper can also be used to manipulate the stereo field to produce original and unexpected sounds. For example, a producer might decide to apply the plugin to a vocal track to produce an unusually stretched and warped effect that is distorted and otherworldly in nature. The producer can produce a variety of effects that give the vocal performance texture and character by experimenting with the plugin's various parameters. Here are some key points to consider:

- Stereo width control:

  - **Fruity Stereo Shaper** enables you to adjust the width or spread of the stereo image. Increasing the width parameter enhances the stereo presence and can make the sound appear wider, while decreasing it narrows the stereo field.

  - By adjusting the stereo width, you can create a more immersive listening experience and make certain elements stand out or blend in with the mix.

- Pan control:

  - The plugin allows you to adjust the panning of individual audio signals. This is useful for placing elements within the stereo field and creating a sense of movement.

  - Use the pan control to position instruments or sounds at specific points in the stereo spectrum. This can help create separation between different elements and add depth to the mix.

- Stereo separation:

  - **Fruity Stereo Shaper** enables you to control the separation between the left and right channels of the stereo signal.

  - Increasing the separation can make the stereo image wider and more pronounced, while decreasing it can create a more centered or mono-like effect.

  - Adjusting the separation parameter allows you to balance the stereo spread and ensure that elements in the mix are appropriately placed within the stereo field.

- Mid/side processing:

  - **Fruity Stereo Shaper** offers mid/side processing capabilities. This allows you to independently manipulate the center (mono) and side (stereo) components of the audio signal

  - By adjusting the mid and side parameters, you can fine-tune the balance between the center and side information, controlling the perceived width and focus of the stereo image

- Creative applications:

  - **Fruity Stereo Shaper** can be used in various creative ways. For example, you can widen the stereo image of a lead vocal to make it more present and immersive.

  - Experiment with automating the stereo width or panning parameters over time to create evolving spatial effects and enhance the dynamic movement of elements in the mix.

  - Use the stereo separation control to create interesting effects on percussive elements, such as widening the stereo spread of a snare drum or making hi-hats more focused and centered.

- Mono compatibility:

  - While stereo enhancement can be desirable, it's important to consider mono compatibility, especially for playback on systems or devices that may collapse the stereo image to mono.

  - Use **Fruity Stereo Shaper** judiciously to ensure that important elements and the overall balance of the mix remain intact when collapsed to mono. Regularly check your mix in mono to verify its mono compatibility.

  - **Fruity Stereo Shaper** in FL Studio provides a range of controls for shaping the stereo image and spatial perception of your audio. Whether you're looking to widen the sound, create separation, or fine-tune the panning, this plugin can enhance the depth and immersive quality of your mix.

  - Experiment with its parameters and use it creatively to achieve the desired stereo effects in your productions.

From a technical standpoint, we can use this plugin to add width and depth to the track. **Fruity Stereo Shaper** can be used to make a mix sound wider and deeper by adjusting the stereo image of individual tracks.

Overall, **Fruity Stereo Shaper** is an effective tool for modifying a mix's audio and adding stereo effects. A producer can use this plugin to increase a song's impact and emotional resonance, as well as its overall impact, with careful experimentation and a willingness to think creatively.

Now, let's dive into the exciting world of my favorite plugin stacks and discover the incredible possibilities they hold for your mixing journey on a purely technical level.

The power of plugin stacks for technical frameworks

Get ready to unlock a whole new level of creativity and finesse as you familiarize yourself with the dynamic plugins discussed in this section and become comfortable with the magic they can bring to your tracks. Whether you're aiming for a pristine and polished mix or an experimental and unique sound, these plugins will be your trusted companions, empowering you to shape and mold your music with precision and artistry. So, buckle up and get ready to harness the true potential of these tools as we embark on this exciting exploration of technical mixing frameworks.

Mixing drums using FL Studio stock plugins

As we described in *Chapter 3*, we can leverage certain mixing techniques to mix for a specific vibe versus mixing for technical outcomes. Let's walk through some mixing theory for drums and percussion instruments now. Creating a well-balanced and impactful drum mix is crucial for radio or commercial release, and as we discussed in the *Why we mix, and why we master* section, FL Studio provides a range of powerful stock plugins to help you achieve professional-sounding results.

Here are the plugins for mixing from a technical standpoint that I recommend:

1. When we are mixing for technical outcomes, we typically start by organizing our drum tracks. Separate each drum element onto its own track (e.g., kick, snare, hi-hats, toms, etc.).

2. Adjust the volume levels of each drum track to create a balanced starting point.

3. Utilize the mixer channel for each drum track.

4. Next, we will open the mixer in FL Studio. Assign each drum track to its own mixer channel by right-clicking on the track and selecting **Route to this track only**.

5. EQ each drum track: Insert the **Fruity Parametric EQ 2** plugin on each drum mixer channel. Use EQ to shape the sound of each drum element:

   - For the kick drum, emphasize the low frequencies by boosting the low end and possibly cutting some muddiness in the low-mid range.

   - For the snare drum, focus on the midrange to bring out the body and snap. Cut any unwanted frequencies that clash with other elements.

   - For hi-hats and cymbals, consider reducing any harsh or piercing frequencies in the high-end.

   - For toms and other drum elements, adjust the EQ according to their specific characteristics to enhance or accentuate frequencies as needed.

6. Apply compression: After we have generally EQed each drum sound, insert the **Fruity Compressor** plugin into each drum mixer channel. Use compression to control the dynamic range and add punch to the drums:

    I. Set an appropriate threshold to capture the desired range of the drum's transients.

    II. Adjust the attack and release settings to shape the drum's envelope and control sustain.

    III. Use a moderate ratio to maintain the natural dynamics while still providing some compression.

7. Add reverb and/or delay: Now, insert the **Fruity Reeverb 2** and **Fruity Delay 3** plugins on auxiliary (send/return) tracks. Route the desired amount of each drum track to these auxiliary tracks to apply effects globally:

    I. Use **Fruity Reeverb 2** to add space and depth to the drums.

    II. Adjust the reverb time, size, and pre-delay to achieve the desired effect.

    III. Use **Fruity Delay 3** to add echoes or rhythmic repetitions to specific drum elements.

    IV. Adjust the delay time, feedback, and other parameters to create the desired delay effect.

8. Balance the drum mix: Continuously adjust the volume levels and panning of each drum track to achieve a balanced and cohesive mix. Pay attention to the relationship between the kick and bass, snare and vocals, and other crucial elements.

9. Fine-tune and automate: Use automation to control parameters such as EQ, compression, and effects over time, creating variations and adding interest to the drum mix. Continuously listen to the mix and make adjustments as needed to enhance the overall sound.

Remember, mixing is a creative process, and these steps serve as general guidelines. Trust your ears and experiment with different settings and techniques to achieve the desired drum mix in FL Studio.

Mixing melodies and progressions using FL Studio stock plugins

When it comes to mixing chords and melodies, the type of instrument you use plays a crucial role in determining the approach to make it seamlessly "fit" into the overall mix. Each instrument has its unique characteristics and tonal qualities that require specific attention during the mixing process. Let's explore a few examples and discuss how to approach mixing them based on their characteristics.

Frameworks for approaching instrument mixing

These are frameworks for mixing I have developed over the years for approaching certain instruments and how we can fit them into productions:

- **Pianos**: Pianos are often rich in harmonic content and can occupy a significant portion of the frequency spectrum. To mix pianos effectively, start by ensuring a balanced EQ. Consider accentuating any excessively low frequencies that might clash with other bass elements in the mix. Pay attention to the midrange to maintain clarity and presence in the piano's tone. You may need to make subtle adjustments using EQ to bring out the desired warmth or brightness. Be mindful of dynamics. Use compression with a gentle touch to control any inconsistencies in the piano's volume levels, ensuring a more controlled and even sound throughout.

- **Synth pads**: Synth pads often contribute to the atmospheric and ambient elements in a mix, creating a lush backdrop for melodies and chords. To mix synth pads, focus on their spatial characteristics. Utilize stereo imaging techniques to create a wide and immersive soundstage. Apply EQ to shape the tonal balance of the pads. Depending on their sonic qualities, you may need to adjust the high-end frequencies to prevent them from becoming too harsh or piercing. Consider using subtle modulation effects, such as chorus or phaser, to add movement and depth to the pads, enhancing their ethereal qualities.

- **Bass instruments**: Bass instruments, such as bass guitars or synthesized basslines, provide the foundation and groove of a track. When mixing bass instruments, it's crucial to ensure clarity and definition while maintaining a solid low-end presence. Begin by focusing on the low frequencies. Use EQ to carve out any muddiness or unwanted resonances, allowing the bass to sit well in the mix. Pay attention to the relationship between the bass and kick drum. These two elements should work together in creating a tight and cohesive low-end foundation. Consider using compression to control the dynamics of the bass, ensuring a consistent level while maintaining the instrument's natural nuances.

- **Lead instruments**: Lead instruments, such as lead synths or solo instruments, often carry the melody and take the forefront in the mix. When mixing lead instruments, prioritize clarity and presence. Use EQ to highlight the frequency range that brings out the instrument's defining qualities. Depending on the instrument's tonal characteristics, you may need to adjust the high frequencies to add brilliance or smooth out any harshness. Consider using subtle effects such as reverb or delay to create space and depth around the lead instrument, allowing it to stand out without overpowering other elements.

Remember, each instrument requires individual attention, and there is no one-size-fits-all approach to mixing. Understanding the sonic characteristics of different instruments and adapting your mixing techniques accordingly will help you achieve a cohesive and well-balanced mix. Trust your ears and experiment with different settings and processing techniques to find the sweet spot for each instrument within the overall mix.

Frameworks for approaching melody mixing

Now, let's explore my frameworks for approaching mixing melody, chords, and composition theory. These concepts are frameworks I developed over the years, and are what I use to approach blending and fitting notes in productions:

1. **Organize your melody tracks**: Begin by separating each melody element onto its own track, such as leads, chords, arpeggios, or pads. This allows for individual control and manipulation. Adjust the volume levels of each melody track to establish a balanced starting point, ensuring none overpower or get lost in the mix.

2. **Utilize the mixer channel for each melody track**: Open the mixer in FL Studio, which serves as the control center for your tracks. Assign each melody track to its own mixer channel by right-clicking on the track and selecting **Route to this track only**. This facilitates independent processing and adjustment for each element.

3. **EQ each melody track**: Insert the **Fruity Parametric EQ 2** plugin on each melody mixer channel. Use the EQ to shape the sound of each melody element to your liking:

   - For lead melodies, consider emphasizing the midrange frequencies to make them stand out and cut through the mix

   - For chord progressions, adjust the EQ to create a balanced frequency spectrum, accentuating the desired tonal characteristics

   - For pads and atmospheric elements, experiment with EQ settings to create a sense of space and ensure they blend harmoniously with other melodies

4. **Apply compression**: Insert the **Fruity Compressor** plugin on each melody mixer channel. Leverage compression to control the dynamic range and achieve consistency in your melodies:

   I.   Set an appropriate threshold to capture the desired dynamic range without squashing the sound

   II.   Adjust the attack and release settings to shape the envelope of each melody element, determining how quickly or gradually the compression is applied

   III. Use a moderate ratio to maintain the natural dynamics of the melodies while providing some control over peaks

5. **Add modulation effects**: Utilize FL Studio's stock modulation effects, such as **Fruity Flanger**, **Fruity Phaser**, or **Fruity Chorus**, to add depth and movement to your melodies:

   I.   Insert the modulation effect plugin into each melody mixer channel or utilize auxiliary tracks for global effects.

   II.   Experiment with different settings to create unique and interesting textures that enhance the character of your melodies.

    III.   Use automation to control the modulation parameters over time, adding variations and enriching the musicality of your melodies.

6. **Balance the melody mix**: Continuously adjust the volume levels and panning of each melody track to achieve a well-balanced and cohesive mix. Pay close attention to the relationship between different melody elements, ensuring they complement each other without clashing or overpowering one another. Make subtle adjustments to panning to create a sense of width and space, allowing each melody to occupy its sonic territory.

7. **Utilize spatial effects**: Enhance your melodies with spatial effects using the **Fruity Reeverb 2** plugin on auxiliary tracks:

- Route a portion of each melody track to the reverb auxiliary track to introduce a sense of ambiance and depth.

- Adjust the reverb parameters, such as room size, decay time, and pre-delay, to match the desired character of your melodies, creating a cohesive sonic environment.

8. **Fine-tune and automate**: Utilize automation to control parameters such as EQ, compression, modulation, and spatial effects over time. Fine-tune the settings of each plugin throughout the track, making precise adjustments to achieve the desired sonic results. Continuously listen to the mix and make subtle or significant changes as needed to enhance the overall sound and bring out the best qualities of your melodies.

Remember, while these steps provide a solid foundation for mixing melodies and progressions using FL Studio stock plugins, it's important to trust your ears and allow your creativity to guide the process. Experiment with different settings, techniques, and combinations of plugins to achieve a mix that best represents your artistic vision. The key is to strike a balance between technical precision and artistic expression, resulting in a captivating and well-crafted musical composition. Enjoy the journey of exploring the vast possibilities that FL Studio and its stock plugins offer, and let your melodies and progressions shine with clarity and impact.

Summary

For modern music production to sound polished and professional, mastering the use of mixing plugins is essential to getting your productions to a point of marketability. A producer can sculpt and shape individual tracks to fit together seamlessly in the mix by using EQ, compression, reverb, delay, panning, and level balancing plugins wisely, resulting in a coherent and dynamic overall sound. Each plugin has its own distinct features and functions, but they can all be creatively combined to produce the desired sonic result. You can develop the technical abilities and intuition necessary to use these tools to their full potential through practice, experimentation, and attentive listening, producing chart-topping mixes that stand out in the current competitive music industry. But as I said in this chapter, being a master at mixing is a whole different set of skills from being a master at producing. It's possible to be great at both, but let engineers who spend their entire careers mastering and mixing shine in a collaborative process. You should learn the lingo and be fluent in what plugins do what. I will say, there have been times in my career when artists liked the beat I made so much that they didn't care about the mix and totally relied on an engineer to re-mix it for release. Learn about the plugins and focus on creative mixing, and if you lean toward the technical side, dive in—but focus on being the best producer. It's a marathon, not a race.

In this chapter, we explored a wide range of topics related to mixing and mastering within FL Studio. We started by understanding the difference between mixing and mastering and then delved into the concepts of creative mixing and technical mixing. We discussed the importance of achieving clarity, balance, and cohesion in a mix, and how FL Studio provides a toolbox of powerful plugins to help us achieve these goals.

Throughout the chapter, we covered various plugins and techniques for shaping the sound of our mixes. We learned about EQ, compression, reverb, delay, panning, level balancing, automation, saturation, parallel processing, high-pass and low-pass filtering, stereo widening, de-essing, sidechain compression, multiband compression, mid-side processing, frequency ducking, exciters, stem mastering, phase alignment, tape saturation, parallel distortion, volume shaping, transient shaping, M/S EQ, stereo width control, dynamic EQ, and distortion blending. Each of these plugins and techniques plays a crucial role in creating professional-sounding mixes and masters. By utilizing the power and versatility of FL Studio's tools, we can shape the frequency balance, control dynamics, add space and depth, position elements in the stereo field, achieve proper volume levels, automate parameters, add character, and enhance the overall impact of our tracks.

As we concluded this chapter, I shared insights into the world of mixing and mastering using FL Studio's plugins. We now have a comprehensive understanding of the tools and techniques available to us, allowing us to take our productions to new heights. In *Chapter 8*, we will uncover the secrets to getting your records placed and ensuring they land on the Billboard charts. We will explore the strategies and techniques I used, and those used by successful artists and producers, to maximize the chances of achieving chart-topping success. Prepare to unlock the secrets of chart-topping success and position yourself for recognition in the music industry.

Exercise

Objective: gain familiarity with essential plugin tools in FL Studio and learn how to effectively use them on every track.

To achieve this objective, follow these steps:

1. Open FL Studio and create a new project, then set up a basic drum loop or import a pre-existing drum loop into the project. Create five additional tracks for instruments or audio samples. Now, apply the following plugins to each track according to the given descriptions:

    I.   Track 1: EQ – **Fruity Parametric EQ 2**. Use the EQ to shape the tonal balance of the track. Experiment with boosting or cutting specific frequencies to enhance the sound.

II. Track 2: Compression – **Fruity Compressor**. Apply compression to control the dynamic range of the track. Adjust the threshold, ratio, attack, and release settings to achieve the desired level of compression.

III. Track 3: Reverb – **Fruity Reeverb 2**. Add reverb to create a sense of space and depth in the track. Experiment with different room sizes, decay times, and early reflections to achieve the desired reverb effect.

IV. Track 4: Delay – **Fruity Delay 3**. Use delay to create echoes or repetitions of the audio. Adjust the delay time, feedback, and other parameters to create rhythmic patterns or spacious effects.

V. Track 5: Panning – **Fruity Stereo Shaper**. Apply panning to distribute the sound between the left and right speakers. Experiment with different panning positions to create width and separation in the mix.

2. Once you have applied the plugins to each track, spend some time adjusting the settings and exploring the possibilities of each plugin. Experiment with different combinations of EQ, compression, reverb, delay, and panning to achieve a balanced and cohesive mix. Pay attention to the individual tracks and how the plugins affect their sound, as well as how they interact with each other in the overall mix. Take notes on your observations and any specific settings or techniques that you find particularly useful or interesting.

3. Once you are satisfied with your exploration and experimentation, save the project and review your notes for future reference.

Remember to trust your ears and use your creativity throughout the exercise.

Have fun exploring the essential plugin tools in FL Studio and discovering the unique soundscapes you can create using EQ, compression, reverb, delay, and panning!

8

How to Get Records Placed So They Land on Billboard Charts

Congratulations on reaching the final chapter of this book! Now, we can delve into my favorite aspect of the music industry: the business side. Those who know me are aware that since my early days of learning how to produce music in FL Studio, I have been equally passionate about the business side of the industry as I have been about becoming a successful composer. The fact is that in the music industry, you must be proficient in both music and business if you want to establish a career. Some producers opt to team up with a business-savvy partner, such as a lawyer or a friend who is passionate about business, but for me, I wanted to have a comprehensive understanding of the entire industry and then partner with businesspeople.

I have an interesting perspective on the business of music. My journey has been filled with high-level creative activity and high-level business execution. Not only have I spent my 10,000 hours in the studio crafting records that ultimately landed in the hands of some of the biggest artists, producers, and songwriters on the planet, but I've also placed, sold, licensed, acquired, published, signed, and negotiated a ton of deals and deal types in the industry. Those deals have ranged from your typical master buy-outs with labels and indie artists and licenses for blockbuster movie trailers, advertising campaigns, and TV networks, composer signings, artists deals, and high stakes catalog acquisitions.

In this chapter, we will cover the following topics:

- My high-level view of the music business
- Why your catalog is an asset
- Copyrights and your rights as a creator of intellectual property
- The types of placements, and avenues for monetizing your catalog
- How to get your records placed and start building your catalog
- The types of deals you can do in the music business

By the end of this chapter, you will have gained a comprehensive understanding of the music business from a high-level perspective. You will recognize the value of your music catalog as a valuable asset and comprehend the significance of copyrights and intellectual property rights in protecting your creations. Furthermore, you will be well versed in the various types of placements and avenues for monetizing your catalog, empowering you to make informed decisions about your music's potential revenue streams. Additionally, you will have acquired knowledge on how to navigate the process of getting your records placed and effectively building your catalog. Lastly, you will be familiar with the different types of deals that exist in the music industry, equipping you with the necessary insights to negotiate contracts and make informed business decisions. With this wealth of knowledge, you will be better prepared to navigate the music business landscape and maximize the potential of your musical endeavors.

Embrace your journey

My journey has taken me from the mixing board to the esteemed boardroom. As I embarked on my journey, the destination seemed hazy, yet my expedition has been adorned with extraordinary and mind-bending experiences, encompassing both exhilarating highs and challenging lows. The realm of hip hop possesses a distinct essence, a vibrant energy that sets it apart from other genres of music. Pursuing music, in particular, demands resilience and tenacity; it is a realm that does not cater to the weak or hesitant. The music business as a whole shares this trait. To thrive, you must be primed to seize the moment and act swiftly when opportunities unveil themselves. Remember the timeless saying, "You miss 100% of the opportunities you don't take." Each individual will embark on their own distinctive character arc, weaving their personal story and embarking on a unique journey. Embrace it wholeheartedly. Resist the temptation to harbor resentment or envy toward the paths of others. Your journey is unparalleled; it belongs to you alone. Embrace it, imprint your mark upon it, and relentlessly propel forward, undeterred by external comparisons.

I believe that it's crucial to fully commit yourself to this journey if you want to succeed. There's a significant difference between being a hobbyist and pursuing music production as a profession. While you can certainly use the technical knowledge in this book to share your tracks with friends and have fun, I wrote this book to help producers who are passionate about making music their career. Once you've defined your vision, focus on it, build on it, and take action on it everyday.

Read this chapter when you have that clear vision and are ready to take action. As we discussed in *Chapter 1*, discovering your chief aim, your ultimate purpose, and establishing a strong foundation for your vision are the fundamental building blocks that shape the character arc of your journey in the music business. It is within this arc that you define your aspirations, clarify your goals, and lay the groundwork for your path forward. By anchoring yourself in a clear vision, you create a solid framework upon which to build your career. It becomes the guiding light that illuminates your choices, actions, and decisions along the way. Embrace this character arc wholeheartedly, for it holds the key to unlocking your true potential in the dynamic world of the music industry.

Once you have crystalized your extraordinary vision, it's time to unleash your inner fire and ignite your talent. Sharpen your vision and refine your skills, for they are the essential elements of greatness. But remember, an unbeatable work ethic is the secret sauce that propels you toward success. Brace yourself to wholeheartedly commit to the exhilarating journey ahead. Always remember, *you never reach perfection- but are always perfecting its reach.*

As you strive to reach new heights and conquer one mountain, another mountain looms on the horizon. It is the evolution of your experiences in life that molds your character. Your moral compass, intentions, and intelligence are shaped and honed through the twists and turns of your character arc. Embrace the challenges that come your way, for they are the crucible in which your true character is forged. Embrace the growth, the transformation, and the constant pursuit of becoming the best version of yourself. Each journey is as unique as the beating heart within you. It is influenced by the place you call home, the relationships you nurture, the art of connecting with others, the genre of music you create, and the bold actions you take. Thanks to the boundless reach of the internet, what used to take years to gain momentum can now be accomplished in a fraction of the time.

Undoubtedly, the path you tread will have its fair share of twists and turns. It won't always be a thrilling roller-coaster ride, yet always remember that nurturing anything valuable brings both peaks and valleys. Be ready to embrace the journey wholeheartedly and never relinquish your grip. You will only regret the swings you chose not to take. If you stumble and fall, gather your strength, rise again, and persist relentlessly, regardless of the challenges that come your way.

These are words that should resonate within your soul, echoing through your being. Absorb them, imprint them in your mind, and revisit them often.

Now let's dive into how you can leverage your creative talent to shape your career, and look at it through a view of creating assets.

In the following sections, I will share with you what placements are and the types, how to start to position yourself to get placements, and the tactics I used to build my career with FL Studio as my foundation. We will then look into using digital mediums, and ultimately getting into the right rooms, which got my productions from FL Studio to the Billboard charts.

Understanding placements

A placement is the use of a specific song or piece of music in an audio or audio-visual medium, such as a sound recording featuring a recording artist, a film, a television show, or a commercial. Your objective as a music producer should be to produce music that is not only compelling artistically but also appealing commercially and able to be used in a variety of media projects. Producing a beat, co-writing a song, or adding instrumentation to a track are just a few examples of placements.

When a producer places their music with an artist, it can result in exposure, fees, royalties, and future opportunities for collaboration with the artist and their team. Placements increase market demand and build your catalog and name recognition in the industry. They are the lifeblood of the producer's repertoire, and what placements you strive for will determine the trajectory of your career. Now, as a heads up, not all placements are created equal. Some will generate a ton of exposure and generate income; others will generate little exposure, or nothing at all. Having a Billboard-charting placement is really about placing your productions with artists who have the best chance of charting through their support systems, such as labels, manager connections, and marketing plans. Every now and then, you will work and as an independent or unsigned (that to a major label) artist, and there is always potential for these records to create exposure or become hits, but it's much rarer just given how the music business operates from a marketing standpoint. The saying "hits aren't made, they are marketed" is true. It was kind of a letdown when I saw the inner workings of the business, but ultimately, the music business is a game, and you need to play it accordingly. So, instead of giving up, take risks, take chances, and work with anyone and everyone you can. You never know who is going to get the spotlight on them in the future.

There are a few key areas of focus when it relates to placements. As a producer, you should attempt to attack each of these verticals. Being optimistic in your approach and knocking on as many doors as you can is the name of the game.

A producer has a variety of music placement options available to them in the music business. From my view, I organize these verticals into these two key areas:

- Record placements
- Sync placements

Each of these verticals has several opportunity lines within them, and each should be explored based upon your goals as a producer, and your skill set.

For example, if your production style is geared toward making music for rappers, taking the record placement route may be more beneficial than focusing on trying to compose music for TV and film. However, there is cross-over potential as a pop producer, as some modern pop music is used in TV and film. However, a film and TV producer will rarely find cross-over in the opposite direction. These are the bread and butter of your sales and business development as a producer.

Record placements

Getting a producer's music to appear on a commercial recording that is released by an artist or a record label is known as a record placement. This can take many different forms, such as creating a beat, writing a song with someone else, or adding instruments to a track.

There are two types of artists you can work with: signed artists and unsigned artists. The only real difference between the two is that signed artists typically have a budget to pay upfront fees to a producer, and the label has financial skin in the game to ensure the project is successful, increasing your chances of landing a Billboard-charting song and securing some up-front money or an "advance." Unsigned artists can range from your friend down the street just starting out to an established artist who has figured out how to maximize their potential without the support of a label. The latter is rarer; most unsigned artists don't have budgets. It's a lot harder to break through on a Billboard chart with these types of artists, but it's not impossible.

The key thing here is knowing the artist—having a relationship with them and knowing what their work ethic and plan are.

Sync placements

Music that is licensed in TV shows, films, advertisements, video games, and other types of media are known as sync placements. For producers, this can be a very lucrative source of income because it frequently involves high-profile placements and ongoing royalties. These types of placements typically pay well and pay upfront fees in almost every scenario, unlike working with artists on record placements that may pay, depending on the project, the label, and status of the artist. The reason is the client typically has a budget for music and needs to ensure they purchase the exact rights to include the music used in their multimedia project.

There are several types of sync placements. Some examples are as follows:

- **Film score placements**: These placements entail the creation of music specifically for use in motion pictures, television programs, or video games. This branch of the music business can be extremely competitive and specialized.

- **Radio placements**: Not to be confused with record placements getting radio play. There is an entire industry of music for ads in the radio world.

- **Commercials**: This is when a producer licenses their music to be used in TV commercials, online commercials, or radio spots. For producers, this can be a very lucrative source of income because it frequently involves high-profile placements and ongoing royalties.

- **Video game placements**: Video game placements involve licensing a producer's music for use in video games, which can be a highly specialized and competitive area of the music industry.

- **Placement in music libraries**: Music libraries are collections of pre-approved music that can be licensed for use in media projects. Producers can also place their music in these libraries. Producers have the chance to eventually generate passive income from their music through the use of music libraries. Libraries or **production music libraries** (**PMLs**) can be a great resource to administer your catalog for sync placements.

Now that you have a firm grasp on the types of placements you can pursue with your catalog, let's look at how to pursue these, and discuss why building a catalog of income-producing songs is your overall goal.

A catalog is a sellable asset

Ultimately, you are creating a catalog of works that you will place with artists and multimedia that will eventually be an asset. Let's walk through this.

First, let's discuss what an **asset** is. An asset, broadly speaking, is anything that has value and that a person, business, or organization may own. Physical assets, such as real estate, machinery, and supplies, as well as financial assets, such as stocks, bonds, and bank accounts, are just a few examples of the many different types of assets that can exist. Assets can also include intellectual property, such as patents, trademarks, and copyrights. In the case of the music industry, songs and beats are assets.

At its core, a catalog is a collection of works that a producer has created over a period of time. This production catalog can be sold, licensed, or exploited in order to generate income from the rights to those works. However, the value of a catalog is not necessarily high until the producer is in demand or has placed a significant number of tracks in revenue-generating verticals.

To view your catalog as an asset, you must consider how it contributes to your financial standing. As a producer, the value of your catalog of work is a crucial factor in determining your financial capability, as it represents a broad collection of songs created and placed over the course of your career. In other words, the more tracks you produce and place, the larger your catalog grows, and the greater your potential for generating income and increasing your financial stability.

Now, let's dive into why building and curating a catalog of income-producing records should be your top priority on the business side. By understanding the significance and value of music catalogs as sellable assets, you can unlock the potential for long-term financial success in the music industry. In the following subsections, we'll explore the alternative asset class characteristics, valuation methods, and diverse rights and income streams associated with music catalogs. This knowledge will empower you to make informed decisions and maximize the value of your catalog. So, let's get started and discover the immense potential of building a music catalog for your business.

Catalogs are an alternative asset class

In 2021, over $5 billion was spent on the acquisition of catalogs. Currently, there is a growing interest from investors, including both traditional music companies and private equity firms, in the income generated from song royalties and catalog collections. These assets are increasingly being viewed as an alternative asset class, providing new investment opportunities for those seeking to diversify their portfolios. As the music industry continues to evolve and adapt to new technologies and business models, the value of music catalogs as a stable source of revenue is becoming more widely recognized. This has led to an increase in the number of buyers and sellers of music catalogs, as well as the development of new financial instruments that allow for easier investment in these assets.

The value of a music catalog is influenced by a variety of elements, including the collection of songs' popularity, how frequently they appear in the media, and the number of revenue streams they produce. Recent years have seen an increase in the sale of music catalogs, with major record labels and independent investors buying catalogs from songwriters, performers, and other rights holders. While buying a valuable music catalog can give buyers a reliable and lucrative source of income for years to come, selling your catalog can give songwriters and music producers a sizeable lump sum of cash.

How catalogs are valued

Once you have a collection of placed songs, your catalog is valued using the **net publisher's share** (NPS) for publishing rights or **net label share** (NLS) for master rights. In order to value a music catalog using the formula, it is typical to take the catalog's revenue over the previous three years as an average. This is due to the fact that the revenue produced by a music catalog can be erratic and subject to changes; therefore, taking an average over several years can help to smooth out those changes and provide a more precise estimate of the catalog's value. The NPS/NLS essentially represents the portion of the income stream that the publisher is entitled to, and it is the sum of money that would be left over after all expenses have been met. The average NPS/NLS is then multiplied by a certain number depending on the age of the songs in review, and the brand name of the songs with whom they are placed. At the time of writing this book, multiples have ranged from 7x to 25x the three years average NPS/NLS.

As a producer, you will be responsible for creating records and generating rights that you will either own or control. As you progress in your career, you will have the opportunity to leverage these assets in an exit sale for retirement or to create a liquidity event. This is your end goal, ultimately.

So, now that we know the importance of building a catalog with strong placements, let's talk about the different types of rights you as a producer have when you place records with artists and other forms of multimedia. I will caveat this by saying that in the music business, everything is negotiable, and it's up to you to make sure you capture all of your rights in the agreement you execute with the other party. I'm going to walk you through how to do this later in the chapter. For now, let's go over the basics.

Rights and income streams

Placements of your productions start with you creating the beat or track, and when you do this, you create what is known as a copyright. In most of the world, copyright law protects the creator and owner of these rights, and there are many different income streams that are generated from a single copyright that you as a producer can benefit from when you land a production as a placement.

When it comes to the types of rights associated with music catalogs, I want you to understand the power of a copyright and the multiple income streams it can generate. Let's explore the various rights and income streams that await you in the music industry.

Copyright sides

Now, let's discuss **copyright sides**. A music copyright has two separate elements:

- **Composition component**: The musical structure and lyrics of a song, including its melody, harmony, and lyrics, are referred to as the composition side. The song's songwriter or publisher is the owner of this portion of the copyright. It grants the owner the sole authority to publish, perform, and reproduce the composition. It also grants the owner the right to adapt the composition into other works.

- **Sound recording component**: The sound recording side refers to the specific recording of the song, including the engineering, production, and performance aspects. The record company or the musician who made the recording is the owner of this portion of the copyright. It grants the owner the sole authority to duplicate, transfer, and perform the sound recording, as well as the authority to produce works derived from the recording.

Even though the two sides of the copyright are connected, they are distinct from one another. Thus, the composition and sound recording copyrights for the same song may belong to different parties. For instance, the composition copyright may be owned by the songwriter or publisher, whereas the sound recording copyright may belong to the record company or the artist. Anyone working in the music business needs to understand how these two aspects of copyright differ because it has an impact on how royalties and licensing fees are distributed and gathered.

The publishing side

For a producer, publishing rights refer to the rights associated with the musical compositions or songs they create. These rights encompass ownership and control over the underlying musical elements, such as the melody, lyrics, and arrangement. As a producer, if you contribute to the creation of a musical composition, whether through writing the melody, adding instrumental elements, or collaborating on the arrangement, you are entitled to a share of the publishing rights. Publishing rights allow you to monetize your contributions to the musical composition, such as mechanical royalties, performance royalties, synchronization licensing, and print rights.

Let's walk through each of these income sources from publishing rights:

- **Mechanical royalties**: Mechanical royalties are paid to the songwriter and publisher for the reproduction and distribution of a song's composition. This includes physical copies of a song, such as CDs and vinyl records, as well as digital downloads and streaming. As a producer, you may be entitled to a share of the mechanical royalties for a song's composition, depending on your agreement with the songwriter(s) and/or publishing company.

- **Performance royalties**: Performance royalties are paid to the songwriter and publisher for the public performance of a song's composition. This includes when a song is played on the radio, in a concert, in a public venue, or on TV and film. As a producer, you may be entitled to a share of the performance royalties, depending on your agreement with the songwriter(s) and/or publishing company.

- **Sync licensing**: Sync licensing refers to the use of a song's composition in film, TV, commercials, and other media. As a producer, you may be entitled to a share of the sync licensing fees, depending on your agreement with the songwriter(s) and/or publishing company. This is a significant revenue source for music producers, especially if a song is used in a major film or TV show.

- **Publishing ownership**: If you own a share of the song's publishing rights, you are entitled to a share of the income generated from the use of the song's composition. This can include mechanical royalties, performance royalties, and sync licensing fees. Owning publishing rights can be a significant source of income for music producers, as the song's composition can continue to generate revenue for many years after its initial release.

The master side

Master rights, for a producer, pertain to the ownership and control over the actual sound recordings of a musical composition. As a producer, if you are responsible for the recording, mixing, and overall production of a track, you typically hold the master rights to that specific version of the song. Having master rights allows you to exercise control over how your recordings are used and monetized. It grants you the authority to license the sound recordings for various purposes, such as commercial releases, streaming services, film and television placements, and advertisements.

One of the primary income streams associated with master rights is licensing. By licensing your sound recordings, you can earn royalties when they are used in different media contexts. For instance, if your track is featured in a movie or TV show, you can negotiate a synchronization license and receive compensation for its usage. Additionally, master rights can also generate income through digital downloads, streaming platforms, physical sales (CDs and vinyl), and other forms of distribution.

It's worth noting that in some cases, the ownership of master rights may be shared between the producer and the artist or label. Understanding and protecting your master rights as a producer is essential for maximizing your potential earnings and maintaining creative control over your recorded works. By leveraging these rights, you can effectively monetize your music catalog and ensure that your recordings contribute to your long-term financial success.

Let's discuss these points further now:

- **Sales and streaming revenue**: The master recording is the actual recorded version of a song, which is owned by the artist or record label. As a producer, you may be entitled to a share of the revenue generated from the sales and streaming of a song's master recording, depending on your agreement with the artist or record label. This can include revenue from physical copies of a song, such as CDs and vinyl records, as well as digital downloads and streaming.

- **Performance royalties**: Similar to the publishing side, performance royalties are paid to the artist and record label for the public performance of a song's master recording. This includes when a song is played on the radio, in a concert, in a public venue, or on TV and film. As a producer, you may be entitled to a share of the performance royalties, depending on your agreement with the artist or record label.

- **Sync licensing**: Similar to the publishing side, you may be entitled to a share of the sync licensing fees for the use of a song's master recording in film, TV, commercials, and other media, depending on your agreement with the artist or record label.

- **Master ownership**: If you own a share of the song's master rights, you are entitled to a share of the income generated from the use of the song's master recording. This can include revenue from sales, streaming, performance royalties, and sync licensing fees. Owning a share of the master rights can be a significant source of income for music producers, especially if the song becomes a hit and is played frequently on radio and TV.

Time and dedication are important factors when building your catalog. In the beginning, your catalog won't be of much value to investors but will be of value to the marketplace of artists, labels, and multimedia companies to start securing placements. Let's explore the essential concept of taking action and how it empowers you to position yourself in the perfect time and place to seize opportunities and achieve your goals.

Taking action – put yourself in the right place at the right time

Placing records is tricky in the beginning because you haven't done it yet—there is a huge learning curve, from finding artists or companies to solicit, to negotiating and signing agreements you have never seen before, to registering and collecting royalties, to getting paid. If you don't have any connections to the artists, the media company, an artist's team, a label, or someone in the inner circle of the business, it is extremely hard to get people to pay attention. All of these stakeholders are constantly being solicited for beats, and they tend to only listen to beats that come through very specific channels. This doesn't mean you can't get a placement if you don't know anyone in the business; it just means it's a longer game that takes patience. Now, here is the thing—you hear this from all of the gurus—you need to be at the right place at the right time. That's true! But the reality is, you create the right time by always being at the right place. What do I mean? I mean, if you make a general effort to put yourself in front of opportunities, you will see opportunities. The reality is, the producer industry is extremely competitive and challenging.

Here are some high-level examples of how you can put yourself in the right place:

- **Networking**: Networking is a key component of being in the music industry. Ultimately, it's a small business at the very top, and everyone knows each other. Producers can attend industry events, connect with A&R representatives (Artists and Repertoire representatives, commonly referred to as A&R reps, are individuals who work within the music industry, specifically within record labels and music publishing companies. Their primary role is to discover and develop musical talent), and reach out to artists and their management teams to build relationships and create opportunities. It's crucial you do this at every chance you have. This can mean hopping on a plane and going to LA or Atlanta, or it can mean befriending an industry stakeholder on social media. The key to networking is you need to add value to the other party first. Most people just think because their music is good, people will give them a chance. But it just doesn't work like that in the real world. You need to make a strategic plan, study the person you want to network with, and figure out how you can exchange value. Life is about give and take—give more and you will eventually get back.

- **Online platforms**: Producers can leverage social media and music platforms, such as SoundCloud, BeatStars, and YouTube, to showcase their work and attract attention from artists and their teams. Building your beat-selling website and YouTube channel will pay off in the long term, and although it's not a quick vertical, if you build it correctly, you will be able to make a living off of your music while you are pursuing major placements and Billboard-charting spots that you can leverage for publishing and label deals later.

- **Collaborations**: Producers can collaborate with other producers, songwriters, and artists to expand their network and gain exposure to new audiences. Today, at the time of writing this book, this has become one of the best ways to secure placements. A lot of chart-topping songs have more than one producer or co-writer on the record, where one producer will supply the melody or chord progression, and others will add drum programming or additional musical effects to the record. Collaborations are a key focal point from the beginning of your career to the advanced stages. Some producers' strengths are drum programming and arrangement style, while some tend to be better at cranking out chord progressions and sound design. The best way you can maximize your efforts in collaboration is to offer value to the other side first, and see how you can help that established producer streamline their own placement process. Find producers that have different strengths than you.

- **Referrals**: Producers can get referrals from industry professionals, such as managers, agents, and record label executives, who may recommend them to artists and their teams. This will typically happen once you have proven yourself in the market; it's up to you in the beginning to build the momentum to get other people to share your name and work.

- **Contests and competitions**: Producers can participate in music contests and competitions, to gain exposure and potentially secure placements with major artists. In my experience, a lot of the participants will be other producers, and this is a great opportunity to network with other producers to create collaboration opportunities within the community.

- **Music licensing**: Producers can license their music for use in film, TV, and advertising, which can help them gain exposure and potentially lead to collaborations with major artists.

- **Producer camps and retreats**: Many producers attend producer camps and retreats, such as the infamous "writing camps" where songwriters, producers, and artists come together to create new music, meet new people, and potentially form relationships that lead to placements.

Now that we have some of the key action items down, and know that we need to maximize our time to start participating in these types of approaches, let's discuss how we can start getting the ball rolling.

Foundation steps – how to position yourself

Positioning yourself correctly is indeed a crucial factor in determining your success as a producer. While I can provide you with comprehensive steps and insights on how to engage with artists, labels, and companies, without a solid foundation, these efforts may yield limited results. It all begins with building a strong foundation for your character arc. Self-esteem plays a vital role in this process. Believing in yourself, having confidence in your abilities, and fostering a positive mindset are essential ingredients for success. Cultivate a genuine sense of belief that you can achieve your goals and turn your dreams into reality. Nurturing a strong self-belief system will empower you to overcome obstacles and persevere through challenges. Additionally, maintaining an unwavering work ethic is pivotal. Dedicate yourself wholeheartedly to your craft, investing the necessary time, energy, and effort to hone your skills and perfect your artistry. Hard work, discipline, and consistency are the cornerstones of your journey in the music business. By aligning these key components—self-esteem; belief in your capabilities; a sense of fulfillment in pursuing your goals, dreams, and desires; and an unbeatable work ethic—you will fortify your path and increase your chances of achieving success in the business of music.

So, let's talk about the tangibles and what you need to do after reading this book before diving into taking the action steps in the next section:

- **Know the music business**: Any music producer looking to place their beats must have an understanding of the music industry's complicated and competitive environment. Obviously, when you start, you don't even know what you don't know, but as long as you are working toward learning everything you can about the business, you will build on this foundation and position yourself correctly. Always keep up with current trends and business developments, and cultivate connections with artists, record labels, and other business leaders anytime you can.

- **Make the best music you can**: Obviously, this book was written to give you the frameworks on how to use FL Studio to start revamping your technical knowledge of making records so you can make the best beats possible, so read and re-read it! Creating beats that are marketable and appealing to artists and ultimately their fanbase is the first step in getting your beats used by artists. Put an emphasis on top-notch production, memorable melodies, and distinctive sounds that set them apart from the competition.

- **Develop relationships**: Never underestimate your ability to create relationships in this industry. It's everything when it comes to having a long-lasting career. I can't emphasize it enough—building relationships with artists is one of the most crucial steps in getting your beats heard and placed. Build relationships with artists, labels, music supervisors, A&Rs, publishers, lawyers, accountants, business managers... anyone who is in the business. Never underestimate the power of having a really good lawyer working with you.

- **Build a digital footprint**: In 2023, having a solid digital footprint will bring you opportunities you never would have had 20 years ago in this business. It's so crucial to use online platforms to promote your beats and find new collaborators in addition to developing personal connections with artists. Build your social media and showcase your beats on websites such as BeatStars, SoundCloud, and YouTube. Not only can you start to monetize your music but you're also building exposure points on each site—you just never know who is watching.

- **Create an identity and brand**: Building on your digital footprint, which is the essence and extension of your brand, in today's music industry, producers stand out just like artists—and some have even taken on the route to DJ and tour just like artists. There are a lot of ways to expand your career once you become a solid hitmaker. Beat tags, logos, graphic design, what you wear, how you speak—all of these things matter. Ultimately, you are selling yourself to the world as a creative, and having a strong brand and allure makes you attract more opportunities.

Now that we have covered the foundation principles of knowing your business, making the best music you can, taking the time to really build relationships, and creating your own brand and digital footprint, we can talk about how to leverage two different approaches to get placements and start building your career.

Two approaches to success

The year is 2006. Myspace is the hottest social media site in the world. I upload beats to my music page and cold DM anyone and everyone who is in the music business to see whether I can get their attention.

I spent hours, days, and months doing this—eventually, I got the attention of a few key people who would end up being catalysts in my career. I was invited to come link up in the studio in LA, so I saved up the few pennies I had at the time by working odd jobs here and there and took a plane from Canada to the US. I stayed at a hostel in West Hollywood called the "Banana Bungalow," an odd place that was filled with eccentrics and tourists. It was a party spot at night, with a dorm feel during the day—but it was $20 a night and I had a place to sleep while I set up meetings with my Myspace contacts.

One thing led to another, and I spent the next two weeks in different studios all around LA, which gave me the opportunity to play my music to some important people that over the next few years (and even today) are still in my life as mentors and conduits to the business. This was the start of my career—and I knew this was a formula I could follow to keep pushing forward.

At this time, getting placements online was kind of an unheard-of thing—you had to have money to rent studios in the hope of running into artists and A&Rs. But I came from a generation that really grew up using technology to leverage our position in the industry, so I did that with insane focus.

I say this to explain that as a music producer getting placements, there are two primary methods for obtaining clientele: networking offline and online, or the digital approach and what I call being in the room.

The in-person strategy is self-explanatory—hop on a plane and head to LA, Atlanta, New York, or any major music market where you can network in person with other creatives, labels, producers, and so on. However, in the beginning, no one knows you, and they probably won't let you crash on their couch or into their studio session, so you need to start networking online first (unless you live in a major market—then, you have a better chance of networking in person. But that wasn't the case for me; I had to start online first). Ultimately, you don't want to spend your entire producer career behind a laptop, but in the beginning, when you don't have any resources, it is costly and time-consuming because you have to travel and spend money on travel expenses, having the right image, and so on.

On the other hand, the digital strategy entails virtually knocking on doors—things such as cold emailing artists, labels, A&Rs, and list-building gatekeepers. Start with a digital strategy to establish yourself and begin developing your market presence in the industry. Especially in 2023, everyone is online, and your digital footprint is an important ticket into the real world. If we look at *Figure 8.1*, the worlds of online networking and offline connections intersect, creating a powerful synergy that opens doors to lucrative placements for music producers. By embracing both the digital approach and the "being in the room" strategy, producers can harness the best of both worlds, maximizing their opportunities for building clientele and securing those sought-after placements.

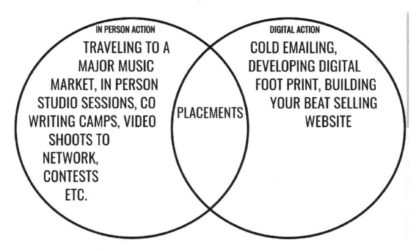

Figure 8.1: Venn diagram of placement theory

Both approaches lead to securing placements if done with focus. If you can leverage your online and digital efforts, you will eventually find yourself in the room—and that's the key. Start by using what you have, focus, and build toward getting in the room.

Now, let's talk about how to leverage digital outreach so you can start connecting with artists, labels, and media companies (among others).

Taking action steps

Following the discussion in the *Foundation steps – how to position yourself* section, you should have an idea of what your brand is, have your social media and BeatStars, and Youtube channel website up, and have some great music ready to go to market. Now, let's talk about taking the digital approach so we can start creating opportunities to get in the room in person.

When it comes to driving growth in any business, there are two types of outreach:

- **Cold outreach**: Reaching out to potential clients who haven't shown any interest in your music is classified as "cold outreach." This includes contacting people or businesses through social media, phone, or email without any prior connection or interaction. Cold outreach seeks to pique interest and initiate dialogue with potential clients.

- **Hot outreach**: On the other hand, hot outreach refers to contacting potential clients who have already expressed an interest in the product or service being provided.

The bigger you get, and the more in demand you become as a producer, the hotter your leads will ultimately become—and you will have to do less and less cold outreach. Until you get to that point, you need to think of making music and placements as your business—ultimately, you are in business for yourself and it's up to you to take responsibility to make momentum happen.

Utilizing cold outreach

If we start with a digital approach, the types of action you can take are based on the following:

- Making unsolicited phone calls to potential customers to introduce a product or service is known as cold calling—it's not likely you will find an artist's phone number, but you may get a hold of a label or A&R rep this way.

- Sending personalized emails to prospective customers who haven't contacted the business or expressed interest in the product or service is known as cold emailing. This is the most effective way to contact artists, labels, and A&Rs in my opinion. Keep your message brief, make it personalized (never spam), and follow up 2-3 times if they don't respond immediately. It's better for them to tell you not to email them rather than to assume they aren't interested. At the end of the day, if you have great music, the world needs to hear it, and your mission is to share it with the world. So, don't be shy about taking action to get it heard.

- Reaching out to potential customers via social media sites such as LinkedIn, Twitter, or Instagram in order to start a conversation or introduce the product or service is known as social media outreach. LinkedIn is a great tool to connect with business people in the music industry. Some producers are on LinkedIn, but most artists don't use it. This is a great platform to connect with music supervisors, label reps, publishers, and managers. Similar to cold email, follow up with a similar personalized but short message to escalate to an email exchange so you can share your beats with them.

I know, it's not appealing, nor does it sound fun; it's the work part. But you need to swing at the plate as many times as possible—it's a pure numbers game. Cold outreach, specifically emailing, is a work-intensive but cost-effective way to secure placements. It's how I got my first placement with G-Units Young Buck in the early 2000s, and it's still a viable way to get placements today. However, because the industry has gotten even more competitive, and there are more producers than ever, this has become a lot harder to measure in terms of output and results. But, I will say, if you can dedicate a significant amount of time to this route, especially if you don't live in a major music market, and you knock on enough doors, you should be able to see results that you can leverage to get in the room. Remember, this is a stepping stone—I'm not saying you are going to be cold emailing forever, just to get in the door and get some momentum going. Now, I will say, it's not likely that the top-signed artists will put their email in the public domain, but it does happen from time to time. Let's talk about specifics on how to use this strategy.

Building a lead list

There are a ton of sites that offer Excel spreadsheets of artists' emails, and some of those can be good, but depending on how old they are, the email inbox will most likely be full. So, I recommend you build your own lead list on Excel by using platforms such as Twitter and Instagram to search artist profiles to check whether they have a beat submission email in their profile, or if they have posted a tweet saying "send beats to X email." The key here is speed—once that post goes up, the email inbox will fill quickly.

There are apps such as Yesware that can help you send mass emails, but I don't recommend using these types of mass cold emailing software to pursue signed artists. Your email should be personalized and attentive to that specific artist, plus the beats you are sending should be selected specifically for that artist.

It might seem fruitless, or you might get a response on your first email—again, right place right time. From my experience, most of these emails will be controlled by the artists' engineers—they will be the ones who hear the tracks and play them for the artist as a heads-up.

Now, most artists who are signed will tend to use producers they have relationships with, or producers who are signed to the same label. This is because those producers have a balance owed to that label in their own respective deals, and the label wants to recoup its investments as quickly as possible. So, it will be rare to find signed artists posting emails, and most of these opportunities will be from artists who may not be signed anymore; that is, they may have been signed to a major label and now are independent.

Cold emailing can be really effective for working with unsigned artists, but remember, most of these artists don't have budgets, and you will be betting on a lot of unknown factors—for example, are they seriously pursuing music, do they have a solid work ethic, and do they have the team around them to exploit the record? These are questions you should ask yourself when you pursue this market. The reality is, very few artists in the unsigned category will make it—it's just as competitive as the producer market, if not more. However, I do recommend you network and build relationships with artists you think have the potential in the beginning. It's good practice for you as a producer to work with as many people as you can in the beginning. Plus, with the advent of platforms such as BeatStars, you can start to build your licensing clientele over time by building relationships with artists.

Summarizing the actions

Now that you understand the concept of cold outreach, let's summarize the specific action steps to follow:

1. **Research music industry professionals**: To get placements for your beats, you need to research and identify music industry professionals such as A&R executives, music supervisors, and independent artists who are looking for beats. Start building an Excel sheet or database of emails and contacts so you can solicit prospects.

2. **Customize your outreach message**: Keep it simple, keep it short—let the music do the talking. Here are some tried and tested scripts that I have used in the past to get placements. You will notice that my approach is different with artists and companies. With artists, I'm straight to the point; with companies, I formally introduce myself and let them know I'm a professional with how I write my email:

- **Music supervisor/sync email script**: *Do not* attach MP3s to these emails; use DISCO, BeatStars, SourceAudio, or SoundCloud with links they can download without needing to log in to a platform—super important.

Recipients

Composer Submission (Urban/ Pop Instrumentals)

Hope all is well, I'm reaching out today in reference to an unsolicited submission of links to my catalog for consideration in a Library capacity.

I'm a self published writer-producer with a current catalog of available tracks north of 300 pieces, I own 200% of all my material, and I'm not in any exclusive deals with anyone else.

I'm looking to connect with more established companies that are focused in sync/and see the value in urban production space.

Track Sample 1 - Big Aggressive Orchestral Hip Hop Track W/ Horns and Strings

Track Sample 2 - Bouncy and Bright Track With Memorising Arpeggio, Synths, 808 Drums

I look forward to hearing from you

[Your Name]

Figure 8.2: A music supervisor/sync email script template

- **Artist email script**: Send artist-specific beat packs. A beat pack can be 3-4 beats, or a ZIP of 20 beats or more. It is a collection of your best beats that you think would fit their style or the style of the artists they work with. You need to attach 3-4 beats in MP3 format so they can hear what you're showcasing.

Figure 8.3: Artist email script template

> **Tip**
>
> Send 2-4 beats in MP3 format, the formula that worked for me is the first beat should be a beat that you don't think they would pick, 2 and 3 should be something you know they would pick, and the fourth beat should be a beat you don't think they would pick. Ultimately, sending beats to artists is a risk—you just don't know what they will pick, and you will often be wrong in what you think they want to hear.
>
> Don't send your BeatStars or SoundCloud link to signed artists; they have too much to pick from and you want them to ideally hear the track you send, and cut the record ASAP. You don't need to introduce yourself in these types of emails; *let the music do the talking!*

3. **Build relationships**: Once you have reached out the music industry professionals, and they like what they hear, keep in contact with them—they are constantly bombarded with music, so you need to stand out! You can follow them on social media platforms such as Twitter and Instagram, attend music industry events, and follow up constantly with personalized emails asking what they are working on and whether you can add value.

4. **Be persistent**: Getting placements for beats requires persistence. You may need to send multiple beat packs and follow up with music industry professionals to get their attention.

5. **Collaborate with producers**: Another way to get placements for your beats is to collaborate with independent producers. You can find independent producers on social media platforms such as Twitter/X, Instagram, and SoundCloud. Collaborating with independent producers can help you get exposure and potentially lead to placements with larger artists. Use a similar approach when cold emailing producers—don't be annoying and don't spam. Every producer who has placements knows you want to ride their coattails. Offer value, be humble, and if they are open to it, they will let you in. Ultimately, when you have been in the game for a while, making thousands of records can get old, and it can be fun working with newer producers who have that passion like you had at the beginning of your career.

6. **Use online marketplaces**: There are several online marketplaces, such as BeatStars and Airbit, where music industry professionals and independent artists search for beats. You can upload your beats to these marketplaces and promote them to potential buyers.

7. **Attend beat battles and producer showcases**: Beat battles and producer showcases are events where producers showcase their beats and compete against each other. Attending these events can help you get exposure and potentially lead to placements.

So, we know what a *catalog is* and *how it's valued*, what a *copyright* is, the types of rights that attribute *income* you can generate, the *types of placements*, how to *secure these placements* by taking the digital outbound approach, and then leveraging those online relationships to meet in person and start networking within those circles. Now, let's talk about the types of *deals* producers can build toward.

Types of deals

A publishing deal is an agreement between a music producer and a publishing company where the publisher will promote, license, and collect royalties for the music producer's compositions. There are several types of publishing deals we will explore. Most notably, in modern times, are the co-publishing deal, the administration deal, being self-published, and the traditional publishing deal. Each of these scenarios has benefits and downsides attached to it. The upside and the downside will be specific to the producer and company practices.

Publishing deals will typically manifest in your life when you're landing placements that have charted, or you have several single releases with signed artists. Record labels all have publishing arms that work in conjunction with their label partners, and it's in the best interests of the record company to have its hand in each side of the copyright.

These can be advantageous for you as a composer or producer, whereas the publishing company should offer you an advance in exchange for assigning a portion of your royalties to the publishing company. Let's discuss the bright side of doing a publishing deal.

A producer typically negotiates a signing bonus or an advance of the estimated income they will generate based upon several factors, including how many current placements they have, what songs are in their placement pipeline, and the market potential over a period of years that the producer has. When they agree to a publishing deal with a well-known publisher, an advance can range on the small end from $15,000 to six or even seven figures depending on the producer's catalog.

This section discusses different types of generic deals, though each of them is nuanced. Let's walk through each one.

Co-publishing deals

This is a partnership between a music producer and a publishing company where both parties share ownership of the copyright and revenue generated from the producer's compositions. The publisher in effect will be taking 50% of the publisher's share of the producer's publishing income, or 25% of the total publishing income.

Administration deals

The publisher will take between 10%-20% to act as the publishing administrator and the producer will remain self-published in the sense that the administrator will typically only offer its collection, registration, and enforcement defense obligations for the producer.

Traditional publishing deals

The original type of publishing deal, which is seldom done anymore, is where the publisher will take the entire publishing share with similar terms and benefits in kind of a co-publishing deal, whereas they will have the entire 50% of the publisher's share, or 50% of the entire publishing income of the producer.

Typically, a major publishing house usually has a wide network of contacts and resources to help promote the producer's music and get it in front of a larger audience, which increases exposure. This should result in more opportunities for the producer to work with other artists and gain fans, as well as greater exposure. The publishing house may offer the producer support, such as assistance with songwriting collaborations, A&R meetings, and meetings with artists. This can aid the producer in honing their craft and creating music of higher caliber in addition to higher exposure and placement opportunities.

The publishing company is also in charge of obtaining royalties on the producer's behalf and the publisher can act as the collecting agent when disputes arise. A publishing company should defend a producer's work, including copyright registration, enforcement, and infringement prevention.

In addition to co-writing and artist placements, a sizable publishing company should have connections with TV and film studios, ad agencies, and other businesses that may want to use the producer's music in their projects. The publisher should support the producer in licensing negotiations so they can land syncs and media placements.

The key downside to doing a publishing deal is the overselling of the extra benefits outside of an advance. You need to properly vet and be comfortable with the executive and their team and keep them accountable for providing placement opportunities and co-writing sessions. Way too many producers get lost in the roster at major publishing companies, and end up never being able to recoup their advance, as well as in certain situations being locked into the agreement for a long period of time. In addition, a publishing company might have specific requirements for the genre of music they want the producer to produce, which might place restrictions on the producer's ability to express themself freely. The company might also have a say in the song's composition and arrangement, which might compromise the producer's artistic intent. The other key issue is, when you share income with a publisher and they don't provide any additional value in the procurement of placements, you might not make as much money overall as you would have if you had self-published your music.

Overall, traditional publishing deals are a great way to launch your career. They can offer you financial stability in the form of an advance with an opportunity to leverage a publishers network to secure placements that you would not have had access to.

Self-publishing

Producers and songwriters who don't have a publishing deal are considered to be "self-published." Being a self-published music producer is both empowering and challenging. Not signing a publishing deal with a major publisher is like running your own musical enterprise. At the beginning of your career, you are by default self-published.

It means taking control of your artistic destiny, handling everything from the creative process to the business side of things. As an independent music producer, you have the freedom to explore your artistic vision without the constraints of external influences. You can release your music when and how you want, allowing you to stay true to your unique style and cater to your niche audience. However, it also comes with a host of responsibilities. You take on a multitude of responsibilities to shape your music career. It starts with creating original music, overseeing the entire production process, and ensuring your compositions are registered with **performance rights organizations** (**PROs**), such as ASCAP, BMI, or SESAC, for proper royalty collection. Handling the distribution of your music across various online platforms, streaming services, and digital stores such as Spotify and Apple Music is crucial for reaching your audience. Additionally, you manage copyrights and explore licensing opportunities for your music in film, TV, commercials, and other media placements.

As your music gains popularity, you may find that staying self-published aligns with your preferences and goals. With each successful release, your fan base grows, and your music reaches more ears. As your audience expands, you have the opportunity to connect directly with your fans, fostering a loyal community around your music. As you generate more income from your music and performances, you'll have the financial resources to run your self-publishing operation effectively; covering the intricacies of being a true self-published producer becomes more manageable. You can invest in and hire professional services for marketing and promotion, and even expand your team with managers, publicists, or booking agents to further elevate your career. Moreover, being self-published means you retain all rights to your music, including the creative and financial aspects. You get to decide where your music is distributed, how it is marketed, and how royalties are managed. Most producers that opt to stay self-published will actually hand off the administration duties to a major publisher, as the back office rights collection and enforcement piece can take just as much focus as creating the music does.

It's a challenging journey, requiring dedication, resilience, and a strong DIY spirit, but the rewards can be immense. Embracing the path of a self-published music producer empowers you to shape your musical career according to your vision and values.

Production deals

A production deal is essentially a contract between a producer and a record label. A producer can collaborate with the label in this way to write and produce music for the label's artists. The producer typically receives a fee for each project or album they work on, as well as a cut of the revenue from the music they create. In some circumstances, the producer may additionally have the choice to sign artists to the label and earn a cut of the sales of their music.

It's important to keep in mind that the terms and conditions of production deals can vary greatly. While some might only last a few months, others might go on for years. A producer's pay can also differ significantly depending on their level of experience, the genre of music they are producing, and the commercial success of that music. In conclusion, production deals can be a great way for producers to get their name out there, collaborate with well-known labels, and make money from their work.

Production deals can undoubtedly provide some great advantages for producers, but there are also some potential drawbacks to take into account. The producer might have less creative control over the music they create, which is one of the main disadvantages. The producer may be expected to adhere to the label's guidelines, rather than pursuing their own artistic vision, if the label has specific ideas about the type of music they want to release. Producers who want to be more involved in the creative process may find this to be frustrating. Production deals may also have the drawback of tying the producer to a lengthy agreement with the label. As a result, while the contract is in force, they might not be able to collaborate with other labels or artists. Producers risk being locked into contracts that no longer serve their interests if their priorities or interests change over time. It's important to remember that not all production deals provide the same level of pay or benefits. Some music producers may only be paid a small percentage of the revenue generated by the songs they create, receiving very little cash upfront.

In modern times, a signed producer may sign an up-and-coming producer to its own production deal, thus creating a second layer of income splits between the actual record company and the intermediary. This is not necessarily a bad thing, but know what you are getting into. If the producer you are doing a production deal with is established, make sure they have a vested interest in making you succeed. I always consider whether it's better to get 50% of something versus 100% of nothing.

Management deals

A producer and a music manager or management company enter into a management deal. The manager or business is in charge of advocating for the producer's interests and assisting them in navigating the music business. In a management deal, the manager or business may be in charge of a variety of tasks, such as contract negotiations, finding venues for the producer's music, and giving suggestions on marketing and promotion. The manager or business typically receives a portion of the producer's earnings in return for these services. A management deal has a number of advantages, one of which is that it frees up producers to concentrate on their music while the manager takes care of the business end of things. Producers who are just starting out in the business and may not have much experience with things such as contract negotiations and marketing may find this to be especially helpful. A skilled manager can aid a producer in establishing their name and reputation in the marketplace.

It's important for producers to carefully consider the terms and conditions of any agreement before signing on because not all management deals are created equal. Some managers may have too many clients and not give each one enough personal attention, while others may lack the skills or connections to support a producer's success. However, a strong management deal can be a useful tool for producers looking to advance their careers and find lasting success in the music business. The manager might not always have the producer's best interests in mind, which is one of the main drawbacks. Some managers might put their own or the interests of their other clients before those of the producer, and they might not always act in the producer's best interests. Conflicts of interest or other issues may result from this, which could be detrimental to the producer's career. A management deal may also have the drawback that the manager may not be as successful as the producer had hoped. Despite their best efforts, some managers might simply lack the knowledge, contacts, or experience required to support a producer's success in the business. This can be annoying and make it harder for the producer to succeed.

Label deals

A producer and record label come to an agreement known as a label deal. In this arrangement, the label agrees to release and market the producer's music in return for a cut of the sales. A label deal has many advantages, one of which is that it gives producers access to a larger audience. Labels can assist in promoting and disseminating a producer's music on a larger scale because they frequently have established connections in the industry. This type of deal is almost always reserved for producers with a proven track record.

Joint venture deals

A producer and record label may enter into a joint venture agreement whereby both parties share the risks and benefits of a project. In essence, the producer and the label collaborate to produce and market music, with both parties taking a cut of the revenue. In a joint venture, both the label and the producer put equal financial and material resources into the endeavor. While the producer contributes their musical and artistic abilities, the label may offer resources such as funding, distribution options, and marketing know-how. Together, the two parties promote the music and split any revenue that is made. One of the main benefits of a joint venture agreement is that it can be a mutually advantageous means of success for both the producer and the label. Both parties are invested in the success of the music because they share in the project's risks and benefits. In contrast to a traditional label deal, the producer might also keep more creative control over their music.

But it's important to remember that joint venture agreements can also be trickier to negotiate than other kinds of contracts. It's possible that the producer and the label have different perspectives on the project or different ideas about how to promote the music. Conflicts or disagreements that result from this may need to be settled in order to move forward.

Distribution deals

An agreement between a record label and a producer known as a "distribution deal" commits the label to distributing the producer's music to stores, streaming services, and other outlets. The label typically serves as a distributor in such a deal, managing the logistics of getting the music into the hands of listeners rather than owning the rights to the music.

A distribution agreement can be a low-risk way for producers to release their music into the world, which is one of its main benefits. The label manages the distribution process, working with retailers and streaming services to get the music in front of listeners as well as producing physical copies of the music (if applicable). The producer may maintain more control over their music under a distribution agreement than they would under other kinds of agreements, which is another benefit. The producer may have more creative freedom and more control over how their music is marketed and promoted because the label typically does not own the rights to the music.

It's important to keep in mind that compared to other types of agreements, distribution deals might not provide as much support or financial backing. The label's primary responsibility is distribution; it does not support the producer's professional development or provide other resources. Furthermore, the producer might still be responsible for some aspects of marketing and promotion for their music, which can be difficult.

Now that we have discussed the most important frameworks on how to land placements that can chart on Billboard, here's a recap of the steps you need to take to chart and build a successful career in the music industry, as well as why building a catalog of solid placements should be your chief aim.

The steps for a successful career

To start, you need to create high-quality music that stands out from the crowd and showcases your unique style and creativity. Once you have your music ready, you should focus on securing placements in movies, TV shows, commercials, and other media. This will help you establish credibility, generate income, and create opportunities for yourself as a producer.

To secure these placements, you need to build relationships with music supervisors, agents, and other industry professionals who can help you get your foot in the door. You can also use online platforms and directories to find opportunities and pitch your music to potential clients. Once you've secured placements, it's essential to negotiate deals that are fair and beneficial for both parties. This involves understanding the types of rights that come with placements and how you can generate income from them.

Finally, you should focus on building a catalog of solid placements over time. This will not only increase your credibility as a producer but also create a steady stream of income and opportunities for you in the future. By following these steps and building a catalog of solid placements, you can chart your music and create a successful career in the music industry. All of these factors combine to create a successful and long-lasting career. Making a name for yourself in the music industry therefore requires building a strong catalog, which should be your chief aim.

Summary

The concepts and actionable steps I presented in this chapter offer a broad overview of how I achieved success, and they can guide you on your own path. As I write this book in 2023, it's important to acknowledge that technology will continue to disrupt the media and entertainment industry, leading to the emergence of new opportunities for building your career. It is your responsibility to embrace these evolving landscapes and seize the chances they present. Remaining focused, pushing forward relentlessly, and never giving up are vital elements in your journey.

Success will be defined uniquely for each individual. Not every producer will follow the path of Dr. Dre or Timbaland, as their character arcs and journeys are distinct. Some producers may find fulfillment in earning a great living by selling beats online, while others may focus on music for film and television. Some may thrive as the kings of their regional music scene. There is no superior position or path; it is your journey to define and pursue according to what you desire to achieve in your full-time music career. Remember, the measure of success will be personal to you. Embrace the diverse opportunities that arise, adapt to the changing landscape, and continue pushing forward with unwavering determination. Stay true to your vision and carve your own unique path in the music industry.

As we draw to a close, I hope you have found the knowledge and strategies presented in this book to be insightful and useful. We've looked into FL Studio's features and how to use them to produce chart-topping productions. I hope that this book has given you a thorough understanding of the software, from the fundamentals to the more complex features.

With this information, you'll be well on your way to creating music that stands out and attracts the attention of the biggest names in the business. Remember that it takes time, effort, and dedication to become a Billboard-charting producer. It requires constant skill development and craft improvement. However, FL Studio is a strong tool that can enable you to realize your musical vision. I urge you to experiment, try new things, and not be afraid to take chances as you set out on your journey. The music business is constantly changing, so success requires a willingness to change and develop. I appreciate you coming along for the ride, and I wish you all the best in your upcoming musical endeavors. I hope your recordings become the next big hits on the radio.

So, go out there with insane focus, and make your dreams a reality.

Index

W

Packtpub.com

Subscribe to our online digital library for full access to over 7,000 books and videos, as well as industry leading tools to help you plan your personal development and advance your career. For more information, please visit our website.

Why subscribe?

- Spend less time learning and more time coding with practical eBooks and Videos from over 4,000 industry professionals

- Improve your learning with Skill Plans built especially for you

- Get a free eBook or video every month

- Fully searchable for easy access to vital information

- Copy and paste, print, and bookmark content

Did you know that Packt offers eBook versions of every book published, with PDF and ePub files available? You can upgrade to the eBook version at packtpub.com and as a print book customer, you are entitled to a discount on the eBook copy. Get in touch with us at customercare@packtpub.com for more details.

At www.packtpub.com, you can also read a collection of free technical articles, sign up for a range of free newsletters, and receive exclusive discounts and offers on Packt books and eBooks.

Other Books You May Enjoy

If you enjoyed this book, you may be interested in these other books by Packt:

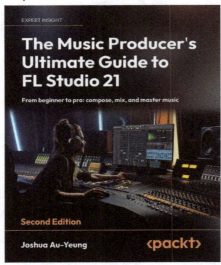

The Music Producer's Ultimate Guide to FL Studio 21 - Second Edition

Joshua Au-Yeung

ISBN: 9781837631650

- Get up and running with FL Studio 21
- Compose melodies and chord progressions on the piano roll
- Mix your music effectively with mixing techniques and plugins, such as compressors and equalizers
- Record into FL Studio, pitch-correct and retime samples, and follow advice for applying effects to vocals
- Develop your brand to promote your music effectively.
- Publish your music online and collect royalty revenues.

Music for Film and Game Soundtracks with FL Studio

Joshua Au-Yeung

ISBN: 9781803233291

- Compose production-ready music for films and video games
- Plan and deliver a soundtrack music score for clients like a professional
- Apply practical music theory using themes, leitmotifs, scales, and modes
- Compose orchestral music with MIDI programming
- Design music for specific emotions
- Create sheet music with MuseScore, score music for films with Fruity Video Player, and make diegetic music.

Packt is searching for authors like you

If you're interested in becoming an author for Packt, please visit `authors.packtpub.com` and apply today. We have worked with thousands of developers and tech professionals, just like you, to help them share their insight with the global tech community. You can make a general application, apply for a specific hot topic that we are recruiting an author for, or submit your own idea.

Peace and Blessings!

I'm Chris Noxx, the creator behind "A Power User's Guide to FL Studio 21." I trust you've enjoyed your journey through these pages, discovering valuable insights to elevate your productivity and streamline your FL Studio experience. My wish is for you to use this book to elevate your production skills and land on Billboard Charts! Your feedback holds immense significance, not just for me, but also for prospective readers.

Please consider leaving a review on Amazon, where you can share your impressions about "A Power User's Guide to FL Studio 21" and contribute to our growing community of music production enthusiasts. Your thoughts are truly appreciated.

Go to the link below or scan the QR code to leave your review:

`https://packt.link/r/1803234385`

Your review will help me to understand what's worked well in this book, and what could be improved upon for future editions, so it really is appreciated.

Best Wishes,

Chris Noxx

Download a free PDF copy of this book

Thanks for purchasing this book!

Do you like to read on the go but are unable to carry your print books everywhere?

Is your eBook purchase not compatible with the device of your choice?

Don't worry, now with every Packt book you get a DRM-free PDF version of that book at no cost.

Read anywhere, any place, on any device. Search, copy, and paste code from your favorite technical books directly into your application.

The perks don't stop there, you can get exclusive access to discounts, newsletters, and great free content in your inbox daily

Follow these simple steps to get the benefits:

1. Scan the QR code or visit the link below

https://packt.link/free-ebook/9781803234380

2. Submit your proof of purchase
3. That's it! We'll send your free PDF and other benefits to your email directly

www.ingramcontent.com/pod-product-compliance
Lightning Source LLC
Chambersburg PA
CBHW080622060326
40690CB00021B/4778